THE PURSUIT OF IMPROVEMENT IN EDUCATIONAL ORGANIZATIONS

Michael D. Richardson
Richard L. Blackbourn
Connie Ruhl-Smith
Joseph A. Haynes

University Press of America,® Inc.
Lanham • New York • Oxford

Copyright © 1997 by
University Press of America,® Inc.
4720 Boston Way
Lanham, Maryland 20706

12 Hid's Copse Rd.
Cummor Hill, Oxford OX2 9JJ

All rights reserved
Printed in the United States of America
British Library Cataloguing in Publication Information Available

Library of Congress Cataloging-in-Publication Data

The pursuit of continuous improvement in educational organizations
/ (edited by) Michael D. Richardson . . . (et al.).
p. cm.
Includes bibliographical references.
1. School improvement programs--United States. 2. Total quality
management--United States. 3. Educational change--United States.
I. Richardson, Michael D. (Michael Dwight).
LB2822.82.P87 1997 371.2'00973--dc21 97-30107 CIP

ISBN 0-7618-0878-7 (cloth: alk. ppr.)
ISBN 0-7618-0879-5 (pbk: alk. ppr.)

⊖™ The paper used in this publication meets the minimum
requirements of American National Standard for information
Sciences—Permanence of Paper for Printed Library Materials,
ANSI Z39.48—1984

Contents

Foreword

**Section One
Definitions**

Chapter 1	**Quality Improvement: Not Another Reform Movement** *Gary Rinehart* Captain, United States Air Force	1
Chapter 2	**Building the Foundation for Quality Education** *Donald F. DeMoulin* University of Memphis	15
Chapter 3	**Total Quality Management and Education: "And if You Can't Come, Send Nobody"** *David Shirley*, Vice-President Tri-County Technical College, Pendleton, SC	35
Chapter 4	**Learning as Continuous Improvement in Educational Organizations** *Michael Richardson* Georgia Southern University *Kenneth E. Lane* California State University-San Bernardino	55

Section Two
Rationale

Chapter 5	**Deming's Philosophy: Implications for Education** *Harbison Pool* Georgia Southern University	75
Chapter 6	**Dewey versus Deming: Implications for Educational Administrators** *Michael D. Richardson* Georgia Southern University *Jackson L. Flanigan* Clemson University *Kenneth E. Lane* California State University-San Bernardino	93
Chapter 7	**Using TQM as A Philosophical and Organizational Framework to Achieve Effective Schools** *Tom Valesky* University of South Florida *Frank Markus* University of Memphis	115
Chapter 8	**Continuous Improvement: A Post Structuralist Critique** *Lars G. Bjork* University of Kentucky	123
Chapter 9	**The Quality Principal** *Dennis W. VanBerkum* Moorhead State University	153

Chapter 10	**Case Studies of Two Schools: A Look at the Stages of Progress Toward Total Quality Management** *Garth Petrie* Georgia Southern University *Gordon Friberg* University of Montana	175
Chapter 11	**Achieving Quality Schools Through Technology Change** *S. John Gooden* University of North Carolina–Charlotte *Randall L. Carlson* Georgia Southern University	195
Chapter 12	**Statistical Process Control in Education: Utilizing TQM to Maintain Curriculum Alignment** *Donald V. Cairns* Montana State University *Roberta D. Evans* University of Montana	207
Chapter 13	**Total Quality Management and the Classroom Teacher** *Connie Ruhl-Smith* Western Michigan University	221
Chapter 14	**Continuous Improvement** *Patricia Lindauer* Hardin County Schools (KY) *Garth F. Petrie* Georgia Southern University	237
Chapter 15	**Total Quality Education: An Epilogue** *Marylyn Granger* Alabama State University	257

Continuous Improvement:
A Foreword
James M. Smith
Indiana University-Southbend

There is seldom a time in my life that I do not ponder organizational quality and quality leadership. As I am delayed in countless airports, I often reflect not on the reason for the delayer but on the treatment of the customer during the course of the delay. Recently, while trying to make a connection at a major transportation hub in the Midwest, I stopped to ask a gate agent if my connecting Sight had already departed. I certainly must have appeared shocked when the young lady responded with the following statement: "How should I know?" Possibly it was not her occupational duty to know of all the connections for that given concourse; nonetheless, in a quality work environment, it is her occupational duty to treat the customer as an important, if not critical, element with regard to the overall success of the organization. As Kaufman (1992) so clearly states:

> TQM is a people process. TQM is an on-going process. It is never complete. Quality and client satisfaction constitute the continuing TQM goal. TQM relies on all of the factors of production, including the most valuable one of all—people consistently producing high quality outputs. They "do it right the first time and every time," so much so that the client is satisfied. TQM operates as if each person M the organization were the actual customer, making things the way they would want to buy it themselves. (p. 150)

Again reflecting upon the aforementioned gate agent, I am wont to consider both her lack of understanding with respect to Total Quality Management, as well as her basic ignorance of the principles of overall quality leadership. Did the employee not know that in a quality organization the customer should be treated with the utmost of courtesy? Did the employee not know that customer satisfaction is never a single event but rather a continuous process? Obviously, I remain uninformed with regard to the answers to these queries. Due to my intense need to rush to the connecting gate, no time existed to discuss these concerns. Likewise, I have not, in subsequent months, taken time to interview the supervisory staff of the airline in question. However, I feel certain that a quality assurance division exists within the overall organizational structure and, concomitantly, that the quality assurance division employees are well versed in the works of Crosby, Deming Imai, Juran and others. Essentially, my final question is a rather simple one—what then went wrong?

This book appropriately entitled The Pursuit of Continuous Improvement in Educational Organizations, is designed to offer ad educators the opportunity to examine the same types of questions concerning what has gone wrong with public school environments (P- 12 and higher education alike). The chapters contained within this text range in scope from a philosophical examination of quality to those offering more pragmatic applications of quality standards to the classroom. The authors of these varied chapters challenge the reader to think about TQM and other quality practices, not in an amorphous sense, but rather in a manner that calls for site specific applications. This edited book calls the reader's attention to the myriad facts that surround public schools of today. It is no surprise to the average educator that many public schools have less than a quality reputation. This text challenges the reader to look beyond the simple assertion that something is wrong to consider the far more critical concern of how to make it right.

This text reifies the fact that TOM is nothing more than an amalgamation of leadership tools. These tools help leaders and followers to focus on basic principles of organizational improvement; (Ruhl-Smith & Smith, 1993). The application of concepts like Deming's Fourteen Points, as frequently discussed throughout this text, is a process that calls for both organizational introspection, as well as organizational improvement. The reader who selects this book for a "quick fix" to present organizational problems inherent to a given school or a given university will immediately become frustrated by almost every chapter contained on this work. As each author has noted, quality improvement is indeed a lengthy process. To improve overall organizational quality, it takes a massive amount of tune to adopt a new philosophy, institute training, institute new leadership, and coordinate the activities of everyone in order to accomplish this transformation (Walton, 1986). Those searching for "quick fixes" will find none within the pages of this work. They will, however, find countless suggestions of how to move an organization into the quality world. These chapters offer ideas, concepts, and rational descriptions for what a school or university can become. In conjunction with these ideas and suggestions comes the implied notion that to assist with this quality transformation, vie all must be willing to dedicate ourselves to the task at hand. Simply stated, what worked or seemed to world yesterday, in all probability, will not work tomorrow. It must be our mission as faculty and staff to make today better and tomorrow even better still.

In closing, as we prepare to read and/or reread this work. It is important to keep in mind the words of Margaret Byrnes (1995):

> In schools and school districts around the nation, where Total Quality Management is in place, students are learning more and faster; the work students complete is of a touch higher quality; discipline problems are reduced; students become active learners; and students, parents, and teachers are much happier. (p. 4)

Toward that end—read, reflect, and then initiate the total quality message, as shared throughout this most useful book.

References

Byrnes, M. A. (1995, March). <u>Educate parents about your quality.</u> Paper presented at the National Conference for Creating the Quality School, Oklahoma City, OK.

Kaufman, R. (1992). The challenge of Total Quality Management in education. <u>International Journal of Educational Reform, 1</u> (2), 149-165.

Ruhl-Smith, C., & Smith, J. M. (1993). Teacher job satisfaction in a quality school: Implications for educational leaders. <u>Journal of School Leadership, 3</u>, 534-548.

Walton, M. (1986). <u>The Deming management method.</u> New York: Perigee Books.

Chapter 1

QUALITY IMPROVEMENT: NOT ANOTHER REFORM MOVEMENT

Gary Rinehart
Captain, United States Air Force

In 1988, the principal of George Westinghouse Vocational and Technical High School in Brooklyn, New York, took a group of teachers to a seminar on the methods and principles of Total Quality Management. This "TQM"— one popular name for the applied principles of continuous improvement—was steadily gaining acceptance among industrial managers, but among educators it was still largely unrecognized. As a result, their adoption of the quality improvement ideas was almost an act of faith, since it represented a drastic change from previous efforts to improve their school. After establishing a clear-cut mission for their school, they moved into applying the newly-learned principles to problems within the school. By 1991, they had reduced class-cutting by 40% and improved successful course-completion by 92%—quite an accomplishment for an inner-city, largely minority-populated school without many of the advantages of more affluent schools. They attribute these and other successes to their adoption of the quality improvement ideas (Schargel, 1992).

The application of what were once solely industrial quality improvement principles to education has been growing across the United States for several years. Like other so-called "reforms," it has not been applied evenly across the nation; rather, some places have adopted the principles fervently while others have ignored them. Like the principal and teachers of George Westinghouse High School, those who championed the cause of quality improvement did so more from faith in the principles than from proof of their efficacy. And they have learned continuous quality improvement is not a quick-fix reform, but rather a long-term change in the culture of schools and districts.

Despite the localized nature of education's transformation to quality principles, evidence indicates these principles can effect remarkable improvements in the learning environment and educational outcomes. Certainly they can do no worse than other reforms. While the hue and cry for improvement has waxed and waned, reform efforts have been applied like bandages to gaping wounds, with predictable results. However, schools adopting continuous improvement principles have not succumbed to the pressure to implement the latest reform, preferring to work diligently to make their vision of a quality school come true. While some schools and districts have fallen prey to the lure of quick results, reform will come slowly and sometimes painfully.[1] Despite the difficulties of changing the culture of their schools and districts, those involved in the change process have pressed on and achieved outstanding results. And few people would argue that such successes, repeated across the nation, would be unwelcome.

Why Quality?

Is it necessary to list educational troubles which have been so well publicized? The ratio of educational bad news to good news in a given week of television news reports and newspaper and magazine articles is usually quite high. This should not surprise us for a number of reasons. First, we are experiencing a rather general period of dissatisfaction with all manner of public institutions and officials; public education, then, becomes a fair target. Second, many authors have pointed out the disappointing state of literacy in the U.S., which some people quickly and inaccurately lay squarely at the feet of education. In addition, good news is often not "news" in the sensationalist sense, so the number of success stories publicized in the news media is understandably small. Before we fall into the trap of laying the blame for this on the media or the public, we must admit that the ratio should not surprise us for at least one more reason: it is easier to tear down a thing than to build it.

Education in the U.S. seems to be in anger of being torn down, almost as much by insiders touting reform as by outsiders demanding it. This is not to imply that tearing down an edifice or institution is necessarily a bad thing, as long as it is replaced by something better, or at least as good. It is important to note that the U.S. education system is not actually broken; rather, it does not exist as a coherent system at all. The "piece parts" are all there, working feverishly to accomplish their individual goals, but they work together coherently only by accident. Grade schools rarely work in concert with high schools to improve each other; colleges and universities usually remain set apart from lower levels of education, except for experimental or other special programs.

As a result of this fragmentation, many students move from one level to the next without adequate preparation, leading many people to perceive education as not doing what it should. This too may be attributed to a number of factors, from the previously mentioned general mistrust of public officials who handle precious tax revenues, to special interest manipulators trying to mold education in the image they worship, to actual experience with education not living up to expectations. It is this third category that should most concern teachers, principals, and administrators, since improving the educational experience—both the experience itself and the results of that experience—should lead to a reduction in the number of dissatisfied students, parents, and citizens, and, therefore, an improved perception of education.

From this perspective, who can not understand the need for quality in education? For education that enriches lives and enables people to be creative, productive citizens? For education that improves cultural understanding and encourages self-esteem? Few people would argue against such an education, and those few would normally be discounted as malcontents or imbeciles. But if such an education is desirable for all students, why are we not providing it?

The question is admittedly quite naive, since the education of a single person is an incredibly complicated endeavor, much less the education of an entire nation. The question is appropriate, however, because it focuses attention in the right direction. It asks why we are not providing the education we wish people to have; in other words, what are the reasons behind our inability to do what we want? Asked in this way, the question leads us to search for those reasons and may lead to improvements in the situation. Too often, however, we do not ask why; instead we ask who is responsible, and having discovered the supposedly guilty party, we commence with their punishment or replacement, expecting a change in attitude or personnel to lead to the improvement we seek. Perhaps asking why is naive but not so naive and simplistic as asking who and ascribing all guilt to that individual.

Having come this far, we should also ask ourselves another question: Are educators working toward quality? Despite the negative publicity education has received in recent years, the answer is clearly yes. The question asks if educators are obtaining the maximum results. We must believe that no teacher walks into a classroom determined to teach deliberate untruths or otherwise thwart children's learning; no principal purposes to damage egos or paralyze learners with fear through application of disciplinary measures; and no administrator maliciously decides to keep computers out of schools or let school buildings fall into disrepair. To believe otherwise would be the height of cynicism. Just as in other professions, a few practitioners may indeed be scoundrels and approach their jobs with malice of forethought, but they are certainly in the minority; we would be forced to question the values and perhaps the rationality of anyone who set out deliberately to sabotage a child's education. In truth, teachers, principals, and administrators are quite simply doing the best they can under difficult circumstances. They want to do better, but often do not know how.

The overwhelming desire for quality education extends far beyond the educator's classroom world. No parent in his/her right mind would want his/her children to fail in school or to grow up ignorant and incompetent. Certainly no school board member campaigns for the position on a platform of making education worse. No employer wants the graduates available for hiring to know nothing and be unprepared for work. It seems safe to say everyone wants education to succeed, wants children to learn as much as possible and be adequately, if not expertly, prepared for adult life. Granting this is true, why are we continuing to have trouble accomplishing this?

As stated above, educators are doing their best—and it may be safely assumed they will continue to do their best in the future. Yet their best has not been enough to achieve desired results, and consequently they have borne the brunt of the public's dissatisfaction with this country's educational system.[2] The system itself is far too complex to reduce to such a simple explanation, but simplicity seems to be the hallmark of news reporting. The authors of news items are not usually predisposed to investigate the details and identify the root causes behind anything. But the desire for quality education—on the part of parents, students, teachers, and everyone else involved in education—is not the product of editorial or literacy license; it is a genuine interest that can be tapped along with the energies and creative powers of the stake holders. This desire for improved education has led many educators to adopt industrial quality improvement practices—but what is this elusive thing called quality?

What Quality Is (And Is Not)

Quality is notoriously difficult to define. It is somewhat like fun: it's hard to say exactly what it is but easy to recognize its absence. In other words, we may not be able to say exactly what "fun" is, but we have a good idea—from the experience of being bored or otherwise not enjoying ourselves—what it is not. So it is with quality. We may not be able to express what constitutes quality, but we can usually differentiate between a quality product or service and one which is mediocre.

Despite the problem of adequately defining quality, having at least a working definition is necessary to achieving it. Phillip Crosby, whose book Quality Is Free did much to popularize quality improvement in the early 1980s, defines quality as conformance to requirements; i.e., a product or service is considered "quality" if it meets the customer's requirements for it (Crosby, 1979). Dr. Joseph M. Juran, one of the U.S. experts who took quality improvement ideas to Japan in the 1950s, defines quality as fitness for use—this means a quality product or service adequately fulfills the purpose for which it was intended (Juran, 1988). Other experts have still different definitions, but not just the experts disagree on the subject.

Part of this difficulty of definition has to do with perception. Because one person's quality may be another's junk, the determination of quality must be based on the client's definition. That is, the client determines when he or she is or is not receiving a quality product or service. Clients base this determination on whether or not the product or service meets their expectations.

A client's expectations may be based on a real need, a perceived need, or an influenced need. Real needs are those requirements the client has in order to survive and get along adequately in the modern world; they include, but go beyond, such things as nutritious food and clean air to things the client needs to cope with modern life (e.g., adequate transportation). Perceived needs go beyond real needs and begin to approach luxury status (e.g., gourmet food as opposed to staples, or a luxury automobile as opposed to an economy car, or a private automobile as opposed to public transportation). Perceived needs often are not actually needs, but desires instead; the same is true for influenced needs. These are things the client has been convinced are needs by some outside source, perhaps by a friend or through advertising or for entertainment.

The influence of perceptions and expectations (both needs and desires) on what is considered quality poses a significant problem for those faced with delivering quality products and services. What does the client need? Can we deliver it, within constraints of time and cost? What does the client want, and is it the same as what he or she needs? If they are the same, will our product or service satisfy them? If they are different, how do we get clients to focus on needs when other influences pull their attention to desires? These are a few of the questions manufacturing and service industries have learned to answer by applying quality improvement principles; education can also apply the principles to answer these questions for its clients.

Educators trying to adapt quality improvement practices first must answer a more basic question: Who are our clients? A little thought will reveal that this question is not as naive as it seems, since a wide range of the populace has a stake in the outcome of education. They are all in some sense clients, if not of education itself then at least of the educational system. However, agreement among educators about the identity of their client group does not come easily.

Many educators and policy makers quickly identify students as the primary clients of education, recognizing the immediacy of the classroom experience and importance of the teacher/student interface in shaping education outcomes. This assertion brings up another, more insidious, question: Has the client been led to desire something antithetical to his or her needs? If the student is identified as a client, this turns out to be the case as often as not. For example, how many students, even good ones, want to do homework? They may want to learn, but at the same time may not want to work at learning. Thus, educators face the double task of improving quality for their clients as well as educating these same clients of the importance of needs as opposed to desires.

Despite the attention we have just paid to this subject, continuous quality improvement consists of more than defining quality and recognizing the client. Beyond these complex issues is the key idea of transformation, of changing not only the systems which make up an enterprise but also the culture which surrounds the system. "Culture" is indeed the proper term for endeavors which "operate on ... principles of shared loyalty and shared risk," such as:

> families, football teams, political campaigns, churches, [and] small town doctors ... The examples of these groups confirms that the qualities that really count for their ... success cannot be "bought," the way a new running back or a petroleum-law specialists might be bought, simply with a better contract and more attractive fringe benefits. The financial incentives matter, but by themselves they will fail to create the human bonds, as surely as big-city school systems fail when they try to "purchase" a more dedicated corps of teachers by sweetening their contract with the teachers' union. Wherever ... service is judged purely by the economist's calculation of marginal tradeoffs and maximized self-interest, it erects a structure of values inimical to be required goals. (Fallows, 1981)

The educational culture can, like those mentioned above, be characterized by shared loyalty (e.g., between educators and students, schools and communities, parents and children) and shared risk (i.e., the risk of discovering and being discovered, of opening to new possibilities and new people). These are the strengths upon which continuous improvement can be built.

Adopting quality principles depends on participants sharing both loyalty to one another and responsibility for change; to be successful, stakeholders must share the risks, as well as the rewards, of the change process. Quality depends on a culture that values commitment to long-term improvement, rather than short-term, cosmetic change. Building a quality culture in education requires treating all participants as professionals, equipped with high ideals and capable of lofty achievements, rather than wage-earners whose only interests are their paychecks. This is as much a transformation of managerial mind set as it is participant attitude, but it is a transformation, a metamorphosis, nonetheless. This change in organizational culture—from traditional to quality—management practices—is the basic thrust of what is known as Total Quality.

How Total Quality Is Different From Quality

A plethora of names have been applied to the idea of continuous improvement of quality. From Quality Control to Total Quality Control to Total Quality Management to Total Quality Leadership, different groups have coined or selected different names for what is essentially the same concept. As with "client" or "customer," the name itself is not as important as the concept; however, school administration pursuing quality improvement must realize choosing the wrong name can cause problems. Especially in education, the idea of using any commercial or industrial method tends to turn off some purists who fear contamination of academic freedom or educational autonomy. So although the idea behind the name is paramount, selecting a name that will be attractive to as many people as possible (or alienate as few as possible) may be vital to successfully transforming the culture. Thus, we are speaking of "clients" and "continuous improvement" rather than "customers" and "TQM."

Leaving the question of the right name for this transformation process (you may debate this with your partners in this enterprise), the central question remains: How is the "Total Quality" approach or idea different from the idea of "quality" itself?

One may argue that the two are not different; in fact, Dr. W. Edwards Deming, the first U.S. expert to lecture on quality to the Japanese, barely recognizes the phrase "Total Quality," and speaks only of quality and its continuous improvements.[3] The two things are, however, generally considered to represent different things. Total Quality (or any of the other possible names) represents a systematic approach to the continuous improvement of a product, service, or organization. Quality, on the other hand, is that nebulous thing we discussed earlier that is a measure of the relative worth of a product, service, or organization (Feigenbaum, 1961).

As intimated above, the idea of continuous improvement is the key element to Total Quality. The basic tenet is that no product, no service, no system, and no organization is so perfect that it cannot be improved in some way, and only by continuously improving the things for which we are responsible can we better our chances of success. This usually requires a drastic change in the organizations culture, from rewarding quick, heroic fixes to honoring small, incremental improvements. That is, many small improvements in processes and systems—what the Japanese call <u>kaizen</u>— reap bigger rewards in the long run for the organization and society than the stop-gap measures that only return a broken system to its previous level (Imai, 1986).

How can we say that improvement of quality yields such returns? The answer for manufacturing and service industries lies in what has become known as the Deming Chain Reaction: improved quality yields improved productivity because less time, material, and effort is being wasted; the improved productivity effectively decreases the unit cost, allowing producers to decrease the price of their products or services; by decreasing price, the producers can increase their share of the market and stay in business (consider the Japanese share of the U.S. automobile and consumer electronics markets) (Deming, 1986). In contrast, allowing quality to fall results in fewer satisfied customers and increased costs from waste and rework, both spell disaster for the profit-minded organization. The benefits of quality improvement, however, are not limited to profit-making ventures; continuous improvement of quality reaps benefits for all manner of public—and private-sector concerns, whether product- or service-oriented. Like George Westinghouse High School, many schools—and school districts—are applying the principles, proving they can be adapted to non-industrial concerns: for example, Mount Edgecumbe High School (Sitka, Alaska), George Stone Center (Pensacola, Florida), Kate Sullivan Elementary School (Tallahassee, Florida), Independent School District 832 (Mahtomedi, Minnesota), Johnston County School District (North Carolina), and many others.

With regard to the change in outlook this transformation requires, we may draw an analogy between managers of complex systems and medical professionals. In the past, it was only required that things which went wrong be fixed: managers were often "fire fighters." Doctors and dentists also followed this principle, prescribing drugs or surgery, filling cavities and pulling teeth—only when the patient's health deteriorated. Today, the changing nature of the workplace makes quick, temporary fixes less appealing, just as the rising cost of health care makes corrective medicine less appealing. Thus, many doctors currently work on preventive medicine and wellness to keep people from getting sick, dentists coat children's teeth to prevent cavities, and managers now look farther to the future and make long-term improvements that will bring greater returns than their fire-fighting efforts ever did.

To achieve this change, this transformation, many organizations and managers—including many schools and administrators—are looking to the principles of Total Quality. The principles combine the idea that every system can be improved with a scientific approach to problem solving and the recognition and development of the potential of everyone who works within the system. The principles have grown since the 1920s, and many books trace this evolution of ideas; we will briefly trace some of the major developments, hopefully whetting your appetite for further study.

Quality Thought Develops

The modern era of quality began with the recognition that the natural variation of a mechanical process could be controlled within limits predicted by theory of probability. While this sounds complicated (and some of the mathematics can be daunting), the concept itself is simple: variation in processes cannot be avoided, so if you know how much variation to expect you can control the process for repeatedly predictable results.

To better understand this concept, an example from everyday life will help: how long does it take you to get ready for work or school each day? The answer you give will probably be an average, since you do not take the exact same time each day. Why not? You can probably identify any number of reasons why the time it takes varies from day to day: your morning routine may be disrupted for some reason, you may get interested in a morning news show or have trouble finding your newspaper, you may not eat the same things for breakfast each day. The key is this: despite those differences that creep into your getting-ready process, you are still able to estimate with some reliability the time it will take you to get ready. In other words, the system is in control. Because of this, you can predict from day to day how long it will take you to get ready, and thereby achieve some measure of control over your life.

Dr. Walter Shewhart explained this in terms of industrial processes in his seminal work Economic Control of Quality of Manufactured Product. In this work he also explained the difference between common and special causes of variation (Shewhart, 1931). In our everyday example, a common cause might be the time it takes your shower to get warm enough or your coffee to brew; it is a cause of variation in your timing, but it is minuscule and affects each day in much the same way. A special cause, however, would throw your routine off significantly. In our example, a special cause might be a breakdown of your hot water heater or a sudden decision to cook steak and eggs for breakfast. The idea that emerges from knowing special and common causes is that one can control process variation by first removing special causes and then gradually working on minimizing the effect of the common causes.[4] This is the approach advocated by Deming, Shewhart's protegee.

Deming took Shewhart's ideas and gradually built a management system around them. He lectured in Japan in 1950 and 1951, but only gained widespread popularity in the U.S. since 1980. His management system was codefined in his "Fourteen Points," to which he added "Seven Deadly Diseases" which he believed could damage attempts to deliver quality products and services. His approach emphasized individual dignity and worth through training an education, pride of workmanship, and removal of fear from the workplace (Deming, 1986).[5]

As discussed earlier, Juran also lectured in Japan and contributed to their adoption of quality improvement principles. Juran's lectures influenced Japan's top managers to emphasize continuous improvement because he convinced them they would lose money if the failed to do so. Other of Juran's major impacts on quality improvement were his popularization of the Pareto Principle—also known as the 20-80 (or 80-20) rule—and his idea of managerial "breakthrough," a method by which organizations could break out of the status quo and reach innovative solutions to their problems (Juran, 1988).[6]

Many other people have contributed to the quality improvement phenomenon: U.S. quality experts like Dr. Brian Joiner, Peter Scholtes, and Dr. Don Wheeler; international experts like Heero Hacquebord, Dr. Kaoru Ishikawa, and Dr. Genichi Taguchi; and popularizers of quality such as the aforementioned Crosby and the inimitable Tom Peters. We will not, however, catalog their contributions here; it should be enough that you know where to look for more information when you are ready to expand your knowledge of quality.

In addition to this text, teachers, principals, and administrators should have no trouble finding information on specifically adapting the quality principles to education. GOAL/QPC, a non-profit partnership between government, industry, and labor, compiled a "resource guide" listing a number of books and articles and including a glossary of quality terms (GOAL/QPC, 1992). The American Association of School Administrators operates a Total Quality Network featuring seminars and information to members. The National Educational Quality Initiative is a non-profit group working to implement quality improvement practices in schools. Deming himself has made education one of his top priorities, including specific educational references in his latest book (Deming, 1993). But despite the ready availability of references and information, adoption of quality improvement principles to individual schools and districts will be a time-consuming and often frustrating process.

Principles and Principals

One common factor in successfully transforming a school or school district to the quality approach seems to be a receptive attitude on the part of the leadership. The principal or administrator need not be an ardent supporter—although it would make the entire enterprise that much easier—but certainly cannot be a vocal opponent of the quality initiative.

Educators will, through no fault of their own, inevitably spend more time on traditional fire-fighting than they do on implementing long-term improvements. Their day is already filled with of preparing for and teaching classes, monitoring extracurricular activities, and fulfilling their administrative requirements. As pointed out in Horace's School, many teachers do not have adequate time even to learn enough about their students to counsel them effectively (Sizer, 1992). Teachers who may want to work on systematic change with long-term results—like those we are discussing—but without the cooperation of their principals and administrators, they will have very little of one precious resource: time.

Time (or the lack of it), however, is not the only roadblock on the way to quality. We can make no promise, stated or implied, that improved quality will mean less work for teachers, principals, or administrators. If anything, working consistently and constantly to achieve a high standard and improve upon what was done previously is actually harder than maintaining the status quo. The results of quality education—seeing the gleam of comprehension in students' eyes, hearing words of thanks from parents, reading about the success of a former student—will come more often, to more educators, from more pupils, making the extra effort worthwhile. For students and educators as for workers and managers, easy work without meaning or fulfillment is merely drudgery; hard work with importance or accomplishment, however, is joy.

This brief chapter cannot hope to cover all the principles and tools of the quality transformation; it can only encourage you, pique your curiosity, and help you overcome any trepidation you feel about this new approach. You may feel better about working toward continuous improvement if you understand its two basic ideas. The first we have already discussed: every process has some room for improvement. Some variation in every process must be expected, and may be controllable for consistent results; in addition, each process effects, and is affected by, other processes in the larger system, and understanding process interactions can help optimize the whole system. The second basic idea of quality improvement has to do with the organizational culture: it is the idea that everyone has something to contribute. People may generally be trusted to do their best and must be encouraged to participate without fear of censure or being ostracized; they must be allowed to take pride in their work and be encouraged to personalize the idea of continuous improvement by pursuing their own learning.[7] Only enlightened leaders can start and maintain this environment conducive to continuous improvement.

Principals and administrators eager to begin their journey toward quality must move purposefully, but not haphazardly. Once again, the quality transformation focuses on continuous, long-term improvements instead of quick fixes. This should be enough reason to approach any changes with caution but here is another: Moving too fast, without establishing a constituency and having a coherent theory to explain the changes, will only alienate people and bog down the process. Imagine the school or district as a vehicle stuck in the mud. Often the first impulse is to press the accelerator, to try to go faster—but the only result is to spin the wheels and work deeper into the muck. A better solution is to get out, find some brush or boards on which to get traction, then move steadily out of the mud—we may get a little dirty, but at least we get moving in the right direction.

Not Just Another Reform

While it may seem the adoption of quality principles to education is only another fad, another reform destined to fail. At its roots, it is quite different. Most other 'reforms' are proposed solutions to discrete problems, solutions that are supposed to be applied at specific places and times which will immediately reverse whatever negative trends are in effect. That such reforms fail should not be surprising; that policy makers continue to pin their hopes on reform after reform of this type should be.

The quality philosophy, however, is not any single program to magically make everything better. As you learn more, you will see that applying the principles will take time and effort, and their results—like the results of education itself—will not be immediate. In addition, applying the principles does not end so long as the phrase "continuous improvement" has any meaning: we may never create perfect schools, but we will constantly build toward them.

References

Crosby, P. (1979). Quality is free: The art of making quality certain. New York: McGraw-Hill.

Deming, W. E. (1986). Out of the crisis. Cambridge, MA: Massachusetts Institute of Technology Center for Advanced Engineering Study.

Deming, W. E. (1993). The new economics for industry, education, government. Cambridge, MA: Massachusetts Institute of Technology Center for Advanced Engineering Study.

Fallows, J. (1981). National defense. New York: Random House.

Feigenbaum, A. V. (1961). Total quality control: Engineering and management. New York: McGraw-Hill.

GOAL/QPC. (1992). Education and total quality management. Methuen, MA: GOAL/QPC. (Available from GOAL/QPC, 13 Branch Street, Methuen, MA 01844-1953)

Henry, T. (1993, October). School goals out of reach by 2000. USA Today, D-1.

Imai, M. (1986). Kaizen. New York: McGraw-Hill.

Juran, J. M. (1988). Juran on planning for quality. New York: The Free Press.

Rinehart, G. (1993). Quality education. Milwaukee, WI: ASQC-Quality Press.

Shargel, F. P. (1992, March). School changes way of doing business. Work America, 3 (1), 2-3.

Shewhart, W. A. (1931). Economic control of quality of manufactured product. Princeton, NJ: D. Van Norstrand Company.

Sizer, T. R. (1992). Horace's school: Redesigning the American high school. Boston: Houghton Mifflin.

Notes

[1] See Quality Education, esp. pp. 96-8, for a prediction and explanation of the eventual failure of the National Goals for Education. See USA Today, 1 Oct. 93, p. D-1, for an admission that they are destined to fail.

[2] This is explained by Deming's Second Theorem: "We are ruined by best efforts." Consider the resulting chaos if everyone did their best, but no one knew what to do.

[3] As this was written, Dr. Deming—at nearly 93 years old—was conducting a final tour of the four-day seminars he has held regularly for over a dozen years; in these seminars he has always been quick to point out that this interest is improving quality and productivity, not promoting "Total Quality."

[4] Shewhart also wrote of a sample demonstration which teachers may use to teach almost anyone about special and common causes. You may try it yourself: write the letter 'a' about two dozen times, compare the differences between individual letters, and think about the common causes of variation between the letters you wrote.

[5] Many books on Dr. Deming's ideas are available. Books by Henry Neave, William Scherkenbach, or Mary Walton are highly recommended.

[6] Dr. Juran has written many books on quality improvement, aimed at practitioners at every level of an organization. His most recent public tour was billed as his

"Last Word" on implementing quality improvement, so he could—at age 86—devote more time to writing.

[7] This is a much-simplified compilation of Dr. Deming's Fourteen Points.

Chapter 2

BUILDING THE FOUNDATION FOR QUALITY EDUCATION

Donald F. Demoulin
University of Memphis

The idea of Total Quality Management, namely doing things in the right manner, does not mean that the right things are being done. History is filled with examples of failed products and services which initially satisfied the needs and wants of the individual but, over time, proved to be an unwholesome, even harmful adventure. These unfortunate conclusions resulted in a short-term, "quick-fix" solution without sufficient attention given to any underlying effect, e.g., morality, socially, ethically, etc.

Unfortunately, the Total Quality Management concept has crept into the educational realm bringing with it a sense of apprehension. Perhaps this apprehension stems from a generic definition of the term "quality." What is viewed as quality in one environment is viewed as below standard in another. What is desperately needed, then, is a universal definition of quality which ensures that districts provide the essential curricular offerings to allow graduates to be self-sufficient, self-reliant, and contribute positively to society (Kaufman & Hirumi, 1992).

In this chapter, I will attempt to provide some points of interest which, if practiced, will maximize district-defined quality of operation. However, to obtain quality of operation, accountability for success must be networked, linked to internal and external components, and fused with vision and commitment. This is a partial formula for determining ongoing strategies and tactics for improvement.

Accountability

Accountability in education is a term that has usually been allocated to those individuals who are answerable to the degree of educational success. However, those individuals who have been answerable have usually been educators. Other members of society may have a somewhat recognized relationship with education but have not or will not share the obligation. Subsequently, accountability carries an educational stigma that implies partitioning of responsibility by a populace who has stereotyped the degree of educational success to individuals affiliated with education—namely teachers and administrators. It has been this conviction that has led to an accountability phobia that is destined to immobilize any true education reform. Perhaps, this phobia has resulted from an ongoing sociological perspective that only educators should be held accountable for student achievement; perhaps it has flourished because educators have been relatively easy scapegoats. Whatever the rationality, accountability in education cannot be isolated to one particular segment of society; rather, all of society must be held accountable for the past, present and future status of education because, "its obligations extend not just to a particular group of share holders or sponsors, but to the public at large" (Berkeley, 1978, p. 11).

Defining an Accountability Network

By expanding the scope of accountability, a sociological network to determine a hierarchy of responsibility for quality education can be established whereby increased student achievement is a function of the degree of performance for:

- **community members** to take an active part in local educational improvement, and for corporate leaders to actively communicate specific needs in order to spawn continuity between the school and business sectors.
- **federal, state and local politicians** to initiate leadership, to create aggressive, clear-cut and long-term educational goals, to determine specific objectives to achieve the established goals, and to construct systematic methods of financing education regardless of which political party is in office.
- **university personnel** to establish explicit standards for students that provide high caliber teacher and administrative training programs in order to supply schools with a skilled work force.
- **administrators** to initiate leadership and to establish guidelines and practices that entice a positive learning atmosphere.
- **teachers** to expand classroom opportunity and to inspire students to discover the potential value of learning and to create effective lines of communication to the home environment.
- **students** to develop productive study habits, to attain a high degree of interest in advancing their level of awareness in education, and to enhance their skills for the duties of citizenship.

This conceptualization of accountability rests with the premise that to increase performance levels of each segment within the accountability network, the attitude of each segment must be directed toward improving the existing structure. If individual or group attitudes within each segment lean toward irresponsibility, the primary effect is incompetency, poor achievement and/or an unconcerned attitude. This improper attitudes yields poor performance quality. However, if individual or group attitude within each segment are directed toward accomplishment and responsibility, achievement is usually synonymous with competence, high performance quality and a concerned attitude. To further illustrate the consequence for educational opportunity associated with an improper attitude, the following **if/then** scenarios are offered.

- If parents as part of the community effort do not undertake an assertive role in their child's education, then the child does not have the positive home environment which is necessary to attain meaningful student achievement.
- If government constituent's energy is primarily geared towards reelection, then true educational progress may be tainted by lip-service, political rhetoric—a state that is all too familiar.
- If university training programs are not rigid enough to properly prepare teachers and administrators, then schools may not receive the caliber of leadership for quality educational opportunity.
- If administrators do not maintain a sound educational environment, promote teacher improvement practices, establish solid school/community relations, etc., then a state of disequilibrium may occur leading to discontinuity of operations.
- If teachers do not strive to teach beyond rudimentary boundaries, then students may not be challenged beyond the basic level of the learning process.
- If a student possesses a lackadaisical attitude toward education, then that student usually does not demonstrate the responsibility nor the competence necessary to surpass certain achievement criteria.

This participatory network must work collectively for the teaching/learning process to be successful. Thus, displaying the proper attitude by the American populace may be one missing component in the quest for educational improvement.

The following model (Figure 1) has been designed to categorize the segments of society previously discussed in the accountability network. The possible outcome in education is therefore contingent upon the magnitude of educational commitment, the direction of that commitment and the educational attitude exhibited by each segment of the accountability network.

This model represents the scope of accountability, the educational establishment is consequently an interlocking, progressive network consisting of community members, governmental agencies, university personnel, school district administrators, teachers, and students. The

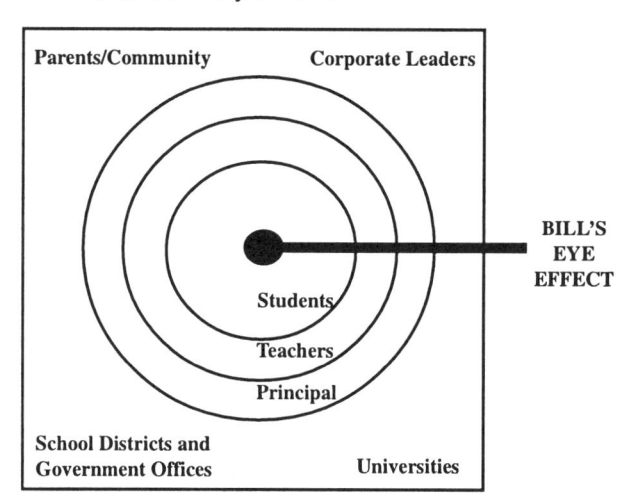

Figure 1. The Accoutnability Network

```
┌─────────────────────────────────────────────┐
│  Parents/Community      Corporate Leaders   │
│                                             │
│            ╱─────────────╲                  │
│          ╱   ╱─────────╲  ╲                 │
│         │   │  ╱─────╲  │  │                │
│         │   │ │   ●   │ │  │────── BILL'S   │
│         │   │ │Students│ │  │        EYE    │
│         │   │  ╲Teachers╱ │             EFFECT
│          ╲   ╲ Principal╱                   │
│            ╲─────────────╱                  │
│                                             │
│  School Districts and                       │
│  Government Offices     Universities        │
└─────────────────────────────────────────────┘
```

success of this network is contingent upon the degree of commitment. Hence, each segment of the network must fulfill its commitment in order for the network to operate in equilibrium.

The ideal situation, therefore, is for the accountability network to work collectively while enhancing the educational opportunity. This is accomplished by instituting consistent and effective measures for obtaining student achievement and success (Bulls Eye Effect). Anything less is unacceptable. Effectiveness, in this instance, is directed toward the outcome of mutually agreed upon long- and short-term goals (one long-term goal being the perpetuation of the network), the processes plus procedures with which to achieve the goals, proper evaluation methods to analyze progress and commitment and responsiveness that accountability will take precedence.

The Role of the Principal in the Network

To fulfill the premise of an effective accountability network, a principal must initiate a good school concept by making it clear that total and effective participation by the whole network is the top priority. The inter-relationship of the principal with the other segments of the network is imperative for each segment to fulfill respective roles. The principal, therefore, must be practical and active to properly facilitate the positive interaction with the other segments of the network. It is through the active role of the principal that each segment of the accountability network can satisfy the necessary commitment toward the ideal outcomes for student achievement.

The principal is in the best position to effectively reach each segment of the network and, through systematic communication, exhibit a visionary outlook which will lead to continual improvement of the school's program. By emphasizing the notion of joint accountability, each segment would work in a combined effort to identify specific community and student needs. An accountability advisory committee, chaired by the principal, would be composed of building, department, and central office representatives from within the school district, corporate professionals outside the field of education, non-professional people (parental and non-parental participants from associations such as parent/teacher organizations, citizen advisory groups, etc.), state representatives or proxy, university professors representing teacher and administrative preparation departments, student council representatives, class presidents, and/or representatives of all minority groups.

The function of this accountability advisory group would be to establish an effective means of communication to the populace and to initiate an effective method of feedback for information concerning the educational operation. The principal, by serving as chair can lead the rationale in determining the difference in "real needs" as opposed to "perceived needs."

When this occurs, the principal can develop meaningful purposes, goals, and objectives in terms of a system-wide, functional plan for providing instruction, resources, and active community participation to meet students' real needs. The enhanced role of the principal involves:

- **parents** by establishing an effectual parent/teacher organization and by arranging efficient lines of communication with the home environment while stressing active participation (home/school partnership) in the decision-making process;
- **corporate leaders** by conducting periodic meetings to identify the needs of the industrial sector, incorporating a curriculum design to meet those needs, and incorporating a school/business partnership—these partnerships are extremely beneficial monetarily and educationally;
- **governmental constituents** by attending, lobbying, and actively participating in meetings that affect the future of the school's operation and by including local and state delegates in the accountability network;
- **university personnel** by working cooperatively to ensure that potential teachers and administrators be given the best training environment necessary for effective exposure to "real-world" duties and by giving feedback to university administration concerning needed liens of study;

- **district-level administrators** by establishing excellent cooperation and working relationships while promoting the school focus to illicit the needed support to achieve the school goals;
- **teachers** by serving as an instructional leader and developing and maintaining a formal work structure which promotes teacher enhancement and job satisfaction, a sound, working relationship and a good climate of trust; and
- **students** by establishing a positive, effective learning climate, by promoting student achievement rather than student existence, and by making the well-being of students the fundamental value of all decision making and actions.

Accountability in education is not a new concept nor is it something pristined to experienced educators. Moreover, most everyone would agree that someone should be held accountable for the status of American education, but few individuals or groups are willing to accept such responsibility. The dilemma in this predicament is that every sociological element has a responsibility for educational success but is willing or incapable of identifying participatory roles.

The principal's purpose in this instance should be the creation of a formal network of operations and the delineation of operational parameters. The installation of an accountability advisory committee would then identify the different roles and expectations, initiate effective participation and maximize communication efforts to the masses.

Successful schools will depend not only upon the circumvention of educational malaise but also upon the collective participation and innovative approaches to school operations. Although adequate funding of school programs is important, it is not the key to educational success. Principals must communicate a tenacious belief in the cause of public education, must initiate a viable collegiality among the staff and actively solicit the support of the surrounding populace. When a principal can accomplish this, the negative aspects of our contemporary culture can be minimized while academic success can be maximized. The essence of this accountability network premise can be delineated as:

> ...a long-range effort to improve an organization's problem-solving and renewal processes, particularly through a more effective and collaborative management of organization culture—with special emphasis on the culture of formal work teams—with the assistance of a change agent or catalyst...(French & Bell, 1984, p. 14)

Even when the accountability network works perfectly, there is no guarantee that it will accomplish the mutually established goals. The scope of society is too vast and too complex to totally satisfy all sectors. However, the network offers a greater opportunity for establishing a consistent direction for advancing educational opportunity and is precisely the area where the issues of accountability become paramount.

For this ideal situation to occur, principals must enhance their management skills by periodic self-evaluations and expand their involvement in establishing a disciplined, positive environment for educational opportunity. The principal's role is becoming increasingly complex and proficiency in role expectation will demand high-tech capability. No longer can a principal be effective without a wide-ranging knowledge of the administrative and educational uses of technology (the importance of the use of technology will be discussed later in more detail).

Effective principals must simulate the learning environment and promote high expectations not only from students, but teachers, community members and local, state and national leaders as well. This undertaking is far more complex than the traditional instructional leader classification. Principals must be willing to identify and recommend individuals with excellent potential to become the principals of the future.

Why Quality Depends on Teamwork

Despite all the reform and upheaval in American education, the one thing everyone agrees on is that education is at a place and time where the rules of the game, as it used to be played, no longer work. Because of specialization of content, we have to learn to play a new game which involves utilizing a total quality management concept. Total quality management is attained by forming and maintaining high-performance teams. These self-directed, self-managed, quality improvement, employment involvement, high-involvement work teams, or whatever name is given to them, has a common purpose: To help provide the best educational opportunity for student success. To accomplish this, smart systems, empowered teachers and incredible teamwork are needed.

Once the network is established, infrastructure teams must be created to ensure proper cohesion and to carry out stipulated goals. These teams are an extension of the network and therefore are responsible for successful implementing procedures. Reasons for developing high-powered teams include:
1. **High-performing teams can respond quickly to change:** Since nothing is stable and predictable, it is imperative that educators keep abreast of changing conditions. This allows a system to respond to change rather than forced to react to it.
2. **High-performing teams can deliver higher quality educational programs which are necessary to meet the Bull's**

Eye Effect: Since the beginning of American education, quality was basically set and determined by non-educators rather than empowering educators for this process. Not only has this been wasteful in terms of money and time, but it underutilized the educational workforce. It is only now that we have determined that teams of multi-skilled workers organized around the concept of building a quality educational environment can design and implement high quality educational programs.

3. **High-performing teams can constantly monitor and improve the existing program:** The Japanese call it <u>KAIZEN</u>: The constant improvement of everything by everyone. Their attitude is basically, "If it is not perfect, improve it." If everyone does something each day to make the educational environment better, everyone reaps the benefits in terms of student attitude, employee satisfaction, etc.

4. **High-performing teams improve the motivation, satisfaction and productivity within the educational environment:** If it has not been clear by now in your experiences, it will be by the end of this manual, only motivation, confidence, and commitment will produce effective productivity. Teamwork can fulfill needs in workers which enhance these areas.

5. **High-performing teams can constantly learn, self-correct, and respond to opportunities:** Only the system which constantly trains and restrains its employees will succeed. In this fast-changing society, educators who do not upgrade their skills will quickly become obsolete and ineffective. This is especially true with technical knowledge which is critical in keeping abreast of changing educational software. As teams constantly learn and teams examine how they operate and self-correct for improvements, they can respond to any opportunity.

Characteristics of Effective Teams

Total quality management teams are a relatively new concept in education. What education is experiencing is a rapid movement toward quality teams in the guise of site-based management. A quality management team is basically a group (from 6-20 selected individuals) who is responsible for the educational process. The team meets regularly (once a week or so) to identify, analyze and solve problems. Effective teams have:

1. **A shared vision which everyone knows, which everyone has agreed to, and toward which everyone has commitment to success:** Team members understand the goals because they have

Building the Foundation

participated in setting them. Team members openly discuss the best avenues to accomplish them. Every member has a feeling of ownership and that s/he is making a difference.

2. **A climate of trust and openness:** The team concept creates an informal atmosphere where members feel comfortable. Trust is established only when fear and rejection are eliminated and members see the advantages of risk taking.
3. **Open and honest communication:** Participants feel free to express their thoughts and ideas without fear of uncontrolled criticism. Members listen to each other's ideas and offer feedback pertaining to its relevance. Conflict is a natural path, however, members self-correct themselves by use of constructive criticism.
4. **A sense of belonging:** One in Maslow's hierarchy for motivation, this area provides a climate for commitment to success. Individualism is present but the good of the team outweighs the good of individual gain. Individual pride is replaced with team pride.
5. **Diversity valued as an asset:** Members are viewed as unique with valuable skills and resources necessary to look at the whole picture. Diversity of opinions, ideas and experiences offers flexibility in analysis of decisions and offers differing views than the traditional opinions.
6. **Creativity and risk-taking:** The value of team diversity is that options which may not have been considered are now a viable part of the process. Risks are viewed as a departure from tradition and mistakes are seen as part of the learning process. Progression comes from change, but change for the sake of change is not encouraged.
7. **Ability to self-correct:** Since the team is constantly seeking different avenues for improvement, the team must be able to discern appropriate actions from inappropriate actions. Team members must analyze the scope of their operation, identify any interference to their operations, and make appropriate modifications. This on-going analysis identifies any potential problem before the problem gets out of hand.
8. **Members who are interdependent:** Members become dependent on each other's knowledge and skill. Individuals do not take action independent from group. Group action supersedes individual wants.
9. **Decision-making is made by consensus:** Decisions are made by the group only after alternatives are presented, discussed, and analyzed for merit. The final decision results from group

participation and is of high quality.
10. Participative **leadership is practiced:** A group may have a designed leader, but that individual does not dominate or does not influence group operations. Each member of the team has an equal share in the group process.

Group composition is important to ensure proper cohesion and to maximize successful outcomes. For this to materialize, group members should assume certain roles. Although the following list is somewhat extensive, group members may assume more than one role. Group make-up should include someone designated as a:

Clarifier: One who breaks things down to simplistic parts so everyone understands. This individual will make a desired outcome of the group clear and understandable.

Pacifier: One who is able to look at extremes and bring everyone back to the center to maintain focus. S/he will be able to provide a calming effect on group members and intervene when discussion is in a tense state.

Encourager: This role requires enthusiasm and needs one who is outgoing; who wants to hear what others say and praises all efforts. S/he makes everyone feel that his/her input is important and necessary to the proper functioning of the group.

Empowerer: This role can also be entitled "involver" because the function of this member is to make sure all members are participating in the process and does whatever is necessary to enable the group to be productive. S/he brings group members who are less involved into the essence of discussion.

Focuser: One who keeps the group on task and has a clear vision of the group's mission. S/he guards against the group shifting to several different subtopics which detract from the original mission.

Process Manager: This role can also be entitled "facilitator" because the main function is to remove barriers that might cause friction among the team members. S/he also increases the ease of performance for the team toward established goals.

Listener: The listener concentrates on what is being said for the purpose of clarification. Although **all** team members should assume this role, not all members do. It is imperative that someone makes it a point to carefully listen to what is being said or presented.

Correlator: This role synthesizes the various ideas contributed by team members. S/he organizes and reviews information presented by the group and makes sure the ideas are complimentary and appropriately related to the task at hand.

Questioner: This role can also be termed "the devil's advocate" because s/he is responsible for forcing the group to critically analyze decisions. This role allows the group members to analyze all sides of an issue to make sure all extenuating possibilities and outcomes are reviewed.

Recorder: This individual writes down the ideas, information, proceedings, conclusions, etc., presented by the team. S/he provides a written record of the group's transactions and processes.

Innovator: This team member offers the group alternative paths to follow and allows for ideas to flow freely. The innovator stimulates creativity within the group and offers challenging solutions.

Doer: When decisions made by the team require implementation or other information, at least one member must be willing and able to follow through with the necessary action. This individual does the leg-work for the group.

Energizer: The person(s) who assumes this role is responsible for keeping enthusiasm high in the group. S/he radiates energy to the team by being invigorating when the group is not progressing and by being enthusiastic when things are going well. This role is very important to keep momentum toward successful task completion.

Informer: This role supplies the necessary information or knowledge base. S/he possesses and shares relevant knowledge or information that will be beneficial to gain insight into the issues being discussed by the group.

Reporter: This person is responsible for disseminating and reporting the findings of the group to outside parties. It is important that the person in this role gets the right information to the right individuals.

Humorist: The person(s) keeps a positive climate by enlightening the group atmosphere and allows the group to function in a less stress-filled environment. S/he must know the limitations of this responsibility to avoid humor over-kill where humor becomes a distracter.

Mediator: Through consent of all involved parties, a mediator is selected to act in a friendly and diplomatic manner to settle differences among team members. His/her main objective is to keep conflict at a minimum and peacefully resolve areas of concern.

It is this type of team design which allows a more relaxed atmosphere and a more productive team effort. It is necessary to know that not all roles are individually assumed. If that were the case, there would be at least 17 team members in every group. Since smaller groups function more effectively, roles are combined.

Staff Development

Emerging statewide and national trends require mandatory continuing education for all staff members. But, more importantly, administrators need to devise better ways of motivating all staff members to improve and continue their education and to acknowledge staff members for their efforts in improving their skills. Where teachers accept the need and desirability of continuing their professional growth, staff development programs thrive.

To implement staff development that works, involved parties should be incorporated into the decision-making process concerning the goals and objectives, experiences, and assessment of the plan. Appropriate and meaningful staff development is accomplished through a five-step process: (a) identifying recipients of the staff development program, (b) conducting a thorough needs assessment, (c) designing a staff development which addresses proposed needs, (d) initiating program(s), and (e) conducting an extensive evaluation to determine effectiveness of program(s) and making appropriate revisions.

The first step is to identify the recipients of staff development and the extent of necessity. For example, staff development programs for non-certified personnel, certified personnel, and administrative personnel, in some cases, may be entirely different. Generic staff development programs, intended for the general populace, are usually ineffective.

Step two requires a thorough analysis of individual needs just as in any basic design plan. Before any program can be designated and implemented, the needs of the client—whether a school, an individual, or a system—must be determined. Individual schools within a school system may not always have the same set of needs. An efficacy profile will provide essential information in determining many of the needs of the certified staff. Staff development programs designed to enhance the personal and professional development of faculty, should not be confused with in-service, programs designed to provide essential information and activities to assist classroom education. Teachers are another important resource in determining specific needs since they are in the classroom daily.

After determining the needs of a school/school system, a staff development program can be effectively designed to meet those specific needs (step three). Through effective design, the principal can assist the group in developing parameters which contribute to a successful staff development experience which is flexible to modifications. The key is to allow flexibility, while avoiding rigidness.

A staff development program is most successful when participants believe that what they are exposed to is valuable; it is least successful when those involved do not think they need the information they are receiving. Participants need to feel ownership of their staff development programs, e.g., they should be involved in decision making, participate in the program itself, perform any follow-up activities, conduct the evaluation of the program, etc.

When designing a staff development program, it is important to determine which resource person(s) will be needed for the designing phase. This individual could be one of an unlimited number of individuals within the building; however, classroom teachers who are highly respected make excellent resource people. Also, community or business leaders, curriculum supervisors, and higher education faculty could also be called upon to design and deliver a staff development program.

Step four is conducting the staff development program. After identifying specific needs and designing an appropriate program, systematic and orderly implementation of the program is essential to ensure proper success. In this case, every participant should contribute as well as gain from it. Participants should be coached to listen with understanding, to be non-judgmental in acceptance, and to respond with consideration of others. These qualities reduce detrimental relationships and encourage the creative forces within each participant. They foster growth of the participants and allow members participation as equals; qualities which are learned from experience.

Evaluation, a crucial process, is step five and should not be overlooked. Every staff development program needs to contain an evaluation of both the content and the presenter(s) conducting the program. It should also determine the effectiveness of the program. The evaluation should provide the designers with valuable information concerning which area or areas of the program need to be improved and the most logical way to implement required changes.

The effectiveness of staff development programs are sometimes difficult to determine. However, Olivia (1989) identified six characteristics which are essential for staff development programs to be considered effective.

1. **In-service education should be designed so that programs are integrated into and supported by the organization within which they function.** A comprehensive plan for in-service education in the school and/or district should be drawn up and funding should be made available.
2. **In-service education programs should be designed to result in collaborative programs.** The plan should include ways to

involve all the constituencies of the school: Teachers, administrators, supervisors, non-teaching staff, students, and lay persons (utilizing the network).
3. **In-service education programs should be grounded in the needs of the participants.** The plan should be developed from an assessment of the needs and interests of the persons to be served.
4. **In-service education programs should be responsive to changing needs.** The plan should allow for changes as conditions change and a research brings forth new knowledge.
5. **In-service education programs should be accessible.** The location, the physical facilities, and the timing are all important factors to be considered in an in-service education plan.
6. **In-service education activities should be evaluated over time and be compatible with the underlying philosophy and approach of the district.** Evaluative data are needed to carry out future planning and implementation.

In essence, staff development can be reduced to a simple formula: **Job Expectation (JE) - Employee Capability (EC) = Necessary Training (NT)** This simple but accurate formula illustrates the type and amount of staff development necessary to meet job expectations. Principals and teachers need to take advantage of existing teams in identifying goals and objectives which will make a positive impact. Principals need to be extremely supportive of the teams and offer viable feedback and input whenever possible. Utilizing this approach will enhance staff development in each of the five steps and maximize the effectiveness of the programs.

Planning for Quality

Constantly changing social and economic conditions make planning a necessity to keep pace. Principals must be able to anticipate these changes and implement strategies which will ensure organizational compliance and progression. Two planning procedures have usually been practiced: long-range and strategic planning.

Long-range planning is basically a closed-system approach in which short-term plans or blueprints are developed. It usually emphasizes internal changes and inside-out planning with focus on organizational goals and objectives up to five years in the future.

Strategic planning differs from long-range planning only in vision and commitment. It can be defined as a mission and goal-finding process that is based on an examination of the environment and an appraisal of organizational strengths and weaknesses. It assumes an open-system approach whereby the organization must constantly change as the need

Building the Foundation 29

to keep pace with society changes.

Strategic planning is also an implementation process that attempts to realize a mission through effective use of resources. It is vital that a mission statement be developed for:
- the district
- individual buildings
- individual departments
- individuals

Strategic planning is basically long-term planning with a VISION. Long-term planning without VISION and COMMITMENT will cause activities to take place <u>which are not cost effective</u> and <u>which are not meaningful in the long run</u>.

Effective Planning

In today's educational situation, it becomes necessary to combine the best of long-range planning and strategic planning into one unique situation called EFFECTIVE PLANNING. Effective planning takes advantage of what long-range and strategic planning have to offer. It not only involves **VISION** of what needs to be, but also **COMMITMENT** to secure the vision. Planning is therefore <u>not</u> limited by designated parameters, but only by individual creativity.

To properly initiate effective planning, the following process is provided.

A Comprehensive Effective-Planning Process

Step 1	—Decide upon the initial focus (social, total organization, etc.)	F
Step 2	— Develop a consensus of beliefs and/or values	E
Step 3	— Identify critical areas which are absolutely crucial for success	E
Step 4	— Conduct formal environmental scan	E
Step 5	— Identify Instructional mission and major objectives (Vision)	D
Step 6	—Identify of external threats and opportunities as well as internal strengths and weaknesses	B
Step 7	—Identification analysis and selection of strategic alternatives	A
Step 8	—Develop specific strategic goals and objectives	A
Step 9	— Develop an operational plan	
Step 10	—Implementation of selected strategic planning operation	C
Step 11	—Continued environmental scanning activities and	K

strategic plan revision as necessary (Monitor and Evaluate)
*Adapted from J. J. Herman and from T. J. Handy

Regardless of the extent of planning, failure occurs. The following list contains reasons why effective planning fails.

Why Effective Planning Fails
1. Leaders of organizations many times want a "quick fix" and effective planning requires time and commitment.
2. Failure of the leader to strongly support the planning activities and be a visible participant in them—(no commitment for success).
3. Failure of the governing board to give strong official sanction to the strategic planning activities and to support them to the public and the media—(no commitment for success).
4. Reluctance to allocate the sufficient human, financial and material resources to accomplish the strategic plan once it is developed—(commitment for success).
5. Inability or lack of desire to involve ALL categories of "stakeholders" in the strategic planning process (NO COMMITMENT FOR SUCCESS).
6. Planning takes place before a vision and mission have been developed (Cart before the horse).
7. Some administrators and planners are not capable of, or do not wish to, specifying clear and measurable strategic objectives for which they can be held accountable.
8. Some planners forget to conduct scanning activities which identify trends to be dealt with during the development of the organization's strategic plan.
9. Some organizations do not know how, forget to conduct, or do not want to take the time to do a strengths, weaknesses, opportunity and threats analysis of their external and internal environment.
10. Planners sometimes do not develop sufficiently detailed action plans, or they do not clearly identify the sub-tasks to be performed, the individuals or groups to perform the sub-tasks, the stipulated measures to be utilized in evaluating the qualitative and quantitative aspects of each task.
11. The organization's leader(s) implement strategic planning by mandate without anticipating the training needs of those who will do the planning or the needs of those who are to operate the plans once they are developed.
12. Most importantly, those involved in strategic planning and operational activities are not clear-cut, identifiable-results oriented

nor are they strategic thinkers.

*Adapted from J. J. Herman

Effective Planning and Change

Effective planning involves change and change is hard to accept by some individuals. Although change is a necessary component, change for the sake of change should be avoided. To initiate change:
1. Conduct a needs assessment to identify areas of concern.
2. Identify needed change as a PROCESS not as an event.
3. Must have COMMITMENT to change.
4. Understand that the principal cannot do it alone.
5. Have a clear mission.
6. Set and define goals and objectives.
7. Decide responsibility for implementation.
8. Provide necessary resources for change.
9. Provide any inservice for participants.
10. Implement the change.
11. Monitor.
12. Evaluate.
13. Make any necessary adjustments.

The final outcome is that the principal must identify the direction needed to keep pace with changing conditions and must be able to initiate effective planning strategies. If the principal does not take the initiative, effective planning becomes nothing more than planning without substance. As the saying goes, "If you do not know where you want to go, any road will get you there."

Program Effectiveness

To begin with, principals need to understand the difference between being efficient and being effective. Efficiency is doing things right or "getting things done." Effectiveness is doing the RIGHT things right or the degree to which the common purposes of the organization are achieved. Therefore, educational program effectiveness is being both precise **and** accurate for attaining the "Bull's-Eye Effect." Our action must be precise (Figure 2) in identifying specific needs and accurate (Figure 3) in taking the appropriate action(s) to ensure fulfillment of those needs. For example, if we create a profile of what a high school graduate should be, the curriculum must be designed according to that profile to attain the "Bull's-Eye Effect." When this occurs, precision of courses and accuracy of content have been achieved. Unfortunately in administration, precision and accuracy are many times neglected in overall analyses.

32   Continuous Improvement

Figure 2. Precise But Not Accurate

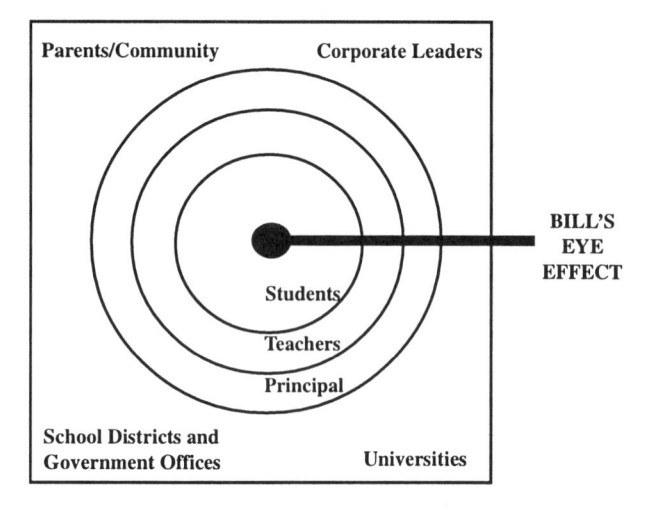

This illustration demonstrates curriculum which is very precise in its focus, but is not conducive for meeting the target set by effective planning. It is basically an out-dated curriculum; the curriculum is precise, but not accurate in reaching stated goals and objectives. Correction involves updating curriculum to match the target.

Figure 3. Accurate But Not Precise

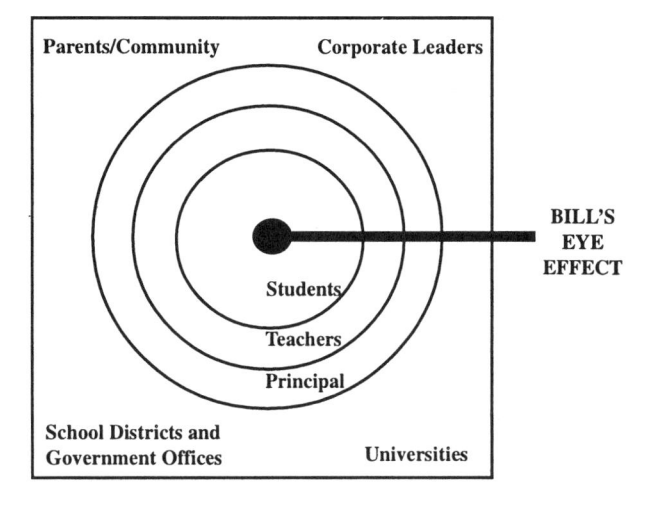

This illustration demonstrates a curriculum without focus. Courses revolve around the stated goals and objectives but do not zero-in on target. Hence, the curriculum contains many non-essential courses which do not conform to stated goals and objectives. Correction involves the elimination of courses which do not fit into the overall plan.

Unfortunately, many times principals become so involved in day-to-day operations that they fail to keep pace with changing times. This failure leads to inappropriate time allotment and ineffectual results. To make sure that the curriculum does not become outdated or too cumbersome, a periodic check of scope and sequence should be performed. Scope is the depth and breadth of the curriculum or how much material is covered and in what detail. Sequence involves the correct order of courses to ensure proper overlap of content. Examination of scope and sequence should be done at the district level, building level and classroom level to assure both precision and accuracy in attaining the Bull's Eye Effect.

Edmonds (1979) recognized, through disaggregating data, that both traditional and effective schools identify some level of expectation resembling excellence. However, traditional schools were found to possess inequity of educational achievement between low socioeconomic students and high socioeconomic students. He concluded that in traditional schools, 40 percent of low socioeconomic students exceeded the established mark for excellence (60 percent fell below the established mark) while 85 percent of high socioeconomic students exceeded the established mark for excellence (15 percent fell below the established mark).

Edmonds (1979) further defined quality as a simple sense of fairness in the distribution of the primary goods and services that characterized our social order and that these current inequities in American education are derived mainly from our failure to educate the children of the poor. It is important to keep in mind that the purpose of quality is to efficiently use the existing resources. To accomplish this, specific influences of the school and outside forces such as student backgrounds and community inputs must be identified (Montero-Sieburth, 1988).

In order to aid educators in altering their essentially negative attitudes and behaviors regarding equity, these attitudes and behaviors must be identified and then removed or their influence negated in some way. Equity in education is an important factor, but equity alone will not ensure an effective school. However, in effective schools, 95 percent of both low and high socioeconomic students exceeded the established mark of excellence. This, he concluded, if held for a period of three years, was the true measure of an effective school (Figure 4).

Figure 4. Measure for Equity in Effective Schools

Traditional Schools		Effective Schools	
Low Socio-Economic	High Socio-Economic	Low Socio-Economic	High Socio-Economic
40%	85%	95%	95%
Minimum Level of Organizational Expectation		Minimum Level of Organizational Expectation	
60%	15%	5%	5%

Conclusion

Because quality is a perception, it becomes imperative that an operational definition be identified as a basis for measurement. Without such a definition, quality of operation will remain multi-dimensional, having different meanings and interpretations in different educational settings. What can be provided are some guidelines which will enhance the essence of the "Total Quality Management" movement and which will provide the integration of the accountability network into the "Total Quality Management" process (Kaufman & Hirumi, 1992).

References

Berkeley, G. E. (1978). The craft of public administration. Boston: Allyn & Bacon.

Edmonds, R. (1979). Effective schools for the urban poor. Educational Leadership, 37 (1), 15-18, 20-24.

French, W. L., & Bell, C. H. (1984). Organization development: Behavioral science interventions for organization improvement (3rd ed.). Englewood Cliffs, NJ: Prentice Hall.

Handy, T. J. (1990). The necessity of environmental scanning prior to long-range planning activities at higher education levels. Educational Planning, 8 (3), 23-30.

Herman, J. J. (1990). Strategic planning: Reasons for failed attempts. Educational Planning, 8 (3), 36-40.

Kaufman, R., & Hirumi, A. (1992). Ten steps to 'TQM Plus'. Educational Leadership, 50 (3), 33-34.

Montero-Sieburth, M. (1988). Understanding the tensions between equity and quality of secondary schooling. Journal of Education, 170, 122-131.

Olivia, P. F. (1989). Supervision of today's schools. Longman Publishing Company.

Chapter 3

TOTAL QUALITY MANAGEMENT AND EDUCATION: "... AND IF YOU CAN'T COME, SEND NOBODY"

W. David Shirley
Vice-President, Tri-County Technical College, Pendleton, SC

Decade of Quality

Perhaps the past decade can be described as the decade of quality. Businesses, industries, and even educational institutions have emphasized quality, continuous improvement, empowerment, evaluating processes, and meeting or exceeding customer needs. According to Seymour (1992), quality includes these concepts, plus much more. Quality is everyone's job. It is leadership, human resource development, fear reduction, recognition and reward, teamwork, measurement, and systematic problem-solving. It is ingrained in the operational system, whatever that system might be.

Following the lead of Japan, which emerged from a state of economic disaster after World War II to its present world class status, such American companies as IBM, Westinghouse, Xerox, and many others began to use the principles of Total Quality Management (TQM) in the early 1980s (Bonstingl, 1992a). Another successful practitioner was Ford Motor Company. Shook (1990) details the transformation of this giant in the automotive industry, from its well-publicized problems in 1978 involving the safety of its top-selling subcompact, the Pinto, to having, from 1986 to 1990, a Ford product selected as:

> Motor Trend Car of the year for an unprecedented four out of five years... [and the number one ranking in 1990] by Fortune magazine

as the most admired U.S. company in the motor vehicles and parts industry. (p. 250)

This emphasis on quality in business and industry has resulted in an "unprecedented public demand for higher quality in colleges and universities" (Chaffee & Sherr, 1992, p. 1). Interest has grown in such things as graduation rates, retention rates of students, placement data on graduates, etc. Outcomes assessment and institutional effectiveness have become buzz words. Coupled with decreased funding, the increased concern for quality presents major challenges for postsecondary education.

Proof of these demands for quality is plentiful. Lively (1992) discusses how several state legislatures are studying or have already placed accountability requirements on colleges and universities. Texas is considering performance-based financing. Arizona is examining the teaching and work loads of faculty. Kentucky and Florida have passed laws requiring efficiency reports on utilization of classrooms and workloads of faculty. Mercer (1993) says that "'report cards' that grade the performance of public colleges are gaining grounds in some states" (p. A39). The purpose of New Mexico's House Bill 4:

is to create a report card for [that state's] educational institutions and to provide information to the citizens of the state on the significant indicators of performance of. . . schools. (p. 1)

Tennessee has implemented a program that allocates "a portion of state funds for higher education on the basis of performance criteria" (Banta, 1988, p. 81). The South Carolina Commission on Higher Education (CHE) (1989) reports that South Carolina, in Section 59-104-650 (B) (1) of its "Cutting Edge" legislation (1988), requires:

each institution of higher learning [to be] responsible for maintaining a system to measure institutional effectiveness in accord with provisions, procedures, and requirements developed by the [CHE]. (Appendix III, p. 10)

The states are not the only ones emphasizing quality in higher education. Two agencies of the federal government have started the process of creating a national test that would assess the analytical skills developed by college students (Zook, 1993). In addition, several regional accrediting agencies have joined the effort of ensuring quality.

The Southern Association of Colleges and Schools (SACS) initiated the movement in 1985-86 when it adopted a new criterion on institutional effectiveness as part of its effort to link outcomes assessment to the process of accreditation. (Bogue & Saunders, 1992, p. 40)

SACS's action was quickly followed by four other regional accrediting agencies.

To meet the challenges of these demands for quality requires a change in philosophy of those in traditional positions of leadership in higher education. Many are advocating that this change should result in increased use of principles of TQM.

History of TQM

TQM traces its beginnings to the 1930s when W. Edwards Deming recognized:

> that if workers could be educated and empowered to manage their own work processes, the quality of their output would improve and the costly and ineffective end-of-line inspection process could be curtailed or eliminated. (Bonstingl, 1992b, p. 9)

Modifying the teachings of Walter A. Shewhart, a statistician from Bell Laboratories, Deming utilized a four-step process, the Plan-Do-Study-Act Cycle (originally and still often known as the Plan-Do-Check-Act Cycle), to ensure quality production. This cycle calls for constant evaluation and revision of processes, as needed.

During World War II, Deming helped the U.S. government apply his philosophy of quality production, resulting in equipment and machinery superior to that of the Japanese. After the war, however, because of heavy demand for goods and services, American industries began to sacrifice quality for higher productivity (Bonstingl, 1992b).

In 1950 the Union of Japanese Science and Engineering Society (JUSE), a group of Japanese scientists that had been assembled for the war effort and had stayed together for the purpose of reconstructing Japan, invited Deming to help them. They had studied Shewhart's <u>Economic control of quality of manufactured product</u> and recognized the potential applications for Shewhart's methods. That summer Deming taught over 400 Japanese engineers from Shewhart's 1939 book, <u>Statistical method from the viewpoint of quality control</u>. Sessions with top management followed, as did additional visits over the years. In addition, Joseph M. Juran, who had also worked at Bell Laboratories, first visited Japan in 1954, adding to what Deming taught (Deming, 1986). Those that learned from Deming and Juran passed on their knowledge to others. The Japanese practiced what they were taught, and the results speak for themselves: the Japanese are considered world leaders in quality and productivity.

After its initial use in America's war effort, Deming's "teachings were largely unknown or ignored in this country" (Bonstingl, 1992a, p. 68) for many years. Seymour (1992), Bonstingl (1992a) and Chaffee and Sherr (1992) credit the June 24, 1980 NBC documentary "If Japan Can... Why Can't We?" with reviving American businesses' and industries' interest in quality. In that television broadcast, Deming "explained that by increasing quality, a company reduced scrap and rework, thereby decreasing costs and increasing productivity" (Seymour, 1992, p. 11). Deming also said that there was a system that could cause quality to happen.

The 14 Points and Seven Deadly Diseases
In an organization in which each employee knows what to do and does his/her best, the results will still be lacking. The reason is because "there is no substitute for teamwork and good leaders of teams to bring consistency of effort, along with knowledge" (Deming, 1986, p. 19).

With this in mind, Deming developed a set of principles, known as the 14 points for management, which he believes will improve quality, productivity, and competitive position. These 14 points emphasize constancy of purpose, building quality into one's product, constantly improving the system, training, leadership, teamwork, improvement, and more. He stresses long-term relationships built on loyalty and trust. All employees must participate in the planning process, make suggestions, and monitor performance. He advocates determining who one's external and internal customers are and then focusing on customer satisfaction.

In addition to the 14 points, Deming says that there are seven deadly diseases and many obstacles that hinder the transformation of management. Among the diseases are emphasis on short-term profits, performance ratings, and job-hopping. Two of the diseases, according to Deming, only apply to American industry, and are beyond the scope of his discussions. These two diseases are excessive medical costs and the excessive costs of liability. The numerous obstacles include desire for instant solutions and obsolescence in schools (Deming, 1986).

Tools for TQM
Of paramount importance to TQM is the concept of continuous improvement. Improvements are made by group processes, data analysis, and the use of such statistical tools as flow charts, fishbone diagrams, scatter diagrams, control charts, Pareto charts, and the Plan-Do-Study-Act Cycle. Both Brassard (1985) and Bostingl (1992b) provide

information on the use of these and other tools of TQM. The purpose of these tools is to enable practitioners to "better perceive, collect, analyze, and understand relevant data" (Bonstingl, 1992b, p. 51). By doing this, leaders can determine when performance falls outside the limits of variation of the system and can take corrective action, perhaps in the form of providing more training or placing the employee in a job appropriate to his skills.

TQM in Postsecondary Education

TQM has implications not only for business and industry, but for education as well. Surveys by Oregon State University (Coate, 1990a; Coate, 1992) and by Seymour and Collett (1991) indicate that TQM is taught in the classroom and used somewhat on the administrative and service side of postsecondary education, but its use is not as widespread on the academic side.

The experiences of implementing TQM at two particular colleges, Oregon State University (OSU) and Delaware County Community College (DCCC), are somewhat similar. Each began with a commitment from the president to improve quality, and teams were established to implement change. Because of expected faculty resistance, initial efforts were on the service side.

OSU started with areas that reported to the vice-president for finance and administration. These included the physical plant, printing, budgets and planning, computing services, business affairs, public safety, the radiation center, and human resources (Coate, 1990a).

> DCCC focused on problems in the following areas: telephone service in the admissions office, academic computing, assignment of students to curricula, staff parking, student employment, photocopying, and facilities usage. (DeCosmo, Parker, & Heverly, 1991, p. 15)

Both schools used the tools of TQM. OSU used surveys and analyzed the data using Pareto diagrams, a special form of vertical bar graph to help determine the order in which to solve problems. They used a flow chart to analyze key processes. They used cause and effect fishbone diagrams to explore barriers to improvement. While working on what was termed the Phone Project, a DCCC team used Deming's Plan-Do-Study-Act (PDSA) improvement process. They also used fishbone diagrams and flow charts to help them reduce the number of lost or abandoned phone calls to the college's admissions office.

Each college stressed the fact that solutions don't come overnight.

It takes time and commitment. Each also expressed confidence in the results of TQM. Evidence of this is found in a quote from an evaluation survey, " 'Total Quality Management seems to be OSU's answer!'" (Coate, 1992, p. 43).

The executive staff at DCCC is convinced that TQM is worth every effort [they] have made. The college is on the leading edge of a management revolution designed to provide higher quality to keep the United States competitive. Success in implementing TQM will allow DCCC to continue to meet the needs of its stakeholders well into the next century (DeCosmo, Parker, & Heverly, 1991, p. 22).

Assessment of TQM

As external demands for quality in higher education became prevalent in the 1980s, the early leaders of the outcomes assessment movement determined:

> that assessment should serve two purposes: Assessment should show that colleges and universities are achieving their intended outputs (the accountability function), and it should provide information that permits faculty and administrators to improve what they do (the improvement function). (Chaffee and Sherr, 1992, 83-84)

The first emphasis of assessment was accountability, which then gave way to the idea of using the results of assessment to plan for change. The changes, therefore, were based on assessments made at the end of the process. "TQM offers an alternative, more effective approach: Ensure quality at every step in the process" (Chaffee and Sherr, 1992, p. 84).

One should not, however, have the mistaken opinion that TQM is not concerned with the end results. It definitely is, but for TQM proponents, outcomes assessment is only part of determining quality. "In the TQM approach, outcomes assessment is conducted for the purpose of refining, managing, and measuring work processes so that customer needs can be met" (Bragg, 1992, p. 34). Therefore, the intent of applying TQM in higher education is to ensure positive student outcomes by improving the processes of education.

Based on the above, it would seem that TQM is more comprehensive than outcomes assessment or performance assessment, for TQM evaluates processes to effect improvement, not simply to ensure accountability. When one applies the principles of TQM and discovers that the outcomes indicators are positive, that signifies the effectiveness of the entire system (Bragg, 1992).

Other Successes of TQM in Education

Many colleges and universities have reported successful implementation of TQM. The following are but a few examples:

1. A DCCC parking team gathered data on parking patterns and habits. This "resulted in $10,000 of modifications on signs and current staff lot" (Stass, 1992, p. 1), and eliminated the need to build a $200,000 parking lot.

2. "Several secretaries have mentioned they now have pride in their work since they are trusted and empowered to act on items that in the past were considered off-limits" (Cornesky, et al., 1990, p. 39).

3. A Sanford University cross-functional energy conservation team conducted duties to identify energy usage in every classroom and an auditorium in a building. A recommendation to use lights only when classrooms were occupied resulted in a projected electrical annual cost savings of over $62,475 (Nobel, 1991).

4. A business affairs team used a flow chart to discover some causes of delays in the grant and contract process. "Eliminating one outside signature loop reduced average processing days for Ag Research Foundation contracts from 12.7 days to 0.3 days" (Coate, 1990b, p. 13).

5. Teams at Fox Valley Technical College were given the task of cutting $1.2-million from the college's $38 million operational budget. Using the TQM tools, the teams developed and carried out "plans without laying off or eliminating any programs" (Mangan, 1991, p. A26).

Pursuing Quality in the Classroom Through TQM

"Although the perceived 'path of greatest resistance' [to TQM] comes from the academic side of the educational house" (Seymour & Collett, 1991, p. 3), there is an increasing number of examples of successful utilization of TQM in the classroom. A brief description of some of these follows:

> After TQM opened communication between students and faculty, several faculty began to experiment with different teaching methods, such as teleclasses, video courses, team projects, case studies, inquiry methods and discussion, rather than using the typical lecture method. (Cornesky, et al., 1990, p. 38)

Ord (1993) tells of an introductory statistics course that is disliked by both professors and students in the M.B.A. program at The Pennsylvania State University. After being assigned to teach the course, he, in an effort to improve the course for the students and for him, decided to apply TQM methodology. At the end of each class he had students respond to three questions: What was the main message of today's class? What did you learn? What did you understand (p. 38)?

The first two questions required each student to review the day's class. The third one helped identify potential problems. Responses were analyzed with the aid of a Pareto chart and were reviewed in the next class. A mid-semester review by the students resulted in positive changes to the class, and end-of-the-semester evaluations over the past three years indicate that the quality of the course and the quality for the instructor have increased.

The improvement, however, did not stop here. Students' suggestions "will impact the major restructuring of our M.B.A. program that is being implemented" (p. 39).

Sokol (1993) discusses the efforts of "increasing the amount of time students spend studying outside of [physics] class" (p. 41). Strategies included assigning more challenging homework assignments that were collected and graded. Because 150 students were enrolled in the class, two home-work problems were randomly selected for detailed grading. Constructive criticism was given to the students. To reward students for the extra effort put forth, the homework assignments accounted for 50 percent of the final grade; grading on the curve was abandoned "to discharge the collective laziness phenomenon" (p. 42).

The effectiveness of the changes were evaluated by applying the Plan-Do-Study-Act Cycle and by using information surveys at mid-semester. Survey results revealed that students were spending nine hours per week studying outside of class, a significant increase, and exam grades improved. Over 60% of the students preferred the emphasis on homework over do-or-die exams. Even though almost 40% of the students did not like the new format, one student's negative remarks were taken as evidence that the professors had achieved their goals: "This is terrible! It's like having a take-home exam every week. I would prefer to just cram for exams and foster about it the rest of the time" (p. 42).

Baur (1993) relates the problems of Sanford University's nursing program and the efforts of the faculty to revitalize it. The initial indicator of trouble was a "sudden and unexpected, dramatic drop in graduates' success rate on the nationally standardized licensing examination for registered nurses (NCLEX-RN)" (p. 45). Continued quality assessment resulted in changes in staffing, revised job descriptions, and the resumption of ongoing academic advisement. Success rates on the nationally standardized licensing examination for registered nurses (NCLEX-RN) rose to the desired level. Enrollment doubled, attrition declined, and accreditation reviews were nearly flawless. Participants agreed that "faculty, staff, and student involvement and a commitment to the quality assessment process are responsible for this transformation" (p. 47).

Rogers (1993) tells of the creation of the University of Montevallo's new general education program, which coincided with involvement in outcomes assessment. Although some departments were already voluntarily implementing assessment activities, there was no systematic approach. In many cases, the results were not being used to bring about change, nor was there documentation of the few changes that were made. To remedy the selection, "a task force recommended an evaluation process based on the Southern Association for Colleges and Schools' guidelines and on TQM principles" (p. 1). Plans also were made to link a classroom assessment model to TQM.

A Delaware County Community College nursing team evaluated its process for teaching the administration of medications.

> Based on results of survey, decision was made to initiate changes . . . Immediate and long-term follow-up of students in study have shown a significant positive difference in the pilot group's competence and confidence in administering medications to patients. (Stass, 1992, p. 3)

Cross (1993) describes how frequent assessment of students maximizes learning. This involves:

> collecting data from students periodically throughout the term or semester and then using that information to modify teaching, constantly experimenting to see how teachers can be more effective in maximizing learning. (p. 16)

She sees this as TQM at work in the classroom.

These few examples should suggest that TQM can be successfully applied in the classroom. To emphasize this belief, Santovec (1993) says that Peter Loehr, professor of educational administration at Western Illinois University, is:

> convinced that the classroom is an ideal place for applying Deming's principles. Why? 'Administrators and board members change. . . Stability in education . . . [comes] from faculty, from quality teaching and learning in the classroom. (p. 1)

Deming's first point of constancy of purpose, when applied to the classroom, relates to the improvement of products and services, the improvement and experimentation with instructional content and techniques, and self-improvement in learning approaches and techniques.

The Importance of Leadership to TQM

Deming's (1986) emphasis that leadership is essential to the successful implementation of TQM is evident in his 14 points. Point seven succinctly says to institute leadership. Points 11a and 11b say to substitute leadership for work quotas and management by objectives. Point 12 refers to the responsibility of supervisors. "Actually, most of [his] book [*Out of the Crisis*] is involved with leadership. Nearly every page . . . states a principle of good leadership. . . or shows an example of good or bad leadership" (p. 248). Perhaps, however, Deming's most empathic acknowledgment of the importance of leadership is seen in a quote from a letter sent by the chief executive officer of the Nashua Corporation to another company's vice-president who had requested to visit Nashua to study their improvement process: ". . . and if you can't come, send nobody" (p. 21).

Documentation of the need for leadership is in virtually every book and article on TQM. "The leadership of an organization must, by word and deed, convey the message that customer satisfaction, through a process of continually improving quality, is the responsibility of every member of the organization" (Seymour & Collett, 1991, p. 1). Leadership, therefore, cannot just give lip service. Words backed up by actions are essential. "The CEO needs to talk the talk—and walk the walk" (LeTarte, 1993, p. 18).

Ewell (1992) recounts the experiences of a group of outcomes assessment coordinators from six public colleges and universities in Tennessee and a private university in Alabama; experiences that were discussed at the end of a three-year Fund for the Improvement of Postsecondary Education (FIPSE) grant. From the perspective of the participants:

> some clear roles for leaders seems apparent, including articulation of the vision, consistent reward and recognition of the TQM process, and active modeling of core values, such as customer focus, valuing people, and use of information. (p. 5)

LeTarte (1993), former president of Jackson Community College, Michigan, discusses the importance of executive leadership in implementing TQM. He describes his personal reluctance to change his old habits and ideas in favor of the principles and concepts of TQM. This change requires:

> a fundamental shift about management, about the way things work, and about life. . . One must be prepared to drop old ideas and

understandings, question old assumptions, and open ourselves to very different ways of thinking. (p. 18)

Executive leadership is not enough, however. According to Coate (1992a):

> TQM requires strong leadership at all levels. Inspiring people to do things differently takes leaders who can communicate what needs to be done and why. It takes leaders who have a clear goal or vision, can impart that vision to others, and then demonstrate through action how to make the vision a reality. Most of all, TQM requires leadership that empowers people to work toward achieving their shared vision. (p. 90)

The significance of leadership is recognized in the criteria for the U.S. Department of Commerce's "Malcolm Baldridge National Quality Award [which is] authorized by Congress and privately funded to recognize the nation's leading practitioners of TQM since 1989" (Chaffee & Sherr, 1992, p. 105). Leadership is the first criterion listed, and it specifically is worth almost 10 percent of the possible points that can be accrued. This criterion requires leaders to be personally involved and visible in the organization's quest for quality. In reality, however, leadership is a major component of almost all seven criteria.

A close examination of these criteria also reminds one of Maxcy's (1991) discussion of the transactional nature of empowerment and of the concept that "leaders should be trying to put themselves out of business by transferring democratic social control of the group to the group intelligence as soon and as smoothly as possible" (p. 164). This analysis is based on the fact that the Baldridge criteria accentuate developing and managing human resources (worth 150 or 1000 possible points) and making commitments to both internal and external customers in terms of heeding their suggestions for improvement and of striving to satisfy these customers (worth 300 or 1000 possible points). Empowered employees at each level working together in an organization characterized by good leadership can achieve constancy of purpose for the improvement of products and services, Deming's first point.

Leadership Versus Management

Because of this emphasis of leadership in Total Quality Management, it is important to differentiate between leadership and management. Even though these concepts are sometimes used interchangeably, Duttweiler and Hord (1987) say that "a clear distinction has been made by many researchers" (p. 63). They quote Ubben and

Hughes as saying that "management is 'composed of those activities concerned with procuring, coordinating, and deploying material and the personnel needed to accomplish the goals of the organization'" (p. 63). They all cite Burns' distinction "between managers, as transactors, and leaders, as transformers. Kouzes and Posner (1987) say that the difference comes from the root origins of the words. The word manage traces its roots to a word meaning hand, while the origin of lead is from a word meaning to go. Thus, management implies handling things, and leadership implies going places. Additionally, "managers... get other people to do, but leaders get other people to want to do" (Kouzes & Posner, 1987, p. 27). Cornesky (1992) quotes Covey as saying that "management is about the bottom-line focus... [while] leadership 'deals with the top line' and entails asking the questions about philosophy" (p. 8). Cornesky (1992) goes on to say that "the Forum Corporation found that successful quality leaders: live in strategy... communicate the vision... believe the people. .. capitalize on teamwork [and] stay the course" (p. 8). Managers without leadership qualities, he says, talk too much and don't listen very often. They try to control people considered to be subordinates, and are often perceived as micro-managers.

Opposing View and Barriers

Not everyone sees TQM as the savior of American business, industry, and education. Albrecht (1992) tells how Florida Power & Light, a recipient of the Japanese Deming Prize, dismantled its TQM program. Brandt (1992) cites Peters' research that shows "that 80 percent of TQM programs in the private sector produce no tangible benefits" (p. 3).

> Additionally, the U.S. Federal Quality Institute has backed off from endorsing the TQM approach, and now recommends that Federal agencies develop their own unique approaches and philosophies for quality improvement. The examiners for the Baldridge Award now look for evidence of customer focus and effective leadership, not the slavish applications of TQM methods. The U.S. Navy has distanced itself from the doctrinaire TQM school by calling its effort 'Total Quality Leadership.' More and more businesses are abandoning the term 'TQM' because of its negative implications and mindless hyper-control and dehumanization, and are moving to more generic terms such as 'total quality'. (Albrecht, 1992, p. 188)

Kohn (1993a), a self-proclaimed TQM enthusiast in the business context, objects to using its principles in education, stating "that a marketplace model, even correctly applied, does not belong in the classroom" (p. 58). Moreover, he says that literature on TQM in education does not include fundamental issues about learning or curriculum. He also cites "the evidence suggesting that excessive emphasis on students' performance can undermine their creative thinking and interest in learning" (1993b, p. 67).

Coate (1992) identified seven barriers that Oregon State University had to overcome. These are:

1. Skepticism: It's only a Fad" (p. 37).
2. Time" (p. 37). It was hard to find time to carry out team assignments between meetings.
3. "Language... Faculty members especially were suspicious of jargon-laden language" (p. 38).
4. "Middle management" (p. 39). Most mid-level managers were unfamiliar with using teamwork to solve problems.
5. "University governance... Especially on the academic side, universities are not hierarchical institutions. Usually, they run more like committees" (p. 39).
6. "Dysfunctional units... Most units in a university fall somewhere along a continuum between the functional and dysfunctional, and some are definitely struggling" (p. 40). TQM is best applied in a functional environment, "where interpersonal relationships are harmonious and people are clearly focused on the work process (p. 40).
7. "Attitude" (p. 31).
    a. "Looking for the big fix" (p. 31).
    b. "Institutional arrogance" (p. 31).
    c. "Suspicion" (pg. 31).
    d. "Unwillingness to change" (p. 31).

Another criticism levied at TQM is that it "disregards strategic thinking" (Pedersen, 1992, p. B4). However,

> Deming's first 'deadly disease' is the lack of purpose in organizations and his first principle of quality is 'to create a constancy of purpose'...[which] is similar to strategic thinking or strategic vision (Johnson, 1992, p. B8).

In addition, a component of TQM known as "Breakthrough Planning is an evolution of strategic planning which adds value statements, reminding us that 'how we got here' is just as important as where we are going" (Coate, 1990c, p. 6).

Common to most educational institutions is resistance by the faculty to adopting TQM's principles. "Faculty know what students need, not the other way around" (Coate, 1990c, p. 12). Some take the view that "neither is the student a 'customer'" (Pedersen, 1992, p. B4). That is why most colleges begin applying TQM on the service side. Additionally, most efforts to involve the faculty with TQM begin with teaching it in the classroom, not utilizing it to improve quality.

A recent chance meeting with a professor from a university whose administration claims to utilize principles of TQM provides an example of the barriers to its use. Noticing a book on TQM in education, he said, "They think TQM is happening here, but it's not. The faculty won't buy it. The faculty approach is, 'I've been doing it this way for years, and I'm not going to change.' That is especially true for those with tenure. TQM just won't work here."

An employee at one institution reported an incident that occurred at the first meeting of a cross-functional team concerned with instructional affairs. When setting the schedule of meetings for the academic year, faculty members of the team insisted on a particular day and time, blatantly disregarding the protests of student and Student Services members that they would be able to attend if the schedule were set as indicated. The faculty held firm, and the other members could not participate, nor were they replaced. Whether the demands of the faculty members resulted from a point of personal convenience or from a disinclination to receive input on instructional affairs from non-faculty is open to interpretation. Whatever the reason, a valuable resource was lost to the committee.

Another barrier are leaders themselves. LeTarte (1993) reports that although he shifted to a positive viewpoint of the benefits of TQM, there are still some concepts of it for which he is not yet ready. He does not reject them; he just is not prepared to use them now. Brandt (1992) says that Peters' "disappointing finding suggests that leaders of many of the organizations never got the message. They weren't prepared to change their basic attitudes" (p. 3). Liebmann (1993) tells of a TQM effort that failed at the University of Pittsburgh because "support from leadership was strong verbally but weak in actions. Leaders made careless remarks that eroded the trust and commitment that had taken months to engender" (p. 120). All too often, "discrepancies [exist] between what leaders say they do and what others see them as doing" (Birnbaum, 1992, p. 54).

Implications

Those colleges and universities that have been successful in the quest for continuous improvement have had strong support from top leadership. Without it, the quest is doomed to fail. A previously-cited failure from the service sector, that of Florida Power & Light, resulted, according to Matthews & Katel (1992), from a change in leadership. The new chief executive officer "eliminated most TQM jobs because 'he wasn't too sure about this quality stuff' allowing him to trim personnel" (p. 49).

Proponents of TQM consistently say that it takes five to ten years to implement it. Graba (1993) says that "many of the private organizations that have applied for the Baldrige award report they needed several years of work before they could become serious applicants" (p. 1). We, however, are a society that demands instant gratification. The dramatic rise in sales and use of fax machines, car phones, and similar devices is an example of, among other things, a aversion to waiting. "In Japan, by contrast, managers enjoy easy relations with labor and a government more concerned with a stable economy and long-term growth" (Matthews & Katel, 1992, p. 49). Indeed, the Japanese initiated their efforts in the early 1950s, and it took twenty to thirty years to produce such dramatic results; so, there are no short cuts.

> Raising the quality of our services through continuous process improvement takes study and time—a great deal of time...There is no magic wand that can create such a process in an instance; patience is required. (Sherr & Lozier, 1991, pp. 6-7)

As for TQM being a business concept not applicable to education, Schmoker and Wilson (1993) say there is a distinction "between <u>adopting</u> W. Edwards Deming's methods—which would be foolish for schools— and intelligently <u>adapting</u> them" (p. 62). Furthermore, even Deming lists education among examples of many service organizations that can benefit from the applications of quality principles.

Many barriers to TQM have been discussed: it is a fad, statistical analysis tools are hard to understand, it takes too long to implement, faculty resistance is strong, it lacks strategic planning, etc. In addition, "higher education organizations are inherently decentralized, especially in the academic administration area" (Winter, 1991, p. 58). Also, some fear that a change in the chief executive officer may mean a change in philosophy. Still, it appears that significant accomplishments can be achieved through TQM, for with proper leadership, these barriers can be overcome. Coate (1992) offers proof of this by listing several examples of successful implementation of TQM, despite the seven barriers he discussed.

Additionally, after completing their work, the aforementioned assessment coordinators participating in the FIPSE grant project identified 68 distinct barriers that they had encountered. They had, however, developed 31 strategies to assist them in overcoming the barriers (Ewell,

1992).

> To succeed, total quality requires the involvement of an organization's leadership. Without an involved leadership, everyone is not involved in whole systems improvement... [Also,] personal change is a fundamental building block of total quality. Everyone in a total quality organization must be open to personal change. (Savage, 1992, p. 195, 197)

This "everyone" includes administrators, faculty, staff, at all levels, trustees, current students, and alumni. For continuous improvement to occur, all must play an active role.

Perhaps it is fitting to have some last words from Deming: "The aim of leadership should be to improve the performance of man and machine, to improve quality, to increase output, and simultaneously to bring pride of workmanship to people" (1986, p. 248).

Conclusion

Perhaps one of the strengths of TQM is also its greatest barrier. Successful implementation of TQM in any organization requires total commitment at all levels. But one wonders how this commitment is created. Top leadership must totally believe in the concept, but top leadership alone cannot simply decide that TQM is the route to take and then suddenly announce a change to TQM. That violates the very principle of TQM. The proper foundation must be laid to reach consensus from all levels. This can be a long, slow process. Likewise, faculty and/or staff can implement TQM principles within their own areas, but if other areas and top leadership do not embrace it, its development will be limited. The solution may be to have a few successes in TQM in some mid-level of the organization. These few can lead to a few more, thereby building confidence in TQM and producing additional applications. Successful implementation of TQM throughout the organization, therefore, becomes an evolution, not a revolution.

Implementing TQM in higher education is a relatively new concept. Indeed, it is difficult to find a college or university that has applied its principles for over five years. Most publications regarding TQM in higher education are less than three years old. Therefore, it is too early to either condemn or to give exultant praise to its applications in academia.

There is, however, evidence that emphasis on quality and continuous improvement can produce positive results. The philosophy may not be called Total Quality Management; it may be called Total Quality Excellence, Total Quality Education, Excellence in Education,

Continuous Quality Improvement, or various other things by those who do not want to be managed or by those averse to having education linked to something from the world of business and industry. Regardless of the name, the successes are still there.

References

Albrecht, K. (1992). Perspective: No eulogies for TQM. Total Quality Management Magazine, 2 (4), 188-190.

Banta, T. W. (1988). Assessment as an instrument of state funding policy. In T. W. Banta (Ed.), Implementing outcomes assessment: Promise and perils. New Directions for Institutional Research, No. 59. San Francisco: Jossey-Bass.

Baur, M. K. (1993). Bringing a nursing program back to life. In D. J. Teeter & G. G. Lozier (Eds.), Pursuit of quality in higher education: Case studies in total quality management. New Directions for Institutional Research, No. 78. San Francisco: Jossey-Bass.

Birnbaum, R. (1992). How academic leadership works: Understanding success and failure in the college presidency. San Francisco: Jossey-Bass.

Bogue, E. G., & Saunders, R. L. (1992). The evidence for quality. San Francisco: Jossey Bass.

Bonstingl, J. J. (1992a). Total quality classroom. Educational Leadership, 49 (6), 66-70.

Bonstingl, J. J. (1992b). Schools of quality: An introduction to Total Quality Management in education. Alexandria, VA: Association for Supervision and Curriculum Development.

Bragg, D. D. (Ed.). (1992). Alternative approaches to outcomes assessment for postsecondary education. Berkeley, CA: University of California, Berkeley, National Center for Research in Vocational Education. (ERIC Document Reproduction Service No. ED 352 553)

Brandt, R. (1992). Overview: Are we committed to quality? Educational Leadership, 50 (3), 3.

Chaffee, E. E., & Sherr, L. A. (1992). Quality: Transforming postsecondary education. ASHE-ERIC Higher Education Report No. 3. Washington, DC: The George Washington University, School of Education and Human Development.

Coate, L. E. (1990a). TQM at Oregon State University. Journal for Quality and Participation, 13 (6), 90-91.

Coate, L. E. (1990b). An analysis of Oregon State University's total management pilot program. Eugene: Oregon State University.

Coate, L. E. (1990c). Implementing Total Quality Management in a university setting. Eugene: Oregon State University.

Coate, L. E. (1992). Total Quality Management at Oregon State University. Eugene: Oregon State University.

Cornesky, R. A. (1992). Leadership versus management. TQM in Higher Education, 1 (2), 8.

Cornesky, R. A. (1990). W. Edward Deming: Improving quality in colleges and universities. Madison, WI: Magna Publications.

Cross, K. P. (1993). Involving faculty in TQM. Community College Journal, 63 (4), 14-20.

DeCosmo, R. D., Parker, J. S., & Heverly, M. A. (1991). Total Quality Management goes to community college. In L. A. Sherr & D. J. Teeter (Eds.), Total Quality Management in higher education. New Directions for Institutional Research No. 71. San Francisco: Jossey-Bass.

Deming, W. E. (1986). Out of the crisis. Cambridge: Massachusetts Institute of Technology Center for Advanced Engineering.

Duttweiler, P. C., & Hord, S. M. (1987). Dimensions of effective leadership. Austin, TX: Southwest Educational Development Laboratory.

Ewell, P. T. (1992). Defining the quality-driven institution. Assessment Update: Progress, Trends, and Practices in Higher Education, 4 (5).

Graba, J. (1993, August). The Malcolm Baldrige Award criteria and higher education. TQM in Higher Education, 2 (8), p. 1.

Johnson, H. H. (1992, October 21). TQM: Clearing up misconceptions [Letter to the editor]. Chronicle of Higher Education, 39 (9), B8.

Kohn, A. (1993a). Turning learning into a business: Concerns about total quality. Educational Leadership, 51 (1), 58-61.

Kohn, A. (1993b). Reply: The trouble with management tools. Educational Leadership, 51 (1), 67.

Kouzes, J. M., & Posner, B. Z. (1987). The leadership challenge: How to get extraordinary things done in organizations. San Francisco: Jossey-Bass.

LeTarte, C. E. (1993). Seven tips for implementing TQM: A CEO's view from the trenches. Community College Journal, 64 (1), 17-21.

Liebmann, J. D. (1993). A quality initiative postponed. In D. J. Teeter & G. G. Lozier (Eds.), Pursuit of quality in higher education: Case studies in Total Quality Management. New Directions for Institutional Research No. 78. San Francisco: Jossey Bass.

Lively, K. (1992, September 2). "Accountability" of colleges gets renewed scrutiny from state officials. Chronicle of Higher Education, 39 (2), A25-A27.

Mangan, K. S. (1992, August 12). TQM: Colleges embrace the concept of "total quality management." Chronicle of Higher Education, 38 (49), A25-A26.

Maxcy, S. J. (1991). Educational leadership: A critical pragmatic perspective. New York: Bergin & Garvey.

Matthews, J., & Katel, P. (1992, September 7). Cost of quality. Newsweek, 120 (10), pp. 48-49.

Mercer, J., & Katel, P. (1993, September 1). States' practice of grading public colleges' performance gets an F from critics. Chronicle of Higher Education, 40 (2), A39.

Noble, P. (1991, April). Sanford University cross-functional energy conservation team (ECT) presentation. Deming style quality improvement: A conference on quality improvement in higher education. Conference conducted at Sanford University, Birmingham, AL.

Ord, J. K. (1993). Total quality management in the classroom: A personal odyssey. In D. J. Teeter & G. G. Lozier (Eds.), Pursuit of quality in higher education: Case studies in Total Quality Management. New Directions for Institutional Research No. 78. San Francisco, CA: Jossey-Bass.

Pedersen, R. (1992, September 23). Perils of total quality management: Bringing business rhetoric to academe [Letter to the editor]. Chronicle of Higher Education, 39 (5), B4.

Rogers, J. (1993, July). Joining assessment with TQM/CQI. TQM in Higher Education, 2 (7), p. 1.

Savage, E. W. (1992, September/October). Fear of change. Total Quality Management Magazine, 2 (4), 194-197.

Schmoker, M., & Wolson, R. B. (1993). Adapting total quality doesn't mean "turning learning into a business." Educational Leadership, 51 (1), 62-63.

Seymour, D. T. (1992). On q: Causing quality in higher education. New York: MacMillan.

Seymour, D. T., & Collett, C. (1991). Total Quality Management in higher education: A critical assessment (Application Report No. 91-01). Methuen, MA: GOAL/QPC.

Shook, R. L. (1990). Turnaround: The new Ford Motor Company. New York: Prentice-Hall.

Sokol, P. E. (1993). Improvements in introductory physics courses. In D. J. Teeter & G. G. Lozier (Eds.), Pursuit of quality in higher education: Case studies in Total Quality Management. New Directions for Institutional Research No. 78. San Francisco, CA: Jossey Bass.

South Carolina Commission on Higher Education. (1989). Guidelines for institutional effectiveness. Columbia, SC: Author.

Stass, S. (1992). Examples: TQ improvement efforts. Media, PA: Delaware County Community College.

State of New Mexico. (1990). House bill 4. Santa Fe, NM: The author.

Winter, R. S. (1991). Overcoming barriers to total quality management in colleges and universities. In L. A. Sherr & D. J. Teeter (Eds.), Total quality management in higher education. New Directions for Institutional Research No. 71. San Francisco: Jossey Bass.

Zook, J. (1993, March 24). 2 agencies start work on national test of college students' analytical skills. Chronicle of Higher Education, 39 (29), A23.

Chapter 4

LEARNING AS CONTINUOUS IMPROVEMENT IN EDUCATIONAL ORGANIZATIONS

Michael D. Richardson and Kenneth E. Lane
Georgia Southern University and California State University—San Bernadino

> If he is indeed wise
> he does not bid you enter the house of his wisdom,
> but rather leads you
> to the threshold of your own mind.
> —Kahlil Gibran from <u>The Prophet</u>

Abstract

Many educators have a problem. Many educators have a cookbook mentality when challenged to critically think for themselves and implement the concepts of continuous improvement. Particularly disturbing is the preponderance of educators who have developed "thinking paralysis." Educators should have the ability to practice continuous improvement and learning in schools. The conceptual base is that what we know is not as important as how we learn. This chapter highlights the need for a belief in continuous improvement and learning for educators and offers suggestions on how such a concept could be implemented.

Introduction

Many people, both educators and others, believe that education is at a crucial crossroads in the United States. According to Eurich (1985, p. 1):

> The dimensions, opportunities and challenges compel us to consider that in the high-tech information age with knowledge-intensive demand, educational agendas—be they public, private, traditional, or alternative—are an urgent public policy issue for today and tomorrow.

Eurich goes on to state that "Our society cannot evaluate its problems, nor certainly consider solution, without taking into account . . . education for productivity" (1985, p. 3). Eurich (1985) questions the basic assumption that a few years' formal education can prove adequate for a lifetime when recognizing the urgency and need for improvement that arise from the rapid growth of a knowledge-intensive industry. Educators, policy makers and particularly politicians have attempted to "reform" or "restructure" education since the mid-1960s with minimal results. The only true change must take place internally, not be imposed by some entity or agency outside the organization. Consequently for lasting, meaningful change in education to occur, the change must be articulated, defined, developed and delivered by the people in the profession. As a result, the concept of continuous improvement is so critical to the change which is being demanded of educational organizations.

Practicing educators have historically complained about the theoretical basis of most instruction at institutions of higher education. They argue that instruction should be "realistic" and "practical." Contrary to popular opinion, practitioners are convinced that professors in educational preparation programs have provided students with exactly what they ask for, a "cookbook" which permits the student or practicing educator to turn to page 73 of a book which contains a recipe for cooperative learning, or to page 102 for a recipe on an upset parent, then view the list of ingredients and determine the length of time necessary to *cook* the correct response. Then, as if by a magic recipe or at least a well-cooked process, the problem will be solved. The "cookbook mentality" strikes again!

As Alderfer (1987) so precisely stated:

> Inadvertently, instructors "teach" students to explain the difficulties and dilemmas of human affairs in organizations by projecting onto others. People so taught are less likely to examine their own behavior and relationships as a means of dealing with situations they face. (p. 217)

Today's educators were not "trained" to think critically. They were exposed to the normative model of the teaching learning process which assumes educational transference of relevant information. As Alderfer (1987) concludes:

> ... the material to be learned ... had the form of a mix of abstract generalizations and concrete applications ... The task of the teacher was to transfer the material ... into the minds of the students. The task of the student was to absorb the material. The learning-teaching process succeeded to the degree that the teacher was able to transfer and the student was able to absorb the material. (p. 216)

This instructional technique predominantly used in educational preparation programs creates difficulty when educators are on the job. George Berkley (1984) addressed the *pathology of conservation* as the reason for individuals and organizations maintaining their traditional ways for doing things. Consequently when preparation focuses only on the training and not the learning then conservation of thinking results, not creative thinking.

The Quality Movement

Educational institutions in the United States are following the lead of corporations and Japanese industrialists in implementing Total Quality Management which argues for "doing it right the first time." Administrators and teachers are asked to adopt the philosophy that American students can perform at world-class standards which is articulated in a constancy of purpose toward continuous improvement in all facets of schooling, particularly student performance.

Potential and practicing educators need the competencies to analyze the organizational environment and their own abilities in order to understand their role and function in the organization. This analytic thinking (organization and self) permits the educator to free their actions "from the legitimating ideologies which mask understanding and prevent change" (Watkins, 1986, 97). Consequently, organizations and individuals change in response to each other. As illustrated by Denhardt (1981) organizations would "be seen as historically constituted, humanly derived institutions, always subject to analysis and reformulation; individuals would be seen as active participants in the process of constructing and modifying these institutions" (p. 73). Using this analytic thinking the educator "should be concerned not with certainty but with possibilities" (Watkins, 1986, 97). As a result, artificial parameters and regulations become constraints within which the educator works, but not "givens" which must be obeyed at all costs (Watkins, 1986; Perrow, 1982).

Continuous Improvement

The one given in continuous improvement specifies that the blame for education's current problems do not rest with incompetent administrators, poor teachers, dumb students, uncaring parents, and disinterested communities. Rather the blame for any perceived problem must be assigned to the process or system of education, not to the participants. According to Deming, 90% of the blame for any perceived failure rests with the system. In Deming's terminology system refers to the functions, activities and efforts within the organization that presumably work together to accomplish the organizational mission.

Continuous improvement is accomplished by the hundreds of small, positive, incremental changes implemented in schools over a multi-year period. Continuous improvement implies that the answers involve asking all the questions about every portion of the educational system. Therefore continuous improvement is about improving systems not attempting to locate or place blame.

The application of the principles of quality and continuous improvement in education takes time, commitment and effort; the results do not come easy. There are no "one best answers" for how to improve each local schools so that the differences between schools become the strengths on which improvement is based, not the excuses used for doing things "the way we have always done them." However, continuous improvement should be the most natural thing imaginable to educators, we deal with it constantly both in terms of student performance and professional performance. Most educators are uneasy about change, it creates anxiety, yet continuous improvement is about change.

Continuous improvement is about empowerment, synergy, encouragement, and the ability and willingness to create an environment where everyone, students, faculty, staff, parents, community, district supervisors, and school board members can participate in the learning process. However, continuous improvement can only take place when everyone concerned with the process is willing to commit to the participate in the process. Commitment becomes action, not talk.

Continuous improvement is about the development and implementation of the planning process for creating learning environments. The theoretical and practical application of continuous improvement holds that everything that a person has learned in the past is valuable and beneficial. It builds on the concepts of andragogy, or how adults learn, which articulates the importance of prior learning to the development of the individual. After all, every person is nothing more than the accumulation of their past experiences and to invalidate past experiences is to diminish the quality of the individual.

Continuous improvement specifies as six step action plan:
1. Construct ideal vision.
2. Develop school mission.
3. Develop performance indicators.
4. Take action.
5. Measure performance.
6. Make decisions.

Continuous improvement is a way of thinking, not a one time reform effort. It means that educators must be willing to analyze new ways of doing things, that the comfortable rut is not the place to be. In addition, all levels of education must be linked for determining quality and delivering quality. Continuous improvement must be seen as a philosophy, as a belief statement that leads to a obsession for delivering quality for all learners. All decisions must be based on data, not intuition. Additionally, people must work together to ensure that quality improvement takes place. Developing a management team and allowing them to have input into decisions is not continuous improvement because the people will be no happier with six or eight people making decisions, than they are for one person to make all the decisions.

The "Cookbook Mentality"

It is an unnerving feeling to realize that many educators, especially beginning ones, operate on a "cookbook mentality" with regard to the decision making process. By "cookbook mentality," we mean that the educator desires an answer for every situation they face rather than processing the information and making a valid, responsible decision. Getzels, Lipham and Campbell (1968) labeled this type of approach as education by technology "applying appropriate techniques to the solution of relevant practical problems" (p. 3).

The educator's world is fast-moving, constantly shrinking, and influenced by a variety of constituents that are not always fully understood. The skills of comprehension, communication, and cooperation are crucial. Educators need the ability to pursue new ideas, solve problems and make better choices in an rapidly changing world (Wynn & Guiditus, 1984). The goal is to increase individual awareness and to stimulate the desire to acquire a broader and more far-ranging knowledge of the organization and its various sociopolitical environments. However, education often responds to reform calls for the "quick fix," the easy answer, and the replication model without critically thinking through the process and making decisions based on the needs of the school, the students, the faculty, and the community. Such "easy" answers reflect the "cookbook mentality" so common in education today. Students and practitioners typically state:

"Don't tell me the theory, tell me how to do it!" The "how to," the "recipes," and a general lack of critical thinking and continuous improvement have invaded the profession.

Educators must have more than the "recipes," they need creative attitudes, well grounded values, factual knowledge, and a belief that schools can become beacons of learning before they can deal effectively with the community of the future. Educators who are "trained" rather than "prepared" have a tendency to view schools from the technical aspect as opposed to the human aspect. In other words, training examines the technical competencies of education through structural frameworks. Preparation for learning forces educators to view schools through the learning frameworks which utilize people to make a difference in the organization. This is the a reiteration of the age old problem of the "integration of theory and practice, the application of knowledge and training ... the combination of conceptual study and actual work" (Eurich, 1985, p. 121).

Wynn and Guiditus (1984) describe this learning mentality as convergent thinking:

> The dominant thrust of almost all educational and training programs in the development of the individual's capacity for convergent thinking... This emphasis is continually reinforced by demands for competency testing and other means of demonstrating accountability. Several difficulties result from this singular focus on convergent thinking. First, it leaves the individual unprepared for the demands of leadership. As the individual assumes greater responsibility within the organization, the performance expectations implicit in these higher-level assignments gradually shift from clarification and application of regulations to providing more-creative solutions to the emerging problems. This, however, requires considerable development of the individuals's capacity for innovative thinking. The result is that many individuals find themselves thrust into leadership roles for which they are largely unprepared because the primary source of their success as they moved up the hierarchical ladder was their capacity for convergent rather than divergent thinking. (p. 164)

As stated by Watkins (1986) this lack of thinking or an over reliance on the scientific method has dominated education literature for the past several decades.

> At the core of these manipulative techniques is the predominance of the metaphor of the school as a factory reflecting the ideology of science and scientific management. This, Kliebard argues, is

responsible for the process-product of rationality that still influences school systems at the present time. The organizational and curriculum models of schooling still reflect the ideology of industrial production. (p. 91)

Thinking About Continuous Improvement

Although there is an insufficient amount of related research on the need for continuous improvement and learning by educators, such should not preclude a examination of the need. The issue of continuous improvement has been addressed in various manners. Convey (1989) concluded that ". . . we sometimes look for a shortcut, expecting to be able to skip some of these vital steps in order to save time and effort and still reap the desired results" (p. 36). Coladarci and Getzels (1955) concluded that:

> The educator who behaves on a hit-or-miss basis, one whose professional arsenal consists merely of pat techniques for specific situations, is operating in intellectual low gear and is denied self-initiated, self-critical inquiry and innovation that are possible with a wider frame-of-reference . . . (pp. 7-8)

Theory versus Practice

This discussion focuses on the ability of educators to use the concepts of learning continuous improvement and not about the seemingly endless debate concerning the dichotomy between theory and practice in education. Bennis (1987) concluded that:

> This problem—how do we translate knowledge into action?—Is both complex and deep, as well as chronically elusive. Perhaps this is why the question is either studiously avoided, or worse, written about in such a boring, monotonously shallow manner, uniformly ending up with bromides about "dire straits," "dilemmas, and resistances of all kinds. . . . What I'm impressed with is not the reality of obstacles (which is self-evident) but the challenge, excitement, and promise of a theory of practice. (p. 30)

Whether this dichotomy is between the discouraged practitioner, the hopeful theorist, or the skeptic, education is rapidly pursuing a usable body of knowledge which will enhance the ability of both practitioner and theorist (Hoyle, 1992; Achilles, 1992). The debate between theory and practice is not new to education, or to science in general. In fact, Kurt Lewin (1948) was preoccupied with the relationship between theory and practice: "The research worker can achieve this [creating a bridge between theory and practice] only if, as a result of a constant intense tension, he can keep both theory and reality fully within his field of vision (p. iv)."

Campbell, Charters, and Gragg (1960) concluded that the dichotomy between theory and practice was superficial and that both had to be used cooperatively by educators. They stated that:

> The words or concepts we use, after all, are our tools for coming to terms with the infinitely complex world in which we must act. They tell us what to notice and what to ignore. In my opinion, the proper function of mid-century social science is to give the man of practical affairs a diversity of concepts to apply, a variety of viewpoints from which to see his problems. If concepts are tools, his toolkit should be full. In this way he achieves a flexibility of vision. (pp. 179-180)

Using Continuous Improvement

Certification standards for future educators should include a positive determination of their ability to understand continuous improvement and learning and actively use them to benefit schools. Quality schools can no longer tolerate the certification of educators who make decisions utilizing a "cookbook" for problem solving. According to Wynn and Guiditas (1984):

> Another difficulty arising from the narrow focus on convergent thinking is that it results in problem solving that is satisfying, rather than optimizing. The basic process involved in decision making based on satisfying is that it produces a satisfactory solution rather than an optimal course of action. (p. 164)

As Getzels, Lipham and Campbell (1964) stated:

> The [educator] who was aware of the context within which . . . decisions were being made, and who had an explicit framework (instead of a bagful of prescriptions and precedents) within which to work, was in a more strategic position not only to understand what was going on but also to decide for himself [herself] rather than follow the crowd, ask someone, or just do nothing at all. (p. 13)

The need for continuous improvement skills by practitioners requires more than a cursory agreement on its importance. The issue of continuous improvement and the ability to apply it in the school setting is the essence of improving schools and increasing student academic performance. The move must be away from educators with a "cookbook mentality" to school leaders with a foundation in continuous improvement and the ability to use it to benefit their schools.

Watkins (1986) stated that educators must move beyond the concept of the "one best way" of doing things and rationally examine the organizational environment in which they operate. He stated that:

> This concern with corporate strategies and control mechanisms has been termed by Gronn Neo-Taylorism. In a survey of eight recent studies of school administrators he found a prevalence of "crude Tayloristic thinking." This included a preoccupation with seeking "the one best methods, and with a concern for efficiency." (p. 93)

Sarason (1991) concluded his examination of administrator preparation programs with the observation that universities have prepared administrators for a world in which the future is a "carbon copy of the past" (p. 69). Rather than prepare future educators for the realities of school for the next generation, preparation programs are stuck in a presentation mode as outdated as the overhead projector. Sure the overhead projector was a great asset thirty years ago, but what will the schools of the twenty.

Metacognition

Metacognition is the ". . . ability to formulate a plan of action, monitor our own process along that plan, realize that we know and don't know, detect and recover from error, and reflect on and evaluate our own thinking processes" (Costa, 1991, p. 14). Further, metacognition can be explained as "the learner's recognition and regulation of his or her own processes of thinking" or analysis (Keefe & Walberg, 1992). For educators this concept can be defined as acute awareness of analysis processes. Metacognition is not an easy concept to develop or to use because it exposes the analysis processes to public scrutiny. However, metacognition is one valuable skill in the arsenal of educators who wish to avoid the "cookbook mentality" syndrome.

Metacognition implies that incrementalism be used as a means for measuring success. Improvement in schools will take place as the result of hundreds of small, positive, incremental changes implemented in schools over a multi-year period, such that the eventual product will not be recognizable in today's terms. Continuous learning and improvement are concerned with analyzing everything in the internal environment which can impact quality, not just selected areas for change. Incrementalism implies that the process of improvement is never complete, it is ever changing, flexible to meet the demands of the environment. Incrementalism encourages participation from every sector inside and outside the organization. Incrementalism is not a one short effort, rather it is a way of life. The conceptual basis for incrementalism must become part of the educational culture for continuous improvement to exist. Incrementalism demonstrates the following characteristics:

(1) Break the mold—get out of the rut, think new thoughts, view new challenges as opportunities, think globally, and think improvement;
(2) Linkages—all the educational organizations must be linked together for learning and continuous improvement;
(3) Passion—mans a "hunger to share" and sharing means learning step by step;
(4) Data—educators must rely on data to make decisions and help eliminate decisions based on "gut-level;"
(5) Teamwork—everyone must be committed to the organizational goals; and,
(6) Accountability—everyone is held accountable for incremental improvement not drastic, one-shot approaches.

Behavior Modification

Educators must move from the concept of "push-button decision-making" to decisions which reflect understanding and the ability "to apply inventiveness and ingenuity" on the job (Getzels, Lipham, & Campbell, 1964). The "push-button" approach to education is reflective of the Skinnerian behavior modification system which enjoyed such wide acclaim in the 1960s. However, the implication is that the educator can push button A, and then push button B, and the student receives a banana as a reward. We need educators who can think, not merely react in a patterned, programmed way. If education becomes totally a stimulus-response profession, why do we need educators? Skinner's monkeys can do the job!

Training versus Learning

Training implies the acquisition of skills necessary for job performance, while learning connotes the ability to learn about and within the environment. Training emphasizes the procedure (how to) as opposed to the process (learning) that is critical to improvement (Rudiger & Krinsky, 1992). Training is a short-term, stop-gap approach, while learning is a life-long process. Senge (1990) states that:

> Generative learning cannot be sustained in an organization if people's thinking is dominated by short-term events. If we focus on events, the best we can ever do is predict an event before it happens so that we can react optimally. But we cannot learn to create. (p. 22)

Missile officers in the U.S. Air Force were trained to handle missile deployment, but what of their skills now that we no longer need the same readiness capabilities? They must be retrained to be useful to the military. Training does not permit the trainee to respond to situations outside the training experience while learning prepares the educator to deal with long-term situations (Stevenson, 1993). Training prepares the educator for today while learning is preparation for tomorrow. If educators are trained and given a bag of tricks or skills those skills will be out-dated in five or ten years. The analogy is not far-fetched, look at the abundance of educators today who were trained fifteen to twenty years ago and see how they are functioning in today's schools. According to Malcolm (1992):

> Even if we run an excellent training program, we're influencing only about 20 percent of the competency development. That means there's a lot that can go wrong outside of our control. If students don't apply the things they learned, we feel the training has failed—and from the organization's point of view, it has. (p. 60)

Rather than training, educators need knowledge concerning continuous improvement and learning and help developing learning attributes. Learning has been defined as three separate functions: (a) Learning can be defined as learning on the job (OJL), or learning by experience; (b) Learning can take place as a result of simulated situations (case study, etc.); and, (c) Learning can take place in formal environment, i.e., courses, institutes, etc. The real key to learning for continuous improvement is the integration of theory and practice. Educators must be able to analyze issues from a multidisciplinary perspective; they must be provided more practical application of theory; and they must understand how teamwork functions in educational organizations. When the primary focus of continuous learning is on the individual, not the organization, the resulting individuality will "lessen a person's ability to contribute cooperatively and work effectively with others" (Eurich, 1985, p. 125). Similarly, total analysis of theory in the absence of application can "handicap a good mind, leaving it in speculative limbo" (Eurich, 1985, p. 125).

Educators report that they learn most of what they know on the job, therefore preparation should concentrate on giving future educators the opportunities and knowledge about how to learn on the job. Most research indicates that principals, teachers and physicians learn most of what they know on the job. Business mangers at Honeywell Corporation also reported that they acquired 80 percent of their critical job skills on the job. However according to Malcolm (1992), "Typical OJT is unstructured or under structured, inconsistent and slow. Time-to-competency figures of 18 months or longer are not uncommon" (p. 58). The real challenge has to be preparation for learning which will produce real outcomes in the lives of children. In fact, the Higher Education Act of 1972 stated that "The American people need lifelong learning to enable them to adjust to social, technological, political, and economic changes." Nowhere can these changes be seen more clearly than in educational organizations. The misfit between educator capabilities and the skills required to do the work has been deplored for decades; however, the cyclical trend of advancement and educational retooling continues, this time at an accelerated pace with greater consequences for failure than ever before.

Educational Reform

Educational reform during the 1980s demonstrated that the impetus for change came from outside education. The implication is that educators must be able to view things in a different light, something which is found in learning not training. We live in a information age, in an age when knowledge doubles every two years, in an age when education's future will be determined by how well we assimilate and use the new information. Training uses current information while learning prepares future educational leaders to deal with changes as they occur, and optimistically, to help create needed changes. According to Eurich (1985):

> A new and different type of retraining is call for—more specific, informed and sophisticated. It is learning of a higher order for understanding conceptual bases essential to the operational control and utilization of information systems. Educational demands of such magnitude require human flexibility and trainability and, as with other complex problems, solutions rest on perceptive, thoughtful policies implemented on a comprehensive basis for practical results. (p. 136)

As Stevenson (1993) asserts:

> This information does not come neatly bound along nineteenth-century lines. It is important that we not be seduced by a direction

which promises short-term gains at the expense of long-term, lasting fulfillment. Training is short sighted. Learning is a life long task ... (p. 5A)

The real danger is that educational reform will force preparation to become so directed to immediate employment and specific skills that those so "trained" will be relegated to continual "retraining" the remainder of their professional life. Strategic personal and professional development for the long term is essential for both educators, society, and the schools.

Management versus Leadership

This dichotomy between training and learning does not speculate on the reported dichotomy between management and leadership in organizations. Some have made the analogy that <u>training is management</u> and <u>learning is leadership</u>. However, in the reality of today's complex school organizations, such a simplistic approach will not suffice. According to Wynn and Giditus (1984):

> These distinctions between managing and leading have led some to believe that the two concepts are incompatible. That is to say, the task of the manager is to maintain the status quo, while the role of the leader is to bring about change. To view these two roles as being counterproductive would be to deny the realities of organizational life. There is no such thing as a condition of ultimate stability. There is never a time without change; nor is there ever a state of total change. If an organization is to survive, it needs to experience simultaneously a condition of stability and a measure of change. One is essential as a measure of the other. The locus of stability and of change will, in a dynamic organization, shift as it responds to its environment. The maxim that an organization is either moving ahead or sliding back is a reality, not a cliche. (pp. 28-29)

Skill Acquisition versus Learning Mentality

Inquiry into the learning process, cognitive as well as affective, is a growing concern for education. According to Eurich (1985) "Higher education has done little to learning about teaching and learning. The university's instructional mode has scarcely changed over the past 50 years" (p. 55). Eurich concludes that "Seldom has interest in the learning process, its difference among individuals, and the implications for classroom methods been expressed in educational halls, much less supported and rewarded" (p. 56). Reif (1974) agrees:

> Nor is this situation surprising, since the university, unlike any progressive industry, is not in the habit of improving its own performance by systematic investment in innovative research and development. Indeed, the resources allocated by the university to educational innovation are usually minuscule or non-existent . . . Is it too farfetched to suggest that the university should take education at least as seriously as the Bell Telephone Company takes communication? (p. 540)

The training mentality is often reflected in organizational analysis where the goals of the individual are not congruent with the goals of the organization (Nord & Durand, 1978). Argyris (1964) speculated that "there is a lack of congruence between the needs of healthy individuals and the demands of the formal organization" (p. 314). Such conflict can only produce an ineffective and inefficient organization more driven to control than consensus (Stern, 1958; Karr, 1978). Educators operating in such an environment become acclimated to organizational concerns are the expense of individual attitudes and often develop inappropriate methods to deal with the frustration. Such a situation often leads to the end of learning and improvement.

Senge (1990) concluded that:

> Most of the outstanding leaders I have worked with are neither tall nor especially handsome; they are often mediocre public speakers; they do not stand out in a crowd; and they do not mesmerize an attending audience with their brilliance or eloquence. Rather, what distinguishes them is the clarity and persuasiveness of their ideas, the depth of their commitment, and their openness to continually learning more. They do not "have the answer." But they do instill confidence in those around them that, together, "we can learn whatever we need to learn in order to achieve the results we truly desire." The ability of such people to be natural leaders, as near as I can tell, is the by-product of a lifetime of effort—effort to develop conceptual and communication skills, to reflect on personal values and to align personal behavior with values, to learn how to listen and to appreciate others and others' ideas. In the absence of such effort, personal charisma is style without substance. It leaves those affected less able to think for themselves and less able to make wise choices. It can devastate an organization . . . (p. 359)

According to Price (1990) "training is imparting, by systematic instruction, of a set of skills. Its purpose is to equip the trainee with the ability to do whatever it is the job requires to be done if it is to be performed effectively." Further, he stated that "a person is <u>subjected</u> to training, is a <u>recipient</u> of it. Training is limiting and confining . . ." By contrast, Price defined education as "the sharing, by organized disclosure and dissemination, of knowledge, understanding and insight." In addition he speculated that "a person is <u>exposed</u> to education, is a <u>experiencer</u> of it. Education is unshackling and liberating" (p. 107). Price concluded that "all education involves some training, but not all training requires education" (p. 108). Price also deducted that skill development was training and that knowledge was education. He stated:

> Skill is the product of practice, and takes time to acquire. Knowledge is immediate, one minute you do not know, the next minute you know. If it is to be effective, skill calls for coaching; knowledge needs nothing more than the imagination and the opportunity to express itself. (p. 113)

Educational Transference

The development of schools as learning communities must be conducted in an environment of collegial and shared purpose. Principals and teachers are not the ultimate dispensers of information and knowledge, rather, they must act as facilitators of educational transference. Gery (1991) discusses the concept of performance support systems which provide access to information, advice and training. "Much can be accomplished simply by adding some structure to the traditional notion of on-the-job learning" (Malcolm, 1992, p. 61).

Educational transference has three components: a) utility—the extent to which information is useful to the recipients; b) knowledge—the extent to which information can be learned or a means of retrieval understood; and c) exchange—the extent to which information can be moved from knowledge to utility or application. In some instances learning is called applications education.

Students, teachers, and principals must have access to information and be able to transfer the knowledge from one application to another. Therefore, the "cookbook" or "one best way" of doing things will not suffice in schools of the 21st century. As Boswell stated in the 15th century, "Knowledge is of two kinds: we know a subject ourselves, or we know where we can find information upon it." There is no way for an administrator or teacher to "have knowledge" of all the information necessary to effective functioning in the school, therefore the teacher and administrator must be able to access the necessary information from whatever sources are available and most effective.

Malcolm (1992) articulates another advantage of learning rather than training due to integration of knowledge or competencies:

that it offers the opportunity to bring together the various competencies and subdisciplines that make up many of today's complex jobs.... [Learning is] a natural means to accomplish the "competency integration" critical to success. (p. 60)

Eddy and Kellow (1977) identified a conceptual framework for learning which can be useful for the development of a school as a learning community. They articulated a model which contains three separate steps:
(1) Conceptual awareness. The student understands the concept involved.
(2) Emotional choice. The student emotionally buys into the concept and vows to employ it.
(3) Behavioral change. The concept, through repetition, is pressed into the student's behavior pattern until it becomes normal behavior. (p. 36)

Conclusions

Our conclusions generate more questions than answers to this dilemma. Is the dichotomy between creativity and "one best way" indigenous to all education activities? Is this dilemma more common in education? Have we, as educators, failed our students by not requiring continuous improvement and learning? Are our students thoroughly prepared, both mentally and emotionally for the trials of life after school? Are there other possibilities or explanations which we have overlooked or failed to address? The questions are easy, the answers involve much more study and research.

References

Alderfer, C. P. (1987). An intergroup perspective on group dynamics. In J. W. Lorsch (Ed.), Handbook of organizational behavior (pp. 190-222). Englewood Cliffs, NJ: Prentice-Hall.

Argyris, C. (1964). Integrating the individual and the organization. New York: John Wiley & Sons.

Bennis, W. (1987). Using our knowledge of organizational behavior: The improbable task. In J. W. Lorsch (Ed.), Handbook of organizational behavior (pp. 29-49). Englewood Cliffs, NJ: Prentice-Hall.

Berkley, G. E. (1978). The craft of public administration. Boston, MA: Allyn & Bacon.

Blumberg, A., & Greenfield, W. (1980). The effective principal: Perspectives on school leadership. Boston: Allyn and Bacon, Inc.

Campbell, R. F., Charters, W. W., Jr., & Gragg, W. L. (1960). Improving administrative theory and practice. In R. F. Campbell & J. M. Lipham (Eds.), <u>Administrative theory as a guide to action.</u> Chicago, IL: Midwest Administration Center, The University of Chicago.

Center for Critical Thinking and Moral Critique. (1992). <u>Critical thinking: Shaping the mind of the 21st century.</u> Rohnert Park, CA: Author.

Coladarci, A. P., & Getzels, J. W. (1955). <u>The use of theory in educational administration.</u> Stanford, CA: Stanford University, College of Education.

Collins, C. (1991). Don your thinking caps. <u>The School Administrator, 48</u> (1), 8-13.

Costa, A. (1991). <u>Developing minds: A resource book for teaching thinking.</u> Alexandria, VA: Association for Supervision and Curriculum Development.

Covey, S. R. (1989). <u>The seven habits of highly effective people.</u> New York: Simon and Schuster.

Denhardt, R. B. (1981). <u>In the shadow of organization.</u> Lawrence, KS: The Regents Press of Kansas.

Eddy, B., & Kellow, J. (1977). What we've learned about learning—A corporate 'university' at Leeds & Northrup Co. <u>Training and Development Journal, 31</u> (5), 32-38.

Ennis, R. (1985). Goals for a critical thinking curriculum. In A. Costa (Ed.), <u>Developing minds: A resource book for teaching thinking.</u> Alexandria, VA: Association for Supervision and Curriculum Development.

Eurich, N. P. (1985). <u>Corporate classrooms.</u> Princeton, NJ: The Carnegie Foundation for the Advancement of Teaching.

Filipczak, B. (1992). Sharing the pain. <u>Training, 29</u> (8), 8.

Gardner, J. W. (1991). <u>John W. Gardner on leadership.</u> Reston, VA: National Association of Secondary School Principals.

Getzels, J. W., Lipham, J. M., & Campbell, R. F. (1968). <u>Educational administration as a social process.</u> New York: Harper & Row.

Greenfield, W. (1982). <u>The effective principal.</u> In S. Thompson (Ed.). Reston, VA: National Association of Secondary School Principals.

Gronn, P. (1982). Neo-Taylorism in educational administration. <u>Educational Administration Quarterly, 18</u> (4), 17-35.

Karr, P. J. (1978). Re-evaluating the human curriculum: The change from bureaucratic to professional. <u>College Student Journal, 12</u> (2), 154-157.

Keefe, J. W., & Walberg, H. J. (1992). <u>Teaching for thinking.</u> Reston, VA: National Association of Secondary School Principals.

Kimbrough, R. (1985). Ethics: A course of study for educational leaders. Arlington, VA: American Association of School Administrators.

Lewin, K. (1948). Resolving social conflicts. New York: Harper and Bros.

Lipham, J. (1981). Effective principal, effective school. Reston, VA: National Association of Secondary School Principals.

Maidment, R. (1986). Decisions. Reston, VA: National Association of Secondary School Principals.

Malcolm, S. E. (1992). Reengineering corporate training. Training, 29 (8), 57-61.

Morgan, G. E. (1993). Finance education needs to return to the basics. The Chronicle of Higher Education, 40 (8), A 56.

Nord, W. R., & Durand, D. E. (1978). What's wrong with the human relations approach to management? Organizational Dynamics, Winter.

Perrow, C. (1982). Disintegrating social sciences. Phi Delta Kappan, 63 (10), 684-688.

Price, F. (1990). Right every time: Using the Deming approach. Milwaukee, WI: ASQC Quality Press.

Reif, F. (1974). Educational challenges for the university. Science, 184 (4136), 537-542

Rudiger, C. W., & Krinsky, I. W. (1992). Getting to 2001. International Journal of Educational Reform, 1 (3), 285-290.

Sarason, S. B. (1991). The predictable failure of educational reform. San Francisco, CA: Jossey-Bass.

Schon, D. (1983). The reflective practitioner: How principals think in action. New York: Basic Books.

Senge, P. M. (1990). The fifth discipline: The art and practice of the learning organization. New York, NY: Doubleday.

Stern, L. E. (1958). Foreman's job: What are the boundaries? Supervisory Management, 3, 18-19.

Stevenson, D. E. (1993, January 15). Educational emphasis creating 'Clemson Tech.' The Tiger, 86 (12), 5A.

Trotter, G. (1986). I thought what? The Clearing House, 60, 76-78.

U. S. Senate Resolution 359. (1979). Washington, DC: U. S. Government Printing Office.

Watkins, P. (1986). From managerialism to communicative competence: Control and consensus in educational administration. The Journal of Educational Administration, 24 (1), 86-106.

Wayson, W. (1988). Up from excellence: The impact of the excellence movement on schools. Bloomington, IN: Phi Delta Kappa

Educational Foundation.

    Zenke, L. (1985, March). <u>Improving school effectiveness by teaching thinking skills.</u> Paper presented at annual meeting of the American Association of School Administrators, Dallas, Texas.

This chapter was originally published as "reforming education through the education of exceptional leaders." <u>New Directions for Education Reform, 3</u> (2), 1-17, 1977. Used by permission.

Learning as Continuous Improvement

ORGANIZATIONAL CONCEPTS	TRAINING	LEARNING
abstract thinking	theoretical	problem-solving
accountability	competency based	performance
administration	control	empowerment
attitude	fear	trust
change	product	process
communication	monologue	dialogue
control	technical	human relations
curriculum	separation	integration
decision making	centralized	decentralized
decisions	intuitive	data-based
evaluation	judge ability	insure quality
feedback	task related	continuous
future	status quo	improvement
group expectations	conform	responsibility
learners	independent	interdependent
learning	passive	active
mood	competition	cooperation
motivation	extrinsic	intrinsic
organization	bureaucratic	professional
orientation	individual	group
people	objects	learners
problem identification	avoidance	analysis
problem solving	satisfying	optimizing
products	outcomes	systems
style	parochial	participative
task orientation	habit	innovation
teaching	isolated	cooperation
the way things happen	chance	planning
thinking	convergent	divergent

© *Richardson and Lane, 1993*

Chapter 5

DEMING'S PHILOSOPHY: IMPLICATIONS FOR EDUCATION

Harbison Pool
Georgia Southern University

Over the past century, the educational system in this country has followed a version of <u>scientific management</u> (Holt, 1993). This approach, developed by Frederick Winslow Taylor (1911), was created to improve productivity in industry. Moreover, most public schools in this country were designed according to a factory model to serve the needs of the industrial age. It is not surprising, then, that the authoritarian nature of scientific management (which Tanner and Tanner [1987] refer to disparagingly as <u>scientism</u>) seemed well-suited to educational management. Initiative and imagination were discouraged, and the idea of one right way prevailed (Bonstingl, 1992c).

Although the Taylorism still appears to be alive and well, America has begun to realize that much of the valuable creativity denied students through such an approach has only put this country behind in terms of quality. By the late 1970s, much of the world had caught up with and even surpassed American industry and education (Bonstingl, 1992c). The task of reversing the vestiges of Taylorism in business and industry, while daunting, pale in comparison to that of tackling its deeply entrenched remains in education, especially at the classroom level (Gray, 1993).

A Time for Change

The need for change has become evident. For more than a decade now, society has held the educational system directly accountable for this country's failure, or at least perceived failure, to prepare young people with attitudes, skills, and knowledge necessary to produce high-quality goods and services. The 1983 report, A Nation At Risk, (National Commission on Excellence in Education, alerted Americans to serious problems plaguing their educational system.

Blame was shifted from students to teachers and ultimately to parents, school leaders, and school boards. Something needed to be done. A total paradigm shift appeared to be in order. But, to what? Everything educational leaders tried seemed to have, at best, limited success. Maybe the time had come to consider not fixing blame on individuals, but on the system (Siu-Runyan & Heart, 1992). Such thinking calls for a complete paradigm shift and the possibility of a whole new philosophy. For some time, major business leaders had begun to examine, and in some cases embrace, the set of principles and practices that had become known as Total Quality Management, or simply as TQM.

Japan's Needs and Deming's Answers

During World War II, Japanese planes were inferior to those of the Americans who had followed the advice of Walter Shewhart (1986/1931, 1986/1939), W. Edward Deming's mentor, in building high-quality, mass-produced goods. Following the war, the Japanese economy was in shambles and most Japanese products were still shoddy. It became clear to Deming that American manufacturers were concentrating on production rather than quality. Frustrated with American industry's abandonment of Shewart's and his work, Deming responded to the invitation from Gen. Douglas MacArthur to help Japan get back on its feet. So it was then, in 1950, Dr. William Edwards Deming (1900-1993), an American statistician and physicist, proposed a new management theory to Japanese business leaders (Bonstingl, 1992c).

Juran (1969, 1974, 1988), Crosby (1980), and Fiegenbaum (1961) in the U.S. and Ishikawa (1985) in Japan are among these mentioned in the literature as pioneers in the TQM movement (by Arcaro, 1995; Bostingl, 1992b, 1992c; Hackman & Wageman, 1995; Ross, 1993; and others). But, one name, that of Deming, tops everyone's list. He is given a lion's share of the credit for revitalizing Japan's war-ravaged economy.

Total Quality Management: An Application of Deming's Ideas

Deming's influence on American industry and education today is tremendous. One only has to look at the Japanese products which are consistently of the highest quality and yet sold at competitive prices to recognize that Deming's ideas merit a close examination (Rhodes, 1990). TQM has been variously defined. Rhode's (1992) "current definition" is: *"Total Quality Management is a value-based, information-driven management process through which the minds and talents of people at all levels are applied fully and creatively to the organization's continuous improvement* [emphasis in the original]" (p. 80).

It should be noted in passing that, curiously enough, Deming himself did not espouse the use of the phrase, total quality management. Quality is an output, according to Deming, and thus cannot be managed, according to Deming; one can, he declared, only manage systems (Blankstein & Swain, 1994). Schenkat (1993b) defends his use of the abbreviation *TQM* and states that there are probably "more productive things to do than engage in semantic debates over labels of movements" (p. vi). This is the phrase employed throughout the professional literature and it will be utilized here.

The last two words in Rhode's definition above, "continuous improvement," are perhaps more important than any others associated with TQM; many of those writing about TQM in business (e.g., Gitlow & Gitlow, 1987; Hackman & Wageman, 1995; Ross, 1993) and in education emphasize this concept. Bonstingl (1992b) says that this is what the Japanese call kaizen, a lifelong commitment to betterment for oneself, family, friends, fellow workers, and, finally, the whole world. H characterizes this concept as idealistic and optimistic, but one that really works. Freeston (1992) says that, "With an emphasis on continuous improvement, there is no rest. This, he notes, "is an important paradigm shift professionals accustomed to annual projects and programs as the definition of change" (p. 13).

Deming's Revolutionary Principles

What exactly is Deming's philosophy and how well does it translate to education? The essence of his philosophy is embedded in his now—famous 14 points, set forth in Deming's most well-known work, Out of the Crisis (1986). The 14 points are listed below, followed by a brief consideration of some of the ways in which experts on TQM find that these principles have applications in education, either to the work that superintendents, personnel directors, principals, and other educational administrators do or, in some cases, to teacher's work with students. In some instances, the connections to Deming's points are obvious, in others less so; some of the applications are universal, would apply equally in business or in education; others are specific to the field of education (except where otherwise credited, these examples are drawn or adapted from Blankstein, 1992; Bonstingl, 1992b, Deming, 1986; and Siu-Runyan & Heart, 1992):

1. *Create constancy of purpose for improvement of product and service.*
    a. There should be a strategic (master) plan in place

(Rebore, 1995).
   b. Teachers, principals, and the superintendent must agree on future goals and priorities.
   c. Ideally, this plan will not be undermined by constant turnover of the district's chief executive officer (its superintendent) and other leaders.
   d. Long-term stability is important. Considerable innovation is in order here.
2. *Adopt the new philosophy.*
   a. All members of the staff are able to contribute to the development and implementation of the strategic plan (Rebore, 1995).
   b. The lead-management, not the boss-management, leadership style should be followed (Glasser, 1990).
   c. A consensus on priorities should exist.
   d. Schools, Glasser (1990) contends, must move beyond an instructional approach that is fragmented to one which challenges students to think and to defend their ideas.
3. *Cease dependence on mass inspection.*
   a. It costs more to fix a problem than to do it right in the first place; the better way is to build in quality from the beginning.
   b. Quality cannot be inspected into a product.
   c. It is a little late in the game to worry about students' lack of preparation when they are 16 years old.
   d. Standardized testing is another way in which educators engage in mass inspection. Test results are after-the-fact.
   e. Standardized tests have become barriers to teachers who are asked to teach creative and critical thinking skills, but are still measured according to tests which emphasize isolated facts.
   f. Observing and interacting with students is the only way to get a full and accurate picture of their needs and what they have learned.
   g. Students best demonstrate what they have learned when they are able to apply information and skills to real-life situations or problems.
4. *End the practice of awarding business on the basis of price tag alone.*
   a. Decisions should be based on quality, not cost; hiring

Deming's Philosophy

high-caliber teachers and purchasing excellent teaching materials, for example, is wise, because the personal and social costs of poor education are greater in the long run.
  b. Positive relationships between teachers and principals will reinforce quality.
5. *Improve constantly and forever the system of production and service.*
  a. Teamwork is critical at all stages. Everyone is encouraged to take initiative and to help solve problems.
  b. Every employee works continuously to improve the system.
  c. Quality circles, involving teachers, parents, students, and the principal, can be formed to solve problems. Relevant data are collected, processed, and evaluated, resulting, ultimately, in a permanent change.
  d. Each child is unique; he or she deserves full attention.
6. *Institute training and retraining.*
  a. It is hard to overcome the negative effects of improper training.
  b. New teachers should not be left to their own devices; a top-quality induction program must be developed with the input and involvement of teachers and administrators.
  c. A good mentorship program should be created for all new and early-career teachers and administrators.
7. *Institute leadership.*
  a. Leadership is what superintendents and principals do. It is their responsibility to find any barriers to teachers, classified personnel, and students taking pride in their work.
  b. Then, of course, they must work to overcome the barriers.
  c. Principals must reduce the distance between themselves and the classroom, periodically teaching classes themselves.
  d. Indeed, the most important prerequisite for becoming a good principal is having first been an excellent teacher.
  e. Principals should stay up-to-date on new instructional practices.
  f. Leading involves assisting, not threatening or punishing.

8. *Drive out fear.*
   a. A school should be (provide) a secure work environment, one with an atmosphere of excitement, possibility, and productivity, not one with the specter of fear in the air.
   b. Employees who are motivated by fear play it as safe as they can; they do not continue to learn nor do they take risks.
   c. Teachers and staff personnel should be encouraged to try new materials and curricula, share concerns and ideas, and ask for assistance when something is not working.
   d. Fear stifles motivation and discourages effective learning.
   e. Two-way communication is essential.
9. *Break down barriers between staff areas.*
   a. Collaborative, team relationships are in order.
   b. Competition should be reduced among employees and between schools.
   c. All people should do their best and help others to do theirs.
   d. Barriers that exist between classified and certificated personnel, students and teachers, or the English and math departments are all counterproductive (causing "sub-optimization").
10. *Eliminate slogans, exhortations, and targets for the work force.*
    a. Slogans and exhortations imposed from on high do not help people do a better job; instead, they tend to assess blame.
    b. Internally motivated personnel who have helped set the school's and school system's goals will be more likely to achieve those goals.
11. *Eliminate numerical quotas for the work force and goals for people in management.*
    a. People should not be reduced to statistics.
    b. Teacher ratings cause frustration, lead to jealously, and generate adversarial relationships between teachers and principals.
    c. Deming (1994) cites the political initiative, America 2000 (Alexander, 1991), championed first by the Bush administration and endorsed by all 50 states' governors,

Deming's Philosophy

and later taken up in the form of <u>Goals 2000</u> by the Clinton administration, and merit pay for teachers as "horrible" examples of "numerical goals in public places" (p. 45).

    d. Incentive pay generally results in few winners and many losers.

    e. Rather, the idea is to pull for each person to do his or her best; every person at every level should be helped to do so by all his or her fellow employees; after all, this helps the organization (whether business or school system/individual school) to achieve its fundamental purpose (swell more widgets or educate children and youth to be happy, productive citizens).

    f. Setting numerical quotas or goals often leads to marginal work.

    g. The long-honored management by objectives (MBO) approach (Drucker, 1977) is basically looking back instead of forward (Aguayo, 1990). This rearview-mirror strategy is fallacious since it stresses only outputs and believes the process can be corrected at the end (by fixing or discarding defective products, etc.). The parallels in education are obvious; for example, teachers are encouraged by principals "to become 'beanies' and count the results of tests and trivialize and distort the activities of teaching and learning" (Holt, 1993, p. 383).

    h. The student (A-F) grading system employed in most American schools s fundamentally flawed. Especially pernicious is the practice pursued by some teachers of basing the grades or marks they award on some version of a bell curve. The traditional A-F grading system is outmoded, negative, and unhealthy, but deeply entrenched and extremely difficult for many educators to live up (Blankstein &A. Swain, 1994; Gray, 993). A child comes to school intrinsically motivated to learn; grades, an external motivator, rob children and youth of their "natural desire to learn and do well" (Blankstein & Swain, 1994, p. 53).

12. *Remove barriers that rob people of pride in workmanship.*
    a. As stated under Point 7, this is what true leaders do.
    b. Teachers want to do a good job. Arbitrary goals, outdated equipment, irrelevant curriculum, and other barriers to good teaching are discouraging. Under such

circumstances, the safest response may be mediocrity.
   c. State mandates often get in the way; good school leaders will have both the courage and the data to question spirit-crushing and inappropriate rules and policies. They will also develop community support for what they are doing with students. Under such circumstances, a state department will usually be receptive to school-proposed, transformational changes (Blankstein & Swain, 1994).
   d. Principals should work directly with teachers, asking them what they perceive needs improvement, and then act on what they have learned.
13. *Encourage education and self-improvement for everyone.*
   a. All school employees benefit from enriching their lives by pursuing their interests beyond their professional and personal worlds (Bonstingl, 1993).
   b. Hackman and Wageman state that "TQM is pro-learning, with a vengeance" (p. 330).
   c. New skills, techniques, and information are needed constantly, even if preservice education was exceptional, if for no other reason, because if the incredibly fast-moving dynamics of today's world.
14. *Take action to accomplish the transformation.*
   a. The leader's role is clear. Individual teachers cannot change the system; the principal must help teachers chart a course for change.
   b. Administrators and teachers must have a shared mission.
   c. There must be enough support built into the system that the drive for needed change is not short-circuited or derailed along the way.
   d. Change is never-ending. Restructuring of schools can never be fully accomplished.
   e. The Deming (or PDSA) Cycle—(1) Plan, (2) Do, (3) Study, and (4) Act (Bonstingl, 1993)—should be helpful as a procedure in seeking improvement.
   f. "The transformation is everybody's job" (Tribus, 1994, p. 11).

The TQM Process at Work in American Schools

The TQM process is complicated and does offer a quick fix. According to Lockwood (1992), "it is more a philosophy than a blueprint for action" (p. 1). Yet, those who study the compelling case made by many who have written on this movement for the application of Deming's philosophy to education cannot help but believe that great possibilities exist for educational leaders who practice his principles.

The professional literature is full of exciting examples of principals and teachers who have put Deming's philosophy to work in their schools, often with exceptional results, though usually not without many bumps in the road. From Alaska (Rocheleau, 1991; Tribus, 1990) to Florida (Blankstein & Swain, 1994), schools report their successes. Public-school examples abound in urban, suburban, and rural schools; day and residential schools; well-heeled and poor schools; and comprehensive and vocational schools. "Regular-education" students have been served in TQM schools, but so have those who fall into such categories as vocational, at-risk, gifted, Native American, and handicapped. Public funds have usually been the source of support for the TQM transformation, but some efforts have been financed through school-business partnerships. Examples come from Connecticut (Freeston, 1992), New York (Schargel, 1991), New Jersey (Abernethy & Serfass, 1992), Ohio (Lockwood, 1992), Michigan (Hixson & Lovelace, 1992), and elsewhere. Indeed, the model has been utilized with good results in higher education (Chizmar, 1994) and at the U.S. Army School of Engineering (Higgins, Jenkins, & Lewis, 1993).

Cautions, Caveats, and Concerns

There are those who make connections or draw parallels between TQM and such models as Outcome-Based Education (OBE), Effective Schools, Accelerated Schools, and Essential Schools (Schmoker & Wilson, 1993b; Valesky, Markus, Willis, & Nelson, 1993). Rhodes (1992) indicates that, while a point-by-point comparison may be helpful, it can also blue the rudimentary distinction that he says should be drawn "between improvement and management processes" (p. 80). TQM, he contends, views change as a natural consequence of people governing their own conduct such that they are able to be a little more effective each day. This, he says, leads to "continual growth in *total* organizational and personal capacity to act differently" (p. 80). By contrast, the other models tend to be perceived, whether or not they should be, as processes with change as the goal.

Holt (1993) is even more pointed in his criticism of OBE. He calls OBE a "warmed-over mishmash of the Tyler rationale, Benjamin Bloom's mastery learning, and competency-based education [that] quite explicitly puts the natural learning process into reverse." Indeed, he says, "behind the high-stepping jargon of transformational outcomes, learning paradigms, and empowerment lurk behavioristic methods that are totally at odds with the Deming quest for quality" (p. 384).

There are also those who raise cautions and concerns about adopting or even adapting a business-based model (Blankstein & Swain, 1994; Kohn, 1993a, 1993b). If proper precautions are taken and excesses avoided (Blankstein & Swain, 1994; Bonstingl, 1993; Schenkat, 1993a; Schmoker & Wilson, 1993a), however, the overwhelming weight of professional opinion appears to be that the promise is great and the possibilities are almost unlimited to engender substantial and real changes in education which will make even the most skeptical detractors take a second look. What is more, over and over TQM advocates observe that it is here to stay and that it is, most definitely, not a fad (Hackman & Wageman, 1994; Holt, 1993; Weaver, 1992).

Changes Substantial and Lasting

If Deming's philosophy is to have the desired effects, those who are advocating it must recognize that TQM provides no quick solution, that it necessitates fundamental rethinking of traditional systems, that it seeks continuous improvement, and that it takes a long-range view and a total commitment to transforming one's organization (Freeston, 1992; Hixson & Lovelace, 1992; Siu-Runyan & Heart, 1992; Tribus, 1990). Further, it is the system that must be transformed, not the individual (Rocheleau, 1991). According to Rhodes (1992), when members of a family believe that they, as individuals, not the family, are in need of fixing, that family is dysfunctional. So it is with most modern organizations, including schools. "Humans," Rhodes observes, "are born as purpose-driven, trial-and-error learning, self-regulating organisms. But most organizational life limits this natural behavior" (p. 76).

What is required, then, is a complete paradigm shift (Bonstingl, 1992b). A paradigm describes how the world is viewed; clearly, there are stark differences between what Bonstingl termed the "old paradigm of teaching and learning" and the "new paradigm of continuous improvement" (p. 83). In the old paradigm, learning and teaching are competition-based, lessons are linear, teachers work in isolation for one another, parents are outsiders, instruction is set up to generate "right" answers, and the discrete-discipline curriculum is controlled centrally. Life has purpose only if goals are reached. Administrators are teachers' natural adversaries. By contrast, in the paradigm, learning and teaching are cooperation-based, learning is spiraling (involving continuous improvement), teachers work together, parents are partners, instruction is designed to generate better questions, and the multi- and cross-disciplinary curriculum is site-based. Life is journey and has intrinsic value. Administrators are teammates and colleagues.

Deming has expanded on his 14 points with his Theory of Profound

Knowledge. There are four areas of <u>profound knowledge</u>, each of which, Rhodes (1992) explains, challenges an existing mental model: (a) Deming's concept of systems calls for interdependency within an organization; (b) He holds that people are psychological beings intrinsically motivated to be effective in their work; (c) Management processes, Deming maintains, cause up to 90% of the variation in results and outcomes; hence it is fruitless to try to achieve positive change in a school by monitoring results, assigning blame, and attempting to remediate individual teachers; and (d) Finally, his theory of knowledge views "humans as cognitive beings trying to construct knowledge from experience within frames provided by theories and beliefs" (p. 79).

Putting Deming's Philosophy to Work in One's Own School or District

It is not clear, then, that the philosophy of W. Edwards Deming has much potential when put to work in U.S. and other schools? The possibilities are, quite obviously, revoluntary. Needy schools desperate for answers are everywhere. Those prepared to make bold excursions into the unknown should get as ready as they can for what promises to be an exciting, probably fulfilling, but certainly not gentle expedition. They will doggedly pursue their objectives over sometimes uncharted and rocky terrain. They will ultimately realize that no pot-of-gold panacea, quick or otherwise, awaits at the end of that elusive rainbow. But, for those willing to study, work, and persist, the promise of positive results is great indeed.

While the map is incomplete and the pathway different for any two travelers, there are a few bits of advice which can be given to voyagers about to embark on their quest for quality. To a school-system (or individual-school) leader who would like to apply the principles of TQM, the writer recommends a ten-step strategy:

1. *Understand the old paradigm.* Assess where you are starting from. Know what it is you want to change and try to determine why you think there is something better for your teachers and students. Recognize that once you start down this road, there will be no turning back.
2. *Understand the new paradigm.* Know, to the extent possible, what you are getting into and be sure that you really want to do this. Read broadly and in-depth on Deming's philosophy. Learn how it has been applied and about challenges that other districts and schools have faced and how they confronted them. Visit schools at various stages of implementation of the TQM approach; got to schools like and unlike yours. Look at other sets of recommendations

too (e.g., Savary, 1992; Bonstingl, 1992b).
3. *Commit to transformation.* Buy into the whole package or leave it alone for another time. Ask a like commitment from everybody connected to the school or school district, including principals, teachers, and students, and parents. Adopting the Deming model is an undertaking of great magnitude. It does not have to—indeed cannot and should not happen—overnight. However, the principle of continuous improvement is critical. Once you have pledged yourself, prepare to stay the course. Remember too that a stable staff is important. Know that the application of Deming's philosophy is *not* a quick fix and *is* a long-term enterprise. Realize that you are ultimately going to revamp your system from top to bottom.
4. *Take cautions into account.* Be aware of questions which have been raised and admonitions which have been proffered by experts and practitioners. Answer these to your satisfaction before proceeding. Realize that other problems will come up along the way. Have a mechanism in place for addressing these problems.
5. *Localize the model.* How do you plan to begin? Where? It may be that you wish to begin in a few classrooms or one school first. Wherever you start, try to have all or at least nearly all of the 14 points in place. Anything which will be left for later should be committed to now, with a timeline as to when the remaining steps will be taken. If there are other classrooms or schools planning to join the network later, involve them in all the preliminary work so they will be ready to come on line at the designated time. Be sure to take into account and accommodate—without abandoning any aspects of Deming's philosophy or principles—any special circumstances and characteristics of your community, professional staff, etc.
6. *Make the change.* Once you have completed all reasonable preparations, proceed apace, beginning the process of becoming a TQM school or school district, expecting and settling for nothing less than success. With adequate preparation; a clear and reasonable plan of action; an optimistic attitude; and a dogged determination, you should experience the level of achievement you expect, desire, and deserve.
7. *Stay alert.* Be ever vigilant. Keep a sense of humor, enlist

everyone's involvement in the enterprise, and tackle problems that still present themselves. Do so with wisdom and dispatch.
8. *Involve students and other interested parties at fundamental levels.* Leave no one out at any level he or she is capable of participating. Most particularly, include students. Even kindergartners are capable of rudimentary goal setting and self-evaluation, for example.
9. *Reap—and build on—results.* Once the fruition is apparent, enjoy it. Congratulate yourself, publish the results, and decide what to do next. Success, of course, breeds more success. Thus, you may wish to take advantage of something good that is happening for some students so that more of them can benefit; that is, you might wish to speed up your original timetable. In any event, you will want to learn from—and build upon—your accomplishments as well as your mistakes. And, of course, you will always want to share with others, as others shared with you when you were getting started.
10. *Do not rest on your laurels.* Your new system should have a built-in dynamic. Recognize that you never fully arrive. Even if one achieved metaphysical perfection at one instance in time, there would still be more to do. Why? Because your conditions, constituencies, and potentials are forever in flux.

A Call to Action

Dr. W. Edwards Deming set something incredible in motion in 1950 when he helped Japan to turn its economy around. The leaders who heard him paid attention and responded to his philosophy point by point. Over time, an amazing transformation took place. Thirty years later, following a white paper on the NBC television network, American business leaders took notice and many started to make the tremendous transformation necessary to commit to quality over quantity. The payoff has been apparent.

Now, in the 1990s, educators are working hard to catch up. They too see many possibilities for the adaption of Total Quality Management (TQM) to education involves changes which are fundamental in nature and large in scope. As Chizmar (1994) put it:

> The total package of TQM attributes can be used successfully to manage the teaching and learning process. The TQM teaching/learning model

> highlights teaching and learning strategies that involve students actively in their own learning through the creation of learning communities and increased use of collaboration. The TQM teaching/learning model features continuous improvement, discerning feedback, empowering teachers, empowered students, and ubiquitous teamwork. (p. 182)

For those engaged in these changes, the stakes are high. The demands are great to be sure, but so are the potential rewards. The time is now! The *way* is clear; but, one must ask, is there the *will?* The jury is still out on this one, but a ground swell for the TQM movement appears to be gaining momentum in diverse places and situations all across the nation. If this trends continues on its present course, it bodes well for American education in the third millennium.

References

Abernethy, P. E., & Serfass, R. W. (1992). One district's quality improvement story. Educational Leadership, 50 (30), 14-17.

Aguayo, R. (1990). Dr. Deming. New York: Simon & Schuster.

Alexander, L. (1991). America 2000: An educational study. Washington, DC: U.S. Department of Education.

Arcaro, J. S. (1995). Quality in education: An implementation handbook. Delray Beach, FL: St. Lucie Press.

Blankstein, A. M. (1992). Lessons from enlightened corporation. Educational Leadership, 49 (6), 71-75.

Blankstein, A. M., & Swain, H. (1994). Is TQM right for schools? Executive Educator, 16 (2), 51-54.

Bonstingl, J. J. (1992a). The quality revolution in education. Educational Leadership, 50 (3), 4-6.

Bonstingl, J. J. (1992b). Schools of quality: An introduction to total quality management in education. Alexandria, VA: Association for Supervision and Curriculum Development.

Bonstingl, J. J. (1992c). The total quality classroom. Educational Leadership, 49 (6), 66-70.

Bonstingl, J. J. (1993). The quality movement: What's it really about? Educational Leadership, 51 (1), 66.

Chizmar, J. F. (1994). Total quality management (TQM) of teaching and learning. Journal of Economic Education, 25 (2), 179-190.

Crosby, P. B. (1980). Quality is free: The art of making quality certain. New York: Mentor/Penguin.

Deming, W. E. (1986). Out of the crisis. Cambridge: Massachusetts Institute of Technology Center for Advanced Engineering Study.

Deming, W. E. (1994). The new economics for industry, government, education (2nd ed.). Cambridge: Massachusetts Institute of Technology Center for Advanced Engineering Study.

Drucker, P. (1977). Management. New York: Harper's College Press.

Fiegenbaum, A. (1961). Total quality control. New York: McGraw-Hill.

Freeston, K. R. (1992). Getting started with TQM. Educational Leadership, 50 (3), 10-13.

Gitlow, H. S., & Gitlow, S. J. (1987). The Deming guide to quality and competitive position. Englewood Cliffs, NJ: Prentice-Hall.

Glasser, W. (1990). The quality school: Managing students without coercion. New York: Harper & Row.

Gray, K. (1993). Why we will lose: Taylorism in America's high schools. Phi Delta Kappa, 74 (3), 379-374.

Hackman, J. R., & Wageman, R. (1995). Total quality management: Empirical, conceptual, and practical issues. Administrative Science Quarterly, 40, 309-342.

Holt, M. (1993). The educational consequences of W. Edwards Deming. Phi Delta Kappan, 74 (3), 382-388.

Hixson, J., & Lovelace, K. (1992). Total quality management's challenge to urban schools. Educational Leadership, 50 (3), 24-27.

Ishikawa, K. (1985). What is total quality control? The Japanese way. Englewood Cliffs, NJ: Prentice-Hall.

Juran, J. M. (1969). Managerial breakthrough: A new concept of the manager's job. New York: McGraw-Hill.

Juran, J. M. (1974). The quality control handbook (3rd ed.). New York: McGraw-Hill.

Juran, J. M. (1988). Juran on planning for quality. New York: Free Press.

Kohn, A. (1993a). Turning learning into a business: Concerns about total quality. Educational Leadership, 51 (1), 58-62.

Kohn, A. (1993b). The trouble with management models. Educational Leadership, 51 (1), 67.

Lockwood, A. T. (1992, Fall). Total quality management. Focus in Change, No. 8. (ERIC Document Reproduction No. ED 372 462)

National Commission on Excellence in Education. (1983). A nation at risk: The imperative for educational reform. Washington, DC: U.S. Government Printing Office.

Rebore, R. W. (1995). Personnel administration in education: A management approach (4th ed.). Boston: Allyn and Bacon.

Rhodes, L. A. (1990). Why quality is within our grasp. . . if we reach. The School Administrator, 47 (10), 31-34.

Rhodes, L. A. (1992). On the road to quality. Educational Leadership, 49 (6), 76-80.

Rocheleau, L. (1991). Mt. Edgecumbe's venture in quality. School Administrator, 48 (9), 14-16, 18.

Ross, J. E. (1993). Total quality management: Text, cases, and readings. Delray Beach, FL: St. Lucie Press.

Savary, L. M. (1992). Creating quality schools. Arlington, VA: American Association of School Administrators.

Schargel, F. P. (1991). Promoting quality in education. Vocational Education Journal, 66 (8), 34-35, 77.

Schenkat, R. (1993a). Deming's quality: Our last but best hope. Educational Leadership, 51 (1), 64-65.

Schenkat, R. (1993b). Quality connections: Transforming schools through total quality management. Alexandria, VA: Association for Supervision and Curriculum Development.

Schmoker, M., & Wilson, R. B. (1993a). Adapting total quality doesn't mean "turning learning into a business." Educational Leadership, 51 (1), 62-63.

Schmoker, M., & Wilson, R. B. (1993b). Transforming schools through total quality education. Phi Delta Kappan, 74, 389-395.

Shewhart, W. A. (1986a). Economic control of quality of manufactured product. Washington, DC: CEE Press Books. (Original work published 1931).

Shewhart, W. A. (1986b). Statistical method from the viewpoint of quality control. Mineola, NY: Dover. (Original work published 1939).

Siu-Runyan, Y., & Heart, S. J. (1992). Management manifesto. Executive Educator, 14 (1), 23-26.

Taylor, F. W. (1911). The principles of scientific management. New York: Harper & Row.

Tanner, D., & Tanner, L. (1987). Supervision in education: Problems and practices. New York: Macmillan.

Tribus, M. (1990). The application of quality management principles in education at Mt. Edgecumbe High School, Sitka, Alaska. Washington, DC: Office of Educational Research and Improvement. (ERIC Document Reproduction No. ED 370 166)

Valesky, T. C., Markus, F. W., Willis, J., & Nelson, J. O. (1993, November). Total quality management as a philosophical and organizational framework to achieve outcomes-based education and effective schools. Paper presented at the annual meeting of the MidSouth Educational Research Association, New Orleans, LA. (ERIC Document

Reproduction No. ED 365 703)

Walton, Mary. (1986). <u>The Deming management method.</u> New York: Perigee/Putnam.

Weaver, T. (1992). <u>Total quality management</u> (Rept. No. EDO-EA-92-6). (ERIC Document Reproduction No. ED 347 670)

Chapter 6

DEWEY VERSUS DEMING: A NEW THEORY DEBATE IN EDUCATIONAL ADMINISTRATION?

Michael D. Richardson, Jackson L. Flanigan, and Kenneth E. Lane
Georgia Southern University, Clemson University, and California State University

Abstract

What is the role of theory in modern educational organizations? Deming states that all the hard work and best efforts of managers and workers will lead to ruin without the guidance of profound knowledge. He states that this profound knowledge only comes from outside the system, and comes only by invitation, that it cannot be imposed on the organization by an outside force. Does this mean a new and fundamentally different concept of organizational theory, radically different from that traditionally practiced in most educational organizations? According to Deming and the disciples of Total Quality Management, the answer is a resounding, yes. Dewey postulated that the purpose of theory was to explain practice. He believed that practice was the key to effective education, not a knowledge of theory. This paper will examine both constructs from the educational administrator's perspective permitting the reader to make substantive judgments about the validity of both arguments in application to modern educational organizations.

> The wicked leader is he who the people despise.
> The good leader is he who the people revere.
> The great leader is he who the people say,
> "We did it ourselves."
> —Lao Tsu

Introduction

This paper is not an attempt to ponder the educational administration theory debate of the 1950s and 1960s (Allison, 1989); rather, this is a brief attempt to explain some of W. Edwards Deming's and John Dewey's postulates which concern educational administration. Dewey has been widely read and even more thoroughly discussed throughout our educational history (Passow, 1982), but Deming has recently presented some new and radical ideas on transforming American education. Deming is not alone in his desire to change the American educational experience. Reformers and politicians have been trying various methods of reform for the past four decades, without measurable success. Deweyan thought has also experienced a revival in recent years, so this examination and contrast of the central tenets of the two men is appropriate at this time, particularly as the profession is attempting to determine whether or not there is a knowledge base for educational administration. One note of caution should be sounded: theory may not be the most operative word for discussion at this juncture in the development of an educational administration knowledge base (Swift, 1971). Learning may be a more realistic term to convey meaning to educators and policy-makers concerning educational administration (Senge, 1990).

Who was John Dewey?

The name John Dewey has been used in educational circles since the 1890s. Like Deming, Dewey has been widely quoted and more often misunderstood (Feng, 1989). Although John Dewey probably influenced modern educational thinking as much as any man (Passow, 1982), his writings are obscure, difficult to read and lead to misinterpretation (Berger, 1959). John Dewey was born in Burlington, Vermont into a family that practiced a "mildly pious form of Congregationalist Protestantism, orthodox without being overly creedal, intense without revivalist overtones" (Shea, 1989, p. 294). Dewey was a philosopher who brought education into the national spotlight during his tenure at the University of Chicago (1894-1904) when he chaired the combined Departments of Philosophy, Psychology, and Pedagogy and founded the University Laboratory School, better known as the "Dewey School" (Rockefeller, 1991).

Dewey was the advocate of the Progressive Education movement and a primary proponent of the pragmatic school of philosophy (Sidorsky, 1977). He spent most of his lifetime attempting to rationalize the dichotomy between the scientific method of knowledge acquisition and the problem of living in a modern world. He viewed education as the promise of American democracy for the common person (Parker, 1981).

Dewey was born in 1859 during the administration of James Buchanan and died in June 1952 during Eisenhower's campaign for president (Wirth, 1989). He was born in the same year that Darwin published his famous Origin of the Species, and that oil was discovered in Pennsylvania. He was a world-wide author and traveler who advocated education as an instrument for human growth and social progress (Passow, 1982). Dewey made significant and long-lasting contributions to American education and democratic thinking as conceived by Roth (1962): "Future thought in America must go beyond Dewey . . . though it is difficult to see how it can avoid going through him" (p. 144). Sidorsky (1977, iii) observed that: "John Dewey was the most influential figure in American philosophical thought in the first half of the twentieth century. His influence was both broad in scope and deep in impact."

Who is W. Edwards Deming?

Many educators have heard the name Deming during the past decade, but relatively few know anything about the man. Who is Deming? What are his experiences and how did he become a advocate for educational change? Why should the educational community pay attention to a 92-year-old man whose greatest claim to fame is the rebirth of the Japanese economy?

Deming was born in Sioux City, Iowa in 1900 and spent most of his early years in Wyoming, graduating from high school in 1917 and from the University of Wyoming in 1922. Deming's academic training was in physics and included a doctorate from Yale in 1927 in mathematical physics. Deming spent many years utilizing his acquired skills, first in the United States Department of Agriculture and later in the Census Bureau (Aguayo, 1990). It was during this time that he met Walter A. Shewhart, who would later become known as the father of quality control (Walton, 1986). Deming had established a national reputation as an expert in sampling and left government service in 1946 to establish his own consulting firm (Walton, 1986). At the request of the War Department, he visited Japan in 1947 and returned in 1950, 1951, 1952, 1955, and 1956. In 1950, he met with the presidents of Japan's leading companies and told them that the establishment of quality was essential to their survival. Due to the condition of Japan after World War II and the need to rebuild a shattered economy, the business leaders listened, implemented his ideas, and the rest is history (Pines, 1991).

While his work was relatively unnoticed in the United States, Deming became the guru of the Japanese quality movement (Oberle, 1991). In fact, the Deming Medal was established to honor the top Japanese companies utilizing his management techniques. A 1980 NBC white paper—"If Japan can, why can't we?" highlighted Deming's work and brought him recognition in this country (Oberle, 1991). Shortly thereafter, Ford and other large corporations employed Deming and the "quality management revolution" was born. At ninety-two years of age, Deming is still active and conducts over twenty seminars each year (Aguayo, 1990).

Dewey vs. Deming

How do the theoretical constructs of Deming match those expressed by Dewey? Are there inherent relationships or contrasts between Dewey's theories and Deming's theories? The following distinctions between the two theorists are presented in the hope that prospective educational administrators gain a better understanding of the two men and their ideas.

Learning
Dewey: Learn by doing   Deming: Learn by theory

Dewey postulated that learning comes by experience; that real learning was developed by doing (Feng, 1990). A common theme throughout Dewey's work was that "we learn from experience, and from the books or sayings of others only as they are related to experience" (Dewey, 1897, 80). Dewey believed that people at any age learned best by practice and by doing the job, not studying about the job (Emans, 1981). For Dewey the learner was the center of the learning process, not the curriculum (Rockefeller, 1991). Dewey also advocated learning as experimentation, "children like to do things and watch to see what will happen" (Dewey, 1956, p. 44). Much of Dewey's belief about learning was tied to his desire for a "natural" learning which he contrasted to the "artificial drills and recitations of formal schooling" (Feng, 1989, p. 13). Dewey (1916) said that:

> There are the two great things in breaking down isolation, in getting connection—to have the child come to school with all the experience he has got outside the school, and to leave it with something to be immediately used in his everyday life. (p. 29)

Deming states that repetition by doing is simply modeling and will not produce learning: rather, Deming (1989) believes that the application of theory is the only opportunity for real learning:

> Theory leads to questions. Without questions, experience and examples teach nothing. Without questions, one can only have an

example. To copy an example of success, without understanding it with the aid of theory, may lead to disaster. (p. 22)

Deming contends that by examining theory, questions are raised which ultimately lead to answers which are the basis for real learning. Deming specifies that managers and school leaders must dispel fear. Fear is constantly present in school: fear of grades, fear of job, fear to be risk takers, etc. (Glasser, 1990b). Deming agrees that fear is a motivator, but motivation by fear is not a constructive action. "Learning and risk-taking cannot take place in an atmosphere where people are afraid to ask questions, take a stand, or make suggestions" (Siu-Runyan & Heart, 1992, p. 25).

Deming believes that competition has helped to destroy the love of learning that students have when they first come to school. He states that "the first step in learning is curiosity" and that schools should be more cooperative in nature and less competitive (Neave, 1991, p. 393). He also advocates a close tie and working relationship between the educational organization and its clientele, including the belief that parents and business partners should be brought into the school for assistance. This point also specifies closer cooperation between schools; middle schools with elementary and high schools, high schools with middle schools and colleges, private schools with public schools. Deming would also seek closer cooperation between and among different departments within the school.

Time perspective

<u>Dewey</u>: Orientation to the present and past

<u>Deming</u>: Orientation to the future

Dewey was concerned with improving the current state of affairs, "We always live at the time and not at some other time, and only by extracting at each present time the full meaning of each present experience are we prepared for doing the same thing in the future" (Dewey, 1939, p. 51). According to Wheeler (1977, p. 388) when Dewey speaks about the future, he speaks "not of fantasy . . . but of the possibilities of a past and present as these may be transformed by reflection." Wheeler (1977) goes further to speculate that Dewey had an interest in the future but his primary concern rested "in the experience of consequences that are the consequence of thought of intelligence working in the world" (p. 388), that is, the current, the here and now, not the future.

Dewey's criticism of education, which he characterized as primarily preparation for the future, specified that "if the environment, in school and out, supplies conditions which utilize adequately the present capacities of the immature, the future which grows out of the present is much taken care of" (Dewey, 1916, p. 65). Dewey was a proponent of acculturation which "is linked to the past: the attitude of education to the past is that which determines the survival of culture; this is the opinion held by the votaries of acculturation" (Lamm, 1986, p. 8). Dewey (1939) believed that an understanding of the past was a prerequisite to knowing the present, "but the achievements of the past provide the only means at command for understanding the present" (p. 376).

The focus for Deming is on "improvement of the processes for the future instead of on judgment of current results" (Tveite, 1991, p. 4). Deming, according to Neave (1991, p. 248), has as his objective "to improve the future . . . the past is gone." Deming has a future orientation and a "faith that there will be a future. . ." He goes on to describe "innovation, [as] the foundation of the future . . ." (Neave, 1991, p. 205). Deming's admonitions about the use of prediction also highlight his concern for the future. His entire theoretical constructural thesis for the development of new economic and educational structures to meet the needs of future citizens is tied to his focus on future concerns (Melvin, 1991).

Education

<u>Dewey</u>: Social process   <u>Deming</u>: Learning

Dewey (1897, p. 78) believed that education was a social process: "The only true education comes through the stimulation of the child's powers by the demands of the social situation in which he finds himself." Dewey was a pragmatist "who believed that the essential function of the mind and ideas is the direction of action ... [and] put special emphasis on teaching children to think by challenging them to solve practical problems arising out of their daily experience" (Rockefeller, 1991, p. 250). Dewey (1946, p. 49) postulated that understanding was the true purpose of education and that "understanding has to be in terms of how things work and how to do things. Understanding, by its very nature, is related to action." Dewey in his classic work, <u>Democracy and Education</u> (1916) wrote that education "has no end beyond itself; it is its own end; and . . . the educational process is one of continual reorganizing, reconstructing, transforming" (p. 94).

Price (1990) states that the Deming definition of education differs from Dewey. Deming believes that:

> Education is the sharing, by organized disclosure and

dissemination, of knowledge, understanding and insight. Its purpose is to open and widen the mind of the pupil, to search out and explore the general principles which underpin the observed phenomena. Its purpose is to enable the person to become an *enabler,* one who can enable others *to do* (those who have been *trained* to do). It is a generalist, non-specific, of diffuse focus. It is maximalist (how *much* can be learned?) It has a *good* to know basis. It is assumed to be measurable. It is infinite, open-ended, unbounded. (p. 107)

A key to Deming's concept of education is teamwork: "Industry desperately needs to foster teamwork. The only ... education on teamwork our people receive in school is on the athletic field. Teamwork in the classroom is called cheating" (Scherkenback, 1986, p. 128). Numerical quotas, according to Aguoya (1990), are more likely to serve as ammunition for frustration and jealousy than to engender the cooperative teamwork that nurtures productivity. Using a quota system for grades, incentive pay, teacher rankings, or student test scores encourages people to produce quantity rather than quality.

Most educators believe that once they complete a certification program or some magical degree that their education stops (Rhodes, 1990a). However, according to Deming: "Education and retraining—an investment in people—are required for long-term planning" (Siu-Runyan & Heart, 1992, p. 26). Schools spend very little of their total budget dollars on staff development or continual training. In contrast, most businesses and industries will spend two to four percent of their budgets on training (Miller, 1991). A recent survey of medical physicians found that 80 percent of their knowledge was learned on the job, which was very similar to a study of school principals. If on-the-job learning takes place, what better indication do we have that in-service training and retraining are constantly needed in an educational organization? According to Deming (1986, p. 86): "What an organization needs is not just good people; it needs people that are improving with education." Deming also states that "a school should be like a laboratory—with excitement in learning" (Neave, 1990, p. 198).

Prediction
<u>Dewey</u>: Impulsive   <u>Deming</u>: Management

To a large extent Dewey ignored the irrationality of man. His writings stress a one-dimensional portrait of man that almost completely ignored certain features of the human condition. According to Feng (1989, p. 15) Dewey's account of the ideal educational situation assumed, to start with, an "impulse" to investigate and experiment, as well as a "social impulse" from which cooperation stems. Maybe most of the children in his Laboratory School had such impulses... Dewey did not make explicit the difference in different levels of learning.

Deming (1989) believes that prediction is an integral part of theory and that "management in any form is prediction" (p. 12); while Dewey believed that predication was a constraint to learning (Feng, 1989). For Deming (1989) "management of a system is action based on prediction. Rational prediction requires systematic learning and comparison of predictions..." (p. 11). According to Neave (1991):

> Deming's whole object is to improve the future. As far as he is concerned, that is the purpose of knowledge. The past is gone. We can learn from it, of course—with the aid of theory.... Is the theory helpful to use, especially for prediction?... And there lies the crux of the matter: prediction. (p. 248)

Management
<u>Dewey</u>: Scientific management   <u>Deming</u>: Leadership

Dewey advocated the use of the scientific method as the primary tool for discovering new knowledge. He speculated that learning resulted from the application of the scientific method to experience (Paringer, 1990). This experiential approach was the foundation of Frederick Taylor's Scientific Management (Rogers & Polkinghorn, 1990). Dewey (1940) also advocated that teachers should be at the heart of the decision making process:

> For Dewey,...decisions about... school organization... should be the domain of teachers, working together at the school site. While Dewey acknowledges that decisions should be placed in the hands of experts, he argues that the expert is not some highly placed official in the central hierarchy... (p. 65)

According to Paringer (1990):

> The empirical analysis and methodology of naturalism and scientific rationality were assigned by Dewey as the fundamental means... for advancing human society.... Science was the activity which removed the scales from our eyes. This was the methodological basis of experience, too, which enabled us to see the connectedness of things. (p. 123)

> Deming argues that unless America moves away from the traditional

Taylorism method of management that decline in the West would continue. Deming sees Scientific Management as a "mechanistic approach to managing people" that was unable to "liberate and harness talents in the workforce" (Price, 1990, p. 52). Deming advocates the intrinsic motivation of mankind, while Dewey and the Scientific Management theorists advocate extrinsic motivation (Gabor, 1990). Deming states that the scientific management philosophy serves to demotivate employees rather than assisting employees to develop their potential. According to the Deming philosophy of management, employees should be permitted to make meaningful contributions to their jobs, increase their self-esteem, increase motivation and reduce blame for systemic problems beyond the control of employees (Gabor, 1990).

Deming states that "leadership is the job of management." It is the responsibility of management to discover the barriers that prevent workers from taking pride in what they do" (Siu-Runyan & Heart, 1992, p. 24). Traditional educational managers (not leaders) have managed American schools by the "management by results" technique. Management by results focuses on an organizational chart and key control points within the organization (Lane, 1983). The school board tells the superintendent, who tells the principals, who tells the teachers, etc. The classic example of this bureaucratic method was described by Max Weber in the 1890s (Hall, 1991).

Deming suggests that slogans and exhortations be eliminated because they have a tendency to blame workers for problems that are not theirs, but the system's (Rhodes, 1990a). According to Siu-Runyan and Heart (1992, pp. 25-26): "The job of management is not to coerce, but to generate support, cooperation, and leadership for a process that brings together the energy of everyone for a common vision."

Deming advocates leadership rather than simply management. Leadership is a way to optimize the abilities of all those inside and outside the organization for the benefit of the organization (Jointer & Scholtes, 1991). Recent critics of public schools have advocated an instructional leadership role for the principal (Chait, 1982); but Deming would see the principal as a transformational leader whose job is to mange so that it is easy for workers (faculty and students) "to see a strong connection between what they are asked to do and what they believe to be worth doing" (Glasser, 1990a, p. 427).

Finally, according to Deming, managers must take action to accomplish the transformation. As Siu-Runyan and Heart (1992, 26) state:

> ... all the personnel in your school must make a commitment to moving toward the shared vision—with you as a manager guiding

and serving as a model for the change process. You must build support for change into the system—so enough people are committed to transformation that it won't be derailed by staff turnover... The process of change never ends. Restructuring schools is never finished.... When you create this kind of honest, mutually respecting attitude among staff members, you have the makings for a powerful learning environment in classrooms.

Deming believes that "one of management's jobs is to manage the required change, and to involve everyone in the change" (Neave, 1991, 407). Without the involvement of everyone in the process, change and improvement will not result.

Experience

<u>Dewey</u>: Is acquired by doing

<u>Deming</u>: Is acquired by theory

"Dewey insists that all knowing and inquiry involves some kind of doing that involves physical modifications, and he denounces all traditional theories that separate knowing and doing, theory and practice" (Rockefeller, 1991, p. 406). Paringer (1990, p. 117) summarized Dewey's definition of experience as "Experience was the interaction of a living being with its physical and social environment."

Dewey identified "the object of knowledge with the consequences of directed operations rather than with something which exists prior to or apart from the operations involved in an act of knowing" (Rockefeller, 1991, p. 405). Dewey (1948, p. 663) speculated that:

> Notions, theories, systems, no matter how elaborate and self-consistent they are, must be regarded as hypotheses. They are to be accepted as bases of actions which test them, not as finalities. To perceive this fact is to abolish rigid dogmas from the world. It is to recognize that conceptions theories and systems of thought are always open to development through use. There is no infallible sources of ideas and ideas themselves are tools to be rejected, accepted or remade in the light of the consequences of their use.

According to Rockefeller (1991), Dewey:

> relies upon an empirical method of knowledge that begins with problematical situations in experience and ends with a return to experience for experimental verification. The problems with nonempirical methods from his point of view is that they do not develop ideas which illuminate the meaning of ordinary life and

its predicaments, and consequently, they fail to realize [the potential for experience]. (p. 397)

Dewey's call for experience in learning has found new disciples in the experiential school of knowledge which flourished during the 1970s and 1980s (Bowers, 1984). According to Walter and Marks (1981), the reason for the success of experiential learning is:

> simple and profound. Effectiveness is increased when learning is based on and directly related to the participants' experience, when there is some participation in designing, and when there is some choice concerning personal behavior. (p. 281)

Deming states that "experience teaches nothing unless studied with the aid of theory" (Neave, 1990, p. 147). Deming often describes his seminars as education, "and the purpose of education is to learn theory. . . . We are going to learn theory. We're going to learn why we have to do what we need to do" (Neave, 1990, p. 245). Neave (1990) goes on to describe what Deming means by theory:

> Insistence on a foundation of theory is one of the things that marks Deming... His teachings are not just a collection of good ideas, or challenging one, or controversial ones... They are rather outcomes and logical deductions based on theory. When that is realized, his work is seen to have a unique unity and credibility.... A theory may be complex. It may be simple. It may only be a hunch, and the hunch may be wrong. We learn by acceptance, or by modification of our theory, or even by abandoning it and starting over. (pp. 246-247)

Deming is quite outspoken about the use of experience without theory:

> Experience teaches nothing unless studied with the aid of theory... Experiences teaches us (enables us to plan, to predict) only when we use it to modify and understand theory... An example teaches nothing unless studied with the aid of theory... No number of examples establishes a theory. (Neave, 1991, pp. 249-250)

Systems

Dewey: Deterants   Deming: Cooperation

According to Paringer (1990):

> Dewey only superficially, . . . considered that the materialized world—structures, institutions, systems—intervenes, conditions, even determines consciousness; the materialized world is the creator of consciousness by putting forth what functions it requires of its membership. By explaining differences and hierarchies as "natural," Dewey's reform pedagogy would set specific parameters for challenging social reality. (p. 90)

Dewey saw systems as a deterant to experience. Systems were roadblocks rather than bridges between experience and the natural world. To Deming, a system:

> is a series of functions or activities . . . within an organization that work together for the aim of the organization. . . The schools of a city, including private schools, parochial schools, trade schools, and universities, provide an example of components that ought to work together as a system for education. (Deming, 1989, p. 13)

Further, a system ". . . consists of components [which are] not to be measured by some competitive measure but by its contribution to the system as a whole . . ." (Gabor, 1991, p. 9).

Deming believes that an understanding of variation is essential to the management of a system. Further, he believes that an understanding of variation among people is essential. Senge (1990) states:

> Our prevailing system of management has destroyed our people. People are born with intrinsic motivation, self-esteem, dignity, curiosity to learn, joy in learning. The forces of destruction begin with toddlers—a prize for the best Halloween costume, grades in school, gold stars, and on up through the university. On the job, people, teams, divisions are ranked—reward from the one at the top, punishment at the bottom. MBO, quotas, incentive pay, business plans, put together separately, division by division, cause further loss, unknown and unknowable. (p. 7)

Philosophy

Dewey: Progressivism and Pragmaticism

Deming: Continuous improvement

According to Paringer (1990): "Dewey's progressivism . . . somewhat benignly appealed to a trust in the advances of scientific thinking and economic expansion (pp. 122-23). Paringer concluded that progressivism lulled people into a false sense of security and a lack of questioning concerning growth and security.

> Progressivism foresaw indefinite prosperity, equalization of wealth and income, and the expansion of equal opportunity and humanitarian concern, as well as democratic participation.... The progressive aim was to harmonize the individual with the social changes being wrought by the new methods of production, with their relocation into urban areas, with the greater intermingling of races, creeds, lifestyles, etc., with scientific innovations, and the ideal of the democratic promise itself... progressivism ... was not distinct from nor in opposition to the capitalist organization of society, its division of labor, and its maintenance of the power/ knowledge hierarchy. (Paringer, 1990, pp. 98-99)

Dewey may have been best known for his developmental work with the philosophy of pragmatism. Pragmatic philosophy attempts to explain behavior and human choices in terms of the context in which the choices are presented (Popp, 1987). According to Bullert (1983, p. 208):

> Pragmatism retains a set of principles but nurtures an openness to the evidence that would enable society to cope with the complex, indeterminate problems that demand action. Dewey advised that attention be paid to the context of the problems. The pragmatic framework establishes both the means and the disposition to foster the qualities of discreteness, truthfulness, and compromise, all of which are necessary for the strength of democracy.... Instead of dogmatic platitudes, Dewey argued that political policies should be judged on the basis of their consequences.

Dewey's (1931) focus with pragmatism was "how thought functions in the experimental determination of future consequences" (p. 26).

The Deming philosophy is one of continual improvement. Deming believes that management's job is to continually work on the system which will optimize the product and improve the process (Gabor, 1990). Deming believes that eliminating performance appraisals is one of the key ways that management can demonstrate this philosophy of continual improvement. He advocates management demonstrate a belief is the ability of the worker and provide the assistance necessary to make that worker productive rather than reducing the worker's incentive by comparing his/her performance to others in the system or to some arbitrary ideal. Deming believes that this demotivates the worker, decreases productivity, and thereby reduces profitability. He also believes that top management should not be as job mobile as they are currently in the United States. According to Deming top management should insure a sense of stability in the workplace by remaining on the job for several years, as in Japan. He also believes that learning management is a lengthy process and not one that is learned in generic isolation (Aguayo, 1990; Walton, 1986; Neave, 1991; Deming, 1986).

Economics

<u>Dewey</u>: Social democracy   <u>Deming</u>: Cooperation

Dewey was often described as a social democrat who fought against big business and political power. His primary targets were the chieftains of big business who controlled American business and industry at the expense of democratic ideals (Bullert, 1983). During the 1940s Dewey's criticism of capitalism diminished, but he continued to believe that "economic progress was dependent upon the growth of scientific . . . knowledge rather than the growth and accumulation of capital" (Bullert, 1983, p. 30). Dewey gradually shifted from an abhorrence for capitalism to a "grudging recognition that the available alternatives were much worse" (Bullert, 1983, p. 31). After visiting Russia and other socialist countries, Dewey was convinced that capitalism might not be the best, but the alternatives were worse. In fact, after 1936, Bullert (1983, p. 32) states that "Dewey's enthusiasm for the possibilities of social engineering waned. He still sought democratic controls in the economy, but . . . he emphasized a mixed system with voluntary cooperation."

Deming speculates that economic growth requires both individual initiative and cooperation (Berger, et al, 1989). The organization must be dedicated to "a culture of unity with flexibility, of autonomy with collaboration, of stability with change" (Baker, 1987, p. 24). The principles of quality management cannot always be captured by existing accounting systems, but must be recognized and taken into consideration if the organization is to survive and be economically viable in the future. Deming believes that many American businesses are in trouble because managers do not understand the economic concepts of high quality, high productivity, more jobs, and better return on investments (Metz, 1984). In fact, Deming speculates that the economic and business practices of the 1900s, largely developed after World War II, will not allow the United States to remain economically competitive during the next decade (Mitroff, 1988). Deming also observes that educators are often bound by the "low bid" and fail to look for the quality in goods and services (George, 1984). He admonishes society to look at the cost of educating a child versus the cost of incarcerating a prisoner (Neave, 1991).

Knowledge

Dewey: Born out of experience

Deming: Profound knowledge

To Dewey (1916) knowledge was attained by experience: "ordinary experience is . . . weighed down and pushed into a corner by a load of unassimilated information" (p. 209). Further, he stated that all knowledge came by experience, often from other individuals, ". . . something of another's experience in order to tell him intelligently of one's own experience" (Dewey, 1916, pp. 5-6). Rockefeller (1991) states that for Dewey "all knowledge is . . . of an individual and that the goal of science and philosophy is to reach an individual object of knowledge which is at the same time thoroughly universal" (p. 102). Shaker (1990) speculates that:

> As educators well know, Dewey made a central theme out of the roles of the scientist and the educator emphasizing the discrete purposes they bring to work with a disciplinary body of knowledge. Such claims about the nature and uses of knowledge seem to evolve spontaneously from philosophy of education. . . . Progressive education is remembered even by its hostile critics as emphasizing interest and activity among children, although educational leaders . . . neglect to incorporate the movement in their analyses. (pp. 12-13)

Dewey (1939) states that:

> The further test or mark of a good activity, educationally speaking, is that it have a sufficiently long time-span so that a series of endeavors and explorations are involved in it, and included in such a way that each step opens up a new field, raises new questions, arouses a demand for further knowledge, and suggests what to do next on the basis of what has been accomplished and the knowledge thereby gained. (pp. 177-178)

Deming's system of profound knowledge has four parts: (1) appreciation for a system; (2) theory of variation; (3) theory of knowledge; and (4) psychology. Deming states that "there is no substitute for knowledge. We continue to ignore and forget that at our peril" (Neave, 1991, p. 273). Deming concludes, "Hard work and best efforts will by themselves not produce quality" (1989, p. 6). Deming goes on to say: "Hard work and best efforts, put forth without guidance of profound knowledge, leads to ruin in the world . . . there is no substitute for knowledge" (1989, p. 10).

Psychology
Dewey: Religion   Deming: Individualization

Dewey's early work Psychology outlined his conceptual analysis of the purpose for psychology and its application to philosophy. According to Rockefeller (1991) "Psychology is a study of the way in which the self finds its true self and union with the divine in and through science, philosophy, art, social relations, and religion" (pp. 100-101). For Dewey psychology was a blend of the study of man (psychology) and the study of man's relationship to God (philosophy). He saw the two as being totally inseparable. He used the neo-Hegelian approach for studying psychology, thereby reducing the dualism offered by psychology and religion. Dewey argues in Psychology that "all natural, healthy feeling is absorbed in some object or in the end of some activity" (Rockefeller, 1991, p. 105). Dewey was careful not to differentiate between means and ends. As reported by Rockefeller (1991), Dewey argues that "true means are the end analyzed into its constituent factors, rather than elements which are only externally and mechanically related to the desired end" (p. 107).

When examining psychology, Deming states that:

> People are different from one another... Management of industry, education, and government operate today under the supposition that all people are alike... People learn in different ways, and at different speeds... No one, child or other, can enjoy learning if he must constantly be concerned about grading and gold stars for his performance, or about rating on the job. Our educational system would be improved immeasurably by abolishment of grading... One is born with a natural inclination to learn and to be innovative. One inherits a right to enjoy his work. Psychology helps us to nurture and preserve these positive innate attributes of people (1989, pp. 23-24).

Neave (1991) states that:

> Intrinsic motivation is a person's innate dignity and self-esteem, and his natural esteem for other people. One is born with a natural inclination to learn . . . Modern management has stolen and smothered intrinsic motivation and dignity. It has removed joy in work and in learning ... Modern management is based on extrinsic motivation . . . [which] is submission to external forces that neutralize intrinsic motivation. (p. 271)

Deming states that quality cannot be inspected into the product at the end of the process. According to Siu-Runyan & Heart (1992):

> Education's version of mass inspection is standardized testing. It's the measure by which we determine the quality of what we do. But standardized testing by its nature diverts us from the true purpose of education—which is to enhance the ability of each student to learn and think constructively, critically, and creatively. Mass testing fails to get an accurate measure of students' abilities to use diverse strategies, skills, and information. Mass testing also judges teachers according to their students' performance on tests— and thereby diverts teachers' attention from creating cooperative communication of effective learners. (p. 24)

Similarly managers and school leaders, according to Deming (1986), must remove the barriers to pride of workmanship. Teachers want to do a good job but often find obstacles in their way: outdated materials and curriculum, nonsupportive personnel practices, insufficient equipment, and unclear goals. When such barriers are present, the safest alternative is often mediocrity.

Implications for Administrators

Professors of educational administration must be on the cutting edge of preparing a new generation of administrators to assume the responsibility for restructuring American schools. Understanding the differences between the traditional (Dewey) model and the transformational (Deming) model may help professors to understand the evolving nature of administrator preparation so that future administrators will better meet the constant and divergent winds of change in a substantial and productive manner.

References

Aguayo, R. (1990). Dr. Deming: The American who taught the Japanese about quality. New York: Simon & Schuster.

Allison, D. J. (1989, March). Toward the fifth age: The continuing evolution of academic educational administration. A paper presented at the annual meeting of the American Educational Research Association in San Francisco, CA. (ERIC Document Reproduction Service No. ED 306 662)

Baker, E. M. (1987). The quality professional's role in the new economic age. Quality Progress, 20 (11), 20-28.

Berger, M. I. (1959). John Dewey and progressive education today. School and Society, 87, 140-142.

Berger, S., Dertouzos, M. L., Lester, R. K., Solow, R. M., & Thurow, L. C. (1989). Toward a new industrial America. Scientific American, 260 (6), 39-47.

Blanton, C. (1991). A principal's vision of excellence: Achieving quality through empowerment. Praxis, 3 (2), 1-2, 9.

Bowers, C. A. (1984). The promise of theory: Education and the politics of cultural change. New York: Longman.

Bullert, G. (1983). The politics of John Dewey. Buffalo, NY: Prometheus Books.

Chait, R. P. (1982). Look who invented Japanese management! AGB Reports, 24 (2), 3-7.

Deming, W. E. (1986). Out of the crisis. Cambridge, MA: Massachusetts Institute of Technology, Center for Advanced Engineering Study.

Deming, W. E. (1989, July). Foundation for management of quality in the Western world. A paper presented at the meeting of the Institute of Management Sciences in Osaka, Japan.

Dewey, J. (1897). My pedagogic creed. School Journal, 54, 77-80.

Dewey, J. (1916). Democracy and education. New York: Macmillan.

Dewey, J. (1931). Philosophy and civilization. New York: Macmillan.

Dewey, J. (1939). Experience and education. New York: Macmillan.

Dewey, J. (1940). Democracy in education. In J. Ratner (Ed.), Education Today. New York: G. P. Putnam's Sons.

Dewey, J. (1946). The challenge of democracy to education. In Problems of men. New York: Philosophical Library.

Dewey, J. (1948). Reconstruction in philosophy. Boston: Beacon Press.

Dewey, J. (1956). School and society. Chicago, IL: University of Chicago Press.

Emans, R. (1981). Analysis of four different approaches to teacher education. College Student Journal, 15 (3), 209-216.

Feng, J. (1989). A re-examination of John Dewey and education. (ERIC Document Reproduction Service No. ED 325 448).

Gabor, A. (1990). The man who discovered quality. New York: Times Books.

Gabor, A. (1991). Deming's quality manifesto. In American Association of School Administrators (Ed), An introduction to total quality for schools. Arlington, VA: AASA.

George, P. S. (1984). Theory Z and schools: What can we learn from Toyota? NASSP Bulletin, 68 (472), 76-81.

Glasser, W. (1990a). The quality school. Phi Delta Kappan, 71 (6), 24-35.

Glasser, W. (1990b). The quality school. New York: Harper & Row.

Hall, R. H. (1991). Organizations: Structures, processes, & outcomes. Englewood Cliffs, NJ: Prentice-Hall.

Joiner, B. L. & Scholtes, P. R. (1991). Total quality leadership vs. management by results. In American Association of School Administrators (Ed.), An introduction to total quality for schools. Arlington, VA: AASA.

Lamm, Z. (1986, November). The architecture of schools and the philosophy of education. A paper presented at the Edusystems 2000 International Congress on Educational Facilities, Values, and Contents, Jerusalem, Israel. (ERIC Document Reproduction Service No. ED 283 287)

Lane, J. J. (1983). Managerial techniques in educational administration. School Business Affairs, 49 (10), 34-35.

Melvin, C. A., III. (1991). Restructuring schools by applying Deming's management theories. Journal of Staff Development, 12 (3), 16-20.

Metz, E. J. (1984). Managing change: Implementing productivity and quality improvement. National Productivity Review, 3, 303-314.

Miller, R. I. (1991). Applying the Deming method to higher education for more effective human resource management. Washington, DC: College and University Personnel Association.

Mitroff, I. (1988). Business not as usual: Rethinking our individual, corporate, and industrial strategies for global competition. San Francisco, CA: Jossey Bass.

Neave, H. R. (1990). The Deming dimension. Knoxville, TN: SPC Press.

Oberle, J. (1991). Quality gurus: The men and their message. In American Association of School Administrators (Ed.), An introduction to total quality for schools. (6) Arlington, VA: AASA.

Paringer, W. A. (1990). John Dewey and the paradox of liberal reform. Albany, NY: State University of New York Press.

Parker, F. (1981). Ideas that shaped American schools. Phi Delta Kappan, 62 (5), 314-319.

Passow, A. H. (1982). John Dewey's influence on education around the world. Teachers College Record, 83 (3), 401-418.

Pines, E. (1991). From top secret to top priority: The story of TQM. In American Association of School Administrators (Ed.), An introduction to total quality for schools. Arlington, VA: AASA.

Popp, J. A. (1987). If you see John Dewey, tell him we did it. Educational Theory, 37 (2), 145-152.

Price, F. (1990). Right every time: Using the Deming approach. Milwaukee, WI: ASQC Quality Press.

Rhodes, L. A. (1990a). Why quality is within our grasp . . . if we reach. School Administrator, 17 (10), 31-34.

Rhodes, L. A. (1990b). Beyond your beliefs: Quantum leaps toward quality schools. School Administrator, 17 (11), 23-26.

Rockefeller, S. C. (1991). John Dewey: Religious faith and democratic humanism. New York: Columbia University Press.

Rogers, J. S., & Polkinghorn, R., Jr. (1990, April). The inquiry process in the accelerated school: A Deweyan approach to school renewal. A paper presented at the annual meeting of the American Educational Research Association, Boston, MA. (ERIC Document Reproduction Service No. ED 323 636)

Roth, R. J. (1962). John Dewey and self-realization. Englewood Cliffs, NJ: Prentice-Hall.

Scherkenback, W. W. (1986). The Deming route to quality and productivity. Rockville, MD: Mercury Press.

Senge, P. M. (1990). The leader's new work: Building learning organizations. Sloan Management Review, 32 (1), 7-23.

Shaker, P. (1990). John Dewey and the knowledge base for the beginning teacher. (ERIC Document Reproduction Service No. ED 329 546)

Shea, W. M. (1989). John Dewey and the crisis of the canon. American Journal of Education, 97 (3), 289-311.

Sidorsky, D. (1977). John Dewey: The essential writings. New York: Harper & Row.

Siu-Runyan, Y., & Hart, S. J. (1992). Management manifesto. Executive Educator, 14 (1), 23-26.

Swift, J. S. (1971). The origins of team management. National Elementary Principal, 50 (4), 26-35.

Tveite, M. D. (1991). The theory behind the fourteen points: Management focused on improvement instead of on judgment. In American Association of School Administrators (Ed.), An introduction to total quality for schools. Arlington, VA: AASA.

Walter, G. A., & Marks, S. E. (1981). Experiential learning and change. New York: John Wiley & Sons.

Walton, M. (1986). <u>The Deming management method.</u> New York: Perigee Books.

Wheeler, J. E. (1977). John Dewey's philosophy as a blueprint for the future. <u>High School Journal, 40</u> (8), 387-397.

Wirth, A. G. (1989). <u>John Dewey as educator.</u> Lanham, MD: University Press of America.

Chapter 7

USING TOTAL QUALITY MANAGEMENT AS A PHILOSOPHY AND ORGANIZATIONAL FRAMEWORK TO ACHIEVE OUTCOMES-BASED EDUCATION AND EFFECTIVE SCHOOLS

Thomas C. Valesly and Frank W. Markus
University of South Florida and University of Memphis

Abstract

The educational establishment is under a great deal of pressure to improve and to prove to its critics that it has done so. This work develops three concepts to support its thesis: effective schools, the change process, and outcomes-based education (OBE). To achieve effective schools, major change must take place. Yet change is not easy for schools. The changes that occur in schools must be accomplished in such a way that the public and the critics are provided the information to judge success. We support the notion that OBE is an excellent tool to provide this information. Recently, the National Study for School Evaluation (NSSE) developed an OBE school evaluation model, which was written by representatives from most of the regional accrediting associations. To effectively implement the NSSE model, this paper supports the concept of Total Quality Management (TQM) as a philosophical and organizational framework. The "Profound Knowledge" necessary for organizational management as expressed by W. Edwards Deming is discussed, and the steps used in the NSSE model are presented and matched to TQM concepts.

Introduction

Is Total Quality Management (TQM) yet another change that has been thrust upon the schools by outside reformers in an attempt to reform the education system. To meet the ever-growing criticism of education, are educators using TQM to show that schools themselves are reforming from within? Or, is it a change that began from linkages among business leaders, educators, the major professional administrator and teacher associations, and change agents that has such face validity to meet the needs of our educational system and satisfy the critics of schools, its use in schools has been quickly growing. This work supports the latter thesis. It also supports the thesis that TQM could be *the* change that will provide the administrative philosophy and organization structure within which radical curricular restructure will be possible.

Schools have always been under fire to improve the quality of their products, particularly since the early 1980s after the publication of the now infamous A Nation at Risk report of the National Commission on Excellence in Education. This report and others (Time for Change, Academic Preparation for College, Educating Americans for the 21st Century, and Action for Excellence), which tended to base their conclusions on perceptions rather than fact, nonetheless had a great impact on the public perception of schools. Are schools really as bad as these reports profess? Bracey (1991; 1992; 1993) provided excellent rebuttals to these reports' conclusions. His articles contain detailed information providing evidence that schools are, in fact, producing better products than they were previously, or at least show that education in the United States is not in shambles when compared with other nations. Concerning A Nation at Risk, he states that it:

> ... launched a crusade for school reform by claiming that America was drowning in "a rising tide of mediocrity." *There is no such tide*. Those who penned this document were sometimes merely naive in their interpretations, but at other times they verged on being criminally uncritical about the misinformation they were fed. (1991, p. 110)

It is not the intent of this discussion to review the details of this debate, suffice it to say that Bracey provides supporting data that reveal schools have been either maintaining or improving their output, not the reverse.

However, regardless of whether or not schools are actually in a state of decline, the public perception is that schools in the United States are doing a poor job—not the schools where their kids go, but "other" schools. The annual Gallup polls commissioned by Phi Delta Kappa continue to show that although the public is essentially very positive about the schools their own children attend and somewhat less positive, but nonetheless positive, about their local school district in general, they believe that schools across the United States are not educating the youth of this nation very well. Also, we continue to hear business and government leaders lament the job that schools are doing to prepare kids to enter the workforce. These perceptions have a great effect on the business of education, not the least of which is a negative attitude on the part of the taxpayers to continue to increase education funding at all levels of government. If schools are continuing to improve as Bracey has been able to demonstrate, then why does the public perceive schools as failing. Perhaps the debate should not be about increases or deceases in test scores or how student achievement in the United States compares to student achievement from other developed nations. To judge our nation's education system solely by such limited methods has received much criticism lately, and there seems to be a growing consensus that other forms of assessment are necessary. Perhaps the debate, then, should focus on alternative measures of assessment, and whether or not schools have implemented the improvements necessary to prepare students for a changed society.

Change is inevitable and necessary for schools to insure continual improvement in meeting the demands of a changing society. There is a wealth of research under the name of "Effective Schools Research" that indicates to schools the characteristics they must acquire to improve. (For some earlier effective schools research see Brookover, Beady, Flood, Schweitzer & Wisenbaker, 1979; Brookover, 1982; Edmonds, 1979; Lezotte & Bancroft, 1985; Purkey & Smith, 1983; Purkey & Smith, 1985. More recently see Levine and Lezotte, 1990). These studies have shown schools how they must change to become more effective. In brief, they indicate that schools must: establish a clear mission; have administration and staff that focus on instruction; continually monitor student progress; have high expectations of student achievement; provide staff development; involve stakeholders in decisions; encourage parental support and involvement; provide a safe and orderly environment; and have a positive school culture in which collaborative planning, collegial relationships, and a sense of community lead to shared goals and a focus on problem solving. However, just showing the public that these characteristics are present is not sufficient. With a focus on accountability (meaning test scores to most people), schools must show that specific outcomes have been achieved. Therefore, in recent years there has been a focus on what has been dubbed Outcomes-Based Education (OBE). OBE seeks to develop alternative outcomes as tools in establishing a framework of accountability and to help establish programs that will focus on the desired outcomes. The discussions about OBE have culminated in an evaluation model developed by the National Study for School Evaluation (NSSE), which publishes the material used by the regional accrediting agencies in school evaluation. The OBE model developed by NSSE, published under the title of <u>Elementary School Improvement: Focusing on Desired Learner Outcomes,</u> was written by a team representing all regional accrediting associations except one, the New England Association of School and Colleges (National Study of School Evaluation, 1992).

We know the characteristics of effective schools and we know that a focus on outcomes should drive our programs and be the accountability tool to the public. We know where we should be going, but do we know how to get there? Unfortunately, schools are notoriously bad at change, because the norms of school culture are difficult to change. To get there, then, the following questions must be answered: (a) How can schools effectively attack the change process, and (b) Is there an organizational, decision-making model that can best help schools achieve the changes that are best for the students in a particular school, in a particular district?

To answer the first question, we turn to the seminal work on educational change by Seymour Sarason, <u>The Culture of the School and the Problem of Change</u> (Sarason, 1982). This work is grounded solidly in the social systems theories so familiar to educational administrators (Getzels & Guba, 1957; Getzels & Thelen, 1960).

Regarding the efforts to change schools, Sarason states:

> Nothing has been more characteristic of efforts to change schools than oversimple conceptions of the change process, an oversimplicity matched only by (indeed, deriving from) a very narrow conception of what a school system is. (pp. 11-12)

Sarason shows us that our narrow view of school change becomes "encapsulated" in the immediate environment where a change is anticipated, and that we fail to view the "encapsulated school" as part of a larger system, with all of its pieces interrelated, where a change in one area affects all other areas. Sarason provides support for our current focus on outcomes:

> . . . any change in a programmatic regularity has as one of its intended outcomes some kind of change in existing behavioral regularities, and these behavioral regularities are among the most important criteria for judging the degree to which intended outcomes are being achieved. (p. 107)

Programmatic and behavioral regularities exist to produce desired school outcomes. However, Sarason shows that, in practice, the school culture

Using Total Quality Management 119

of existing programmatic and behavioral regularities are so difficult to change that we have all become aware that "the more things change the more they remain the same" (p. 58). He speaks to the evaluation of outcomes:

> Conspicuous by its absence in the school culture, or so low in priority as to be virtually absent, is evaluation of the regularities. . . . We hear much talk today about "accountability," which reduces to achievement test performance of pupils. . . . I in no way downplay the importance of achievement. . . it is at the expense of recognizing the significance (fiscal and psychological) of behavioral and programmatic regularities in the school culture. (pp. 116-117)

He eloquently shows the need for the change process to examine the interrelatedness of instructional and organizational norms when changing desired outcomes. The NSSE model of OBE evaluation seems to do this very well by evaluating both instructional and organizational norms (or regularities) in terms of their support of desired outcomes.

To answer the second question concerning an organizational, decision-making model that can best help schools change, we submit that Total Quality Management (TQM) is the current "best practice" available. TQM takes a "systems" view of organizational change which addresses some of Sarason's criticisms of the modal process of change in schools. TQM is more than a management process, it is a philosophy of organizational leadership that uses the scientific method and the contributions of everyone in the organization to continuously improve everything the organization does to consistently meet or exceed its stakeholders' needs. The system in this case refers to those elements that impact on the organization in question. For example, TQM in an elementary school would involve not only the students, faculty, staff, and parents of that school, but also other educational institutions, government, and businesses at the local level, and even at state, regional, and national levels. TQM identifies those stakeholders and attempts to understand the cultures involved, the attitudes of the stakeholders toward changes in the behavioral regularities, and uses this information to establish outcomes that address stakeholders' needs. TQM does this by implementing the four philosophical beliefs, which comprise the "Profound Knowledge" necessary for a system to improve, as expressed by its originator, W. Edwards Deming (Deming, 1989; Rhodes, 1990):

1. Psychological Belief: People are purposeful, cognitive beings with an intrinsic desire to learn and be innovative. Each individual has the right to enjoy his or her work and be

successful. The emphasis in this belief is on human resources.
2. Systems Belief: All organizations should be viewed as systems in which subcomponent activities must be aimed at fulfilling the mission of the larger organization. The task of management is to optimize the whole. The emphasis here is on the dynamic character of organizations.
3. Perceptual Framework Belief: Knowledge is constructed from experience bound within a framework of theories and beliefs. Everyone within the organization needs the same theoretical roadmap. The emphasis in this belief is on alignment of goals.
4. Causes of Variation Belief: 80% to 90% of the variation from expected outcomes is a result of problems within the system or process, not the worker. To lessen the occurrence of variation, the system's programmatic and behavioral regularities must be modified. The emphasis here is on the scientific method and data collection.

Within this philosophy, there is room for various management/leadership structures, however, participatory leadership is required. School-based decision making (SBDM) fits very nicely in this framework, and TQM will provide the sometimes wavering school site councils with the tools necessary to get the job done. Decision-making in TQM organizations is based on data, not hunches, and it provides tools necessary to collect and make decisions. Other core values of TQM relate to empowerment, teamwork, long-range and strategic planning, and accountability. These are all concepts that most educators and certainly the literature on school administration and change support.

Table 1

A Side-by-Side Comparison of the Steps for the NSSE, OBE Model for School Evaluation and TQM Concepts.

NSSE	TQM

As indicated in the table, there is a direct match of steps in the NSSE outcomes-based model and TQM concepts. Implicit in both the NSSE and TQM models is that they are both continuous—i.e., when item number seven is completed, they loop back to item number one and begin the process again. A school that uses TQM as its philosophical and organizational framework, is already poised to implement an outcomes-based education model to develop an effective school. TQM focuses on the entire "system", ensuring that all of the stakeholders' needs are considered. By focusing on the system in this manner, any effort to change programmatic and behavioral regularities will more likely succeed. TQM can provide the organizational framework to implement the NSSE model, for it has the necessary philosophical framework to provide sustained direction—that is, it has the "Profound Knowledge."

References

Bracey, G. W. (1991). Why can't they be like we were? Phi Delta Kappan, 73 (2), 105-117.

Bracey, G. W. (1992). The second Bracey report on the condition of public education. Phi Delta Kappan, 74 (2), 104-117.

Bracey, G. W. (1993). The third Bracey report on the condition of public education. Phi Delta Kappan, 75 (2), 105-117.

Brookover, W. B. (1982). Creating effective schools. Holmes Beach, FL: Learning Publications.

Brookover, W. B., Beady, C., Flood, P., Schweitzer, J., & Wisenbaker, J. (1979). School social systems and student achievement: Schools can make a difference. New York: Praeger.

Deming, W. E. (1989, July). Foundation for management of quality in the western world. Paper presented at a meeting of the Institute of Management Sciences, Osaka, Japan.

Edmonds, R. R., (1979). Effective schools for the urban poor. Educational Leadership, 37, 56-60.

Getzels, J. W., & Guba, E. G. (1957). Social behavior and the administrative process. School Review, 65, 423-441.

Getzels, J. W., & Thelen, H. A. (1960). The classroom group as a unique social system. In The dynamics of instructional groups, N. B. Henry (Ed.). Chicago: University of Chicago Press.

Levine, D. U., & Lezotte, L. W. (1990). Unusually effective schools: A review and analysis of research and practice. Madison WI: National Center for Effective Schools Research and Development.

Lezotte, L. W., & Bancroft, B. A. (1985). Growing use of the effective schools model for school improvement. Educational Leadership, 42 (6), 23-27.

National Study of School Evaluation. (1992). Elementary school improvement: Focusing on desired learner outcomes. Fall Church, VA: National Study of School Evaluation.

Purkey, S. C., & Smith M. W. (1983). Effective schools—A review. The Elementary School Journal, 83 (4), 427-452.

Purkey, S. C., & Smith M. W. (1985). School reform: The district policy implications of the effective schools literature. The Elementary School Journal, 85 (3), 353-389.

Rhodes, L. A. (1990). Why quality is within our grasp. . . If we reach. The School Administrator, 47 (10), 31-34.

Rossmiller, R. A., & Holcomb, E. L. (1993, April). The effective schools process for continuous school improvement. Paper presented at the annual meeting of the American Education Research Association, Atlanta, GA.

Sarason, S. (1982). The culture of the school and the problem of change. Boston: Allyn and Bacon.

Chapter 8

TOTAL QUALITY MANAGEMENT: A POSTSTRUCTURALIST CRITIQUE

Lars G. Björk
University of Kentucky

During the last two decades, the United States grappled with fears that heightened international competition, slow economic growth, and demographic changes threatened the nation's well being. These concerns placed the need to redefine expectations for public schooling into sharp focus and led to an intense examination of the purpose, condition, and student achievement in American schools. The steady stream of education commission reports released since 1983 indicted public schools for failing the nation's children and contributing to the nation's "economic decline." These national commission reports captured the public's interest, secured corporate backing, and helped to mobilize political support for reforming American education. The extraordinary pressure for improving educational outcomes and the inability of school leaders and policy makers to find viable solutions forced many reformers to look beyond education for guidance. The corporate sector provided alternative modes of organization (decentralization, site based management), market driven solutions (choice), performance contracting (charter schools), management ideology (TQM, and empowerment), and modern business practices (Murphy 1991). During the era of reform that followed (1983-1995), considerable pressure was brought to bear on educators to redesign the structure and practices of schooling consistent with emerging private sector management initiatives. Some reformers envisioned school systems that were operated as efficient corporations and advocated that corporate management ideology and practices be adopted. The strong desire to emulate corporate sector practices, however, led to the routine transfer of many business practices to public schools. During the past decade, Total Quality Management (TQM) was adopted by a wide array of corporations and touted as a promising approach to lead schools out of bureaucratic inefficiency and disarray. TQM encompasses a number of praiseworthy elements that may hold promise in facilitating productive change in schools. Its emphasis on efficiency, control and quantitative methods, which are reminiscent of the principles of scientific management, however, may also be used as tools of coercion, domination and control. In this regard, TQM may not be the solution to problems in American education and its uncritical adoption by many districts is troubling. The following discussion will examine the educational reform reports, and the emergence of private sector influence on school reform, compare TQM with scientific management and their implications for school practice.

The Educational Reform Reports

For more than a decade, widespread concern over the nation's declining economy raised serious questions about the efficacy of a wide array of public and private organizations. Following the release of A Nation At Risk by the National Commission on Excellence in Education in 1983, an unprecedented number of national commissions and task forces were convened to examine the purpose, condition, and performance of American public schools. These national commission and task force reports helped to initiate and sustain the education reform initiative that has continued well into the 1990s. Even though these reports didn't fall in an orderly fashion into three "waves" (Firestone, Furhman, & Kirst, 1990), many used this framework for analyzing the educational reform movement of the 1980s (Bacharach, 1990; Lane & Epps, 1992; Murphy, 1990). The commission reports which shaped the characteristics of the first wave of educational reform (1982-1986) included The National Commission on Excellence in Education (A Nation at Risk, 1983), the Twentieth Century Task Force on Federal Educational Policy (Making the Grade, 1983), Carnegie Foundation for Advancement of Teaching (Boyer, 1983, High School), the Education Commission of the States', Task Force for Economic Growth (Action for Excellence, 1983), and the Commission on Precollege Education in Mathematics, Science and Technology, (Educating Americans for the 21st Century, 1983). Reports released during the first "wave" of reform captured public attention (Plank & Ginsberg, 1990) by demanding that schools improve achievement, raise standards, mandate assessment, and increase educational accountability. The regulatory environment created by states during the first wave of educational reform strengthened bureaucratic, "top down" management prerogatives which further constrained district and school administrative discretion.

The characteristics of the second wave of educational reform (1986-1989) were largely defined by reports released by the Carnegie Foundation for the Advancement of Teaching (A Nation Prepared: Teachers for the Twenty-first Century, 1986); the Committee for Economic Development (Investing in Our Children, 1985) and Children in Need, 1987); the Holmes Group (Tomorrow's Teachers, 1986), and the National Governors Association (Time for Results, 1986). The recommendations included in these reports exceeded those proposed earlier (Plank & Ginsberg, 1990) and presumed that intractable school bureaucracies created conditions in which children failed and constrained efforts to improve schools. As a result, the focus of reform shifted towards enhancing the professionalization of teachers and administrators. They persuasively argued that increasing the level of professional discretion at the district and building levels would enhance state directed policy initiatives.

In addition, these reports alerted reformers that proposed school changes must be consistent with profound social and economic changes that were recasting America as a post industrial society (Bell, 1978). They were instrumental in directing attention to the need for advancing technological competency, higher order thinking skills, collaboration, and problem solving among students and insightfully discussed the implication of these new competencies for reforming and restructuring schools. These second wave reports also focused attention on American demographic trends. They observed that the nation's minority youth constituted the fastest growing segment of the population and would constitute a significant proportion of its future work force. The implications were clear. Those segments of society which had been least well served by the education system in the past would have to be included in any future reform initiatives. Taken as a whole, these reports made compelling arguments for addressing the needs of all children particularly minority, "at risk" children (Murphy, 1990). The emphasis placed on organizational structures, professional issues, and the narrow scope of restructuring schools that characterized second wave reports were criticized by those which followed. Child centered themes dominated reports released during the third wave of educational reform. In 1991, the National Commission on Children released the report, Beyond Rhetoric: A New American Agenda for Children and Families, which observed that the United States needed to reconcile the incongruity of one of the world's most prosperous nations failing so many of its children. This analysis was broadened by several reports released during 1989 and 1990. Several reports clarified these important issues and championed decisive action on behalf of the nation's forgotten children including: Turning Points released in 1989 by the Carnegie Council for Adolescent Development; Ready to Learn (1991), prepared by the Carnegie Foundation for the Advancement of Learning; Visions of a Better Way: A Black Appraisal of Public Schooling, released by the Committee on Policy for Racial Justice of the Joint Center for Political Studies in 1989; and Education That Works: An Action Plan for the Education of Minorities (Quality Education for Minorities Project, 1990); and One Third of a Nation (1988) presented by the Commission on Minority participation in American Life which was jointly sponsored by the American Council on Education and the Education Commission of the States.

In addition, the United States Department of Education released a report, National Excellence: A Case for Developing America's Talent, during November 1993 that reflected growing apprehension that children at the other end of the learning continuum, the gifted and talented students, also be addressed by public school reform initiatives. This key report identified the "quiet crisis," the benign neglect of students, that prevented the best and brightest students from fulfilling their full potential in schools. If schools abdicate their responsibility to nurture these children, the nation may forfeit their potential future contributions to society. This report departed from similar reports released twenty years earlier in its candid censuring of the failure gifted and talented programs to include culturally different children, students with disabilities, underachievers, female students, and artistically talented students. Although third wave reports identified numerous factors that contributed to the failure of children in public schools, they also called for more fundamental changes in the structure of schools to ameliorate this problem. Proposals calling for restructuring schools as "integrated interorganizational service" systems (Murphy, 1990, p. 29) emerged and called for radically altering the structure of schools. These new configurations placed schools at the hub of a network of community services that could be coordinated to better serve the needs of children and families.

These new child centered structures would require considerable interagency and interorganizational coordination which has significant implications for modifying the role of school administrators. The transformation of school leaders to meet the demands of emerging contexts and new demands were discussed in a parallel set of educational reform reports including Leaders for America's Schools, (1987); School Leadership Preparation: A Preface for Action, (1988); and Report Card on School Reform: The Teachers Speak, (1988). These and other documents discussed the changing context of leadership in schools and the need to adopt new administrative roles. Leaders in these reconfigured schools would serve as advocates for children in mediating services from among a wide array of local, state and federal agencies (Björk, 1993); share instructional leadership roles with other educational professionals in the school; work with teachers as colleagues and be skilled political stewards of school-based, shared governance mechanisms.

During the Bush administration, the United States Department of Education with great fanfare ushered in its report, America 2000: An Education Strategy (1991), that proposed to accomplish prominent education goals through decidedly different means. This report bore all the hallmarks of a skillfully constructed political package. It was an amalgamation of programs that were supported by the nation's governors that coincided with the education interests of the democratic majority in Congress. The creation of 535 "new American schools" served as the center piece of the proposal, however, it also called for the formation of national standards; institutionalizing national achievement tests, and supporting parental choice. This report contended that the education needs of the nation's children, regardless of special need, could be best served through elevating standards and establishing rigorous quality control mechanisms. This broad based solution moved the nation in the direction of a national system of education and naively assumed that it could be established within present state and federal funding levels (Doyle, 1991; Howe, 1991).

Goals 2000: Educate America Act (Public Law 103-227), proposed by the Clinton Administration and signed into law during April 1994, focused on stimulating systemic reform requiring states to develop plans for new curricula, student performance standards, and new initiatives in teacher preparation. The final version of this act used the six national education goals that were announced by President Bush and the Governors in February 1989 at the University of Virginia in Charlottesville as the core of America 2000: An Education Strategy (1991). Two additional goals, however, were added to the act that focused on the professional development of teachers and parent involvement. Both America 2000: An Education Strategy (1991) and Goals 2000: Educate America Act (1994) reports reflected themes that cut across the first two waves of reform, however, their only commonality with the third wave reports was their dates of release.

New Expectations for Schools

Although the rhetoric of reform was harsh in both tenor and in its indictment of public schooling, the magnitude and duration of the demand for improving and even transforming education indicated wide spread conviction of its importance. Americans have long held, as an article of faith, a belief that education is essential for both personal attainment and national well being. Brogan (1962) referred to this fundamental belief as "the formally established national church of the United States" (p. 137). This deep-seated conviction helps to partially explain why Americans have frequently turned to public schools and universities to resolve dilemmas whenever the nation is threatened by international conditions or domestic social change. When these situations arise, it is commonplace for public officials and political leaders to indict public schools and then make strident demands for their reform. These public challenges have led to repetitious reexaminations and calls for redefining the nation's schools. In retrospect, these endeavors have resulted in increasing educational opportunities to increasing numbers of children at successively higher levels (Boorstin, 1975) and enabling larger segments of society access to and participation in the social, economic, and political life of the nation. This trend toward inclusiveness has been a dominant characteristic of educational reform efforts launched during the past century and is a significant departure from rather narrow perspectives that assert that the nation only nurture the intellectual development of the few (Katz, 1971). Although the reports released during the decade of reform (1983-1993) and beyond indicted public schools and made them more susceptible to external intervention, the "overall strength of the country's beliefs in the political, social economic, and individual benefits of supporting public schools persists" (Cuban, 1990, p. 268).

One of the most significant developments during this period involved the blurring of the issues of access and excellence. The emergence of this line of convergent reasoning occurred concurrently with demographic projections which indicated that during the next century a significantly larger proportion of the workforce would be non-white and that all workers would require higher levels of education. Corporate executives and policy makers understood the critical need to attend to human capital development strategies and their being intrinsically linked to school reform. The notion that public education impacts the social and economic well being of the nation (Reich, 1983, 1990: Snyder, 1984) elevated discussions about human capital development from esoteric university enclaves to corporate executive suites, Congress, and the office of the president. Thus, these concepts became an important reference point in redefining public education (Björk, 1995; Wirth, 1992). This new emphasis made past distinctions between access and excellence incompatible with profound economic and demographic realities of the next century. Access and excellence were no longer perceived by prominent policy makers and corporate executives as being separate but intrinsically related. In this dynamic context, morality became pragmatic (Henderson, 1977, p. 235) and remarkably, the interests of liberals and conservatives in educating all children coincided.

The involvement of American corporate executives in the educational reform movement influenced its tenor, direction, and content. Their influence in linking the nation's economy and long-term human capital development strategies with school reform was conspicuous during the decade of reform (1983-1993). These issues challenged deep-seated educational practices and had significant implications for the future of schooling. As noted by Spring (1986) in the past, schools served as "sorting machines" selecting children by both ability and potential fit with industrial and corporate life. Schools prepared them to perform in these settings by stressing the need to obey superiors, comply with bureaucratic rules and regulations, display formal knowledge, and accept current practices. With the emergence of a global, technologically-based economy, American society became aware of the need to change its expectations for schools. Now schools were being asked to educate all children by employing appropriate learning strategies, emphasizing critical thinking skills, employing technology to access information sources, applying knowledge in problem solving situations, and working independently as well as collaboratively on important projects. These changes had significant implications not only for reconfiguring teaching and learning but for altering organizational structures and administrative practices in schools.

The Casual Linkages Between Education and the Economy

During the decade of reform, prevailing public opinion held that the American economy was faltering and trailing behind other industrialized nations in terms of economic growth, quality, and productivity (Underwood, 1990). The rhetoric of impending crisis began with the watershed report A Nation at Risk (1983) which stated, "the education foundations of our society are presently being eroded by a rising tide of mediocrity that threatens our very future as a nation and people" (p. 5). This theme was advanced in other educational reform reports that followed including Action for Excellence: A Comprehensive Plan to Improve Our Nation's Schools (1983); Educating Americans for the 21st Century, (1983); Making the Grade, (1983); A Nation Prepared: Teachers for the 21st Century (1986); Got to Learn to Earn (1991); and America 2000: An Education Strategy (1991). In addition, these arguments were carried forward in influential "think tank" reports released by the Hudson Institute, Workforce 2000 (1988), and the National Center on Education and the Economy, High Skills or Low Wages (1990). The publicity which accompanied the release of these reports combined with persistent and aggressive media coverage helped to formulate the impression that, "public education has put this nation at a terrible competitive disadvantage" (Kearns, 1988b, p. 566); that it "contributed to the decline in performance of the American worker" (Association for Supervision and Curriculum, 1986, p. 20), and diminished the nation's ability to maintain its "once unchallenged preeminence in commerce, industry, science, and technological innovation" (National Commission on Excellence in Education, 1983, p. 5). American corporate executives and others who sought to arrest this decline (Kearnes, 1988a, 1988b; Perry, 1988) thrust a powerful bromide on the American public characterized by Mitchell (1990) as, "economic salvation through educational excellence" (p. 28).

The perception of economic decline placed extraordinary public pressure for improving educational outcomes. The inability of school leaders and policy makers to find viable solutions forced many reformers to look beyond education for guidance and provided an opportunity for corporate executives to foist business ideology and practices on the education enterprise. The pervasive involvement of business in educational reform was facilitated and sustained by corporate leaders, federal policy makers, and journalists who advanced the notion of causal linkages between the nation's economic decline and the failure of public schooling. Cuban (1992), however, noted that the widely accepted myth that America's competitiveness in the international economy, the shrinking purchasing power of the American dollar, declining worker productivity, and rising unemployment were caused by inadequate knowledge, limited skills, low standardized test scores, and poor work ethic of high school students (pp. 157-158) was without foundation. Many authorities noted that "schools have become a convenient scapegoat for our economic problems" (Carnevale, 1992) and that American corporations used the school issue as "an avenue of convenience" (Mishel & Texeira, 1991) to draw attention away from more fundamental corporate, financial, and political reasons for the economic decline. As Lawrence Cremin (1989) observed:

> American economic competitiveness with Japan and other nations is to a considerable degree a function of monetary, trade, and industrial policy, and of decisions made by the President and Congress, the Federal Reserve Board, and the federal departments of the Treasury and Commerce and Labor.
> Therefore, to contend that problems of international competitiveness can be solved by educational reform, especially educational reform defined solely as school reform, is not merely Utopian and millenialist, it is foolish and at worst a crass effort to direct attention away from those truly responsible for doing

something about competitiveness and to lay the burden on the schools. It is a device that has been used repeatedly in the history of American public education. (p. 103)

For more than a decade public education has been blamed for the failure of the nation's economy, however, prominent scholars have examined the data and drawn rather different conclusions. Rather than experiencing a precipitous decline, the nation's economy experienced slow growth. Contrary to popular opinion, there was no causal relationship between education and the condition of the American economy. Both the decline in industrial productivity and proficiency of the American worker were groundless allegations. In fact, the productivity of American industry and workers leads the industrialized nations of the world (Björk, 1995).

While the national commission reports from A Nation At Risk (1983) to National Excellence: A Case for Developing America's Talent (1993) were viewed as an indictment of public education, they also declared the importance of American's "durable faith in the power of public schooling to resolve national problems" (Cuban, 1990, p. 268). While they affirmed the public's support for the efficacy of schooling, they also demonstrated the capacity to misinform public policy makers and misdirect their efforts in unproductive directions (Boyd, 1988; Fowler, 1985). In some cases commission reports contained weak evidence, presented dubious interpretations, and exaggerated the value of simplistic solutions (Peterson, 1985). The aura of authenticity created by the commission reports contributed both to the misperception that public schools had failed but that they were culpable for the decline of the nation's economy (Weisman, 1991). Bracey (1991), however, observed that "so many people said so often that schools are bad that it is no longer a debatable proposition subject to empirical proof" (p. 106). School-bashing, which appears to be part of America's rich heritage (Jaeger, 1992), took on all the earmarks of a public flogging (Bracey, 1993; Fox, 1993; Kaplan, 1992). Although eminent researchers systematically confronted the popular "truths" (see Björk, 1995 for a detailed discussion), the media's sensationalist reporting of the deplorable condition of public schools continued to "fire passions, grab headlines, and lead off the evening news" (Cuban, 1993, p. 183).

Lessons from the Corporate World

The intrusion of business ideology and the imposition of private sector management practices is not a recent phenomenon. At the beginning of the twentieth century, the nation was confronted with two significant issues: unparalleled growth of the population and massive industrialization.

States dramatically expanded their K-12 systems and common schools to serve as important mechanisms for assimilating vast numbers of immigrants into social, economic, and political mainstream of the nation. The common school helped to forge a commonality of language, values, economic views, and political perspectives that enabled immigrants and the nation to prosper.

The expansion of the public education system created larger and more complex organizations. Successful businessmen and professionals in communities across the nation saw the need for increasing the efficiency of schools and being in prominent positions on school boards encouraged superintendents and principals to adopt modern business practices. American industry had been captivated by the notion of efficiency espoused in Taylor's principles of scientific management and implemented these methods to increase productivity. Proponents of scientific management asserted that schools like other organizations could increase productivity by adopting these private sector management practices. Although it is questionable whether schools were made more cost efficient or students performed at higher academic levels, it was abundantly clear that superintendents and principals were, like their predecessors, vulnerable (Callahan, 1962) to the intrusion of business ideology and management practices. It was equally clear that acquiescing to the wishes of business leaders to adopt these approaches enhanced their authority within districts and schools (Guthrie & Reed, 1991).

During the 1980s, widespread anxiety about the state of the economy and increasing international competition raised questions about the ability of American workers to meet the challenges of the twenty-first century; reform reports indicted public schools for failing to adequately prepare the nation's youth to function in a changing and complex job market. The need to compete economically provided business leaders with a powerful rational for becoming involved in the educational reform movement. Koppich and Guthrie (1993), suggest that "business leaders took up the educational reform challenge because they could see the economic handwriting on the corporate wall" (p. 61). Business leaders were not interested in education for altruistic reasons but in procuring highly-skilled employees that could help them meet their future goals.

Prior to the 1980s, business interests in education were limited to more prosaic finance issues such as opposing expensive state "reforms" and opposing tax increases. Their entrance into the educational policy arena during the 1980s, however, was both conspicuous and noteworthy. Corporations and executives working through national business organizations such as the National Alliance of Business, the United States

Chamber of Commerce, and the National Association of Manufacturers played important roles in stimulating interest in educational reform, sustaining its vitality, and defining its direction (McGuire, 1990). In addition, state level business roundtables and partnerships set up commissions, task forces and study committees that released reports and advanced proposals for school reform and became core members of reform coalitions (Borman et al., 1993; Mazzoni, 1995). Business involvement in the education policy arena, however, was not uniformly influential as might be assumed by their historically privileged access to the policy making elite (Linbloom, 1977). While business interests were often fragmented (Thomas & Hrebenar, 1991) and their influence constrained by other reform proponents such as teacher unions, parent coalitions, and conservative advocacy groups (Cibulka & Derlin, 1992), their impressive resources and privileged access enabled them to become key actors in national and state reform arenas (Hayes, 1992).

Corporate leaders viewed the changes occurring in the economy, technology, and the population with apprehension and argued for schools to emulate successful private sector business practices and adopt dramatically different organizational structures that were both post-bureaucratic and post-industrial (Beare, 1989). During the last several decades, American corporations were faced with a number of product quality and employee morale issues (Peters & Waterman, 1982) that were not unlike those confronting public schools (NASSP, 1988). In their search for solutions, corporate leaders found that the most successful companies had resolved their issues by decentralizing their management operations driving decision making down to the lowest level of production, focusing on serving the customer (Maccoby, 1989), shifting management emphasis from top down control to empowering workers through authentic participation in decisionmaking (Beare, 1989), and building reputations for both quality and service (Kanter, 1983; Peters & Waterman, 1982). These exemplary corporations transformed their organizations from centralized, hierarchical organizations to decentralized systems. Corporate leaders used these examples as blueprints for educational restructuring and pressured educators to adopt these structural models for school systems (Kearnes, 1988a, 1988b). In addition, modern management methods such as transformational leadership, worker empowerment, and Total Quality Management (TQM) adopted by a broad spectrum of businesses and industry (Walton, 1990) were acclaimed as indispensable in correcting the deficiencies of both business and schools.

Scientific Management: The Gospel of American Industry

At the end of the nineteenth century, Frederick Taylor presented

American business leaders with a concept designed to standardize production processes that would later become known as scientific management. His concept of the science of work pointedly criticized the disorganized nature of traditional, labor intensive production practices. He believed that conventional forms of control, communication, and measuring worker productivity were conspicuously ineffective in dealing with American industrial problems such as disorder, dissension, and inefficiency. He believed that new ways of measuring and controlling work was essential in bringing about regularity and consistency in the factory production. Frederick Taylor and his associates, believed that workers were motivated by personal economics, limited physiologically, and required constant supervision to maintain high levels of efficiency and production. Taylor's application of time and motion studies to analyzing job operations lay the foundation for the development of a differential rate system in which workers would be paid on the basis of piece work production. His "progressive manifesto" (Nelson, 1980, p. 170) was rapidly adopted as a blueprint for industrial reorganization and management practice. American industry, as Taylor (1911) noted, should strive for "a complete revolution in the mental attitudes and the habits of all those engaged in the management, as well [as those] of workmen" (p. 131).

Taylor's notion of a management revolution, concerned dramatically increasing the productivity of each worker and increasing corporate profits. His recommendations for improvement included several key elements including the identification of "one best method" for workers undertaking each task throughout the factory. Although the systematic analysis of job tasks was directed towards improving performance, it depended heavily on the ability of management to persuade rank and file workers that these new methods were in their best interest. Scientific management's concept of piece work was linked to the notion of a fair day's pay for a fair day's work. Theoretically, this method of restructuring work and linking it to economic rewards had the potential for increasing the compatibility between the interests of management and labor and reducing management conflict.

Scientific management had profound implications for factory supervisors and managers. Rather than relying on a single foreman to represent workers and supervise operations, Taylor advised that several functional foremen oversee specific segments of the manufacturing process and represent the interests of management thus ensuring greater control over production. Taylor's efforts to discover the natural laws of work, described by Campbell et al., (1987) as a new "social physics" (p. 26), focused on systematically analyzing worker tasks concentrating on narrow physiological factors. His work ignored important psychological and sociological components of human behavior. He was also a true believer in the golden rule (Hoy & Miskell, 1991) of management that in effect states that "He who has the gold makes the rules" (p. 23). Thus, he placed responsibility for the ultimate success of the scientific management approach with administrators and their willingness to use these methods. Administrators needed to understand the assumptions and implications of the fourteen principles of scientific management (Hansen, 1991) and apply them in standardizing and controlling production to improve efficiency. Several key concepts illustrate his managerial theory: (a) clearly defining tasks, (b) standardizing conditions associated with task accomplishment, (c) rates of pay should be tied to rates of successful completion, (d) failure to accomplish assigned tasks should have personal costs, and (e) tasks in large, sophisticated organizations should have a high level of difficulty requiring skilled workers.

The principles of scientific management became the gospel of American industry and pressures from many sectors of society demanded that public schools adopt this private sector management orientation (Hansen, 1991). The "cult of efficiency" (Callahan, 1962) that arose indicted public schools for being disorganized and inefficient. John Bobbitt (1913), an influential educator, recommended that teachers be given explicit instructions for undertaking their work, informed of the standards to be used to judge their performance, apprised of the instructional methods to be used, and told what materials to use (p. 89). Ellwood Cubberly (1916) concurred and argued further that business ideology and a production orientation be adopted by educators and that specifications for teaching, tools, and continuous measurement of production, be employed to eliminate waste. His characterization of the schools "as a factory processing [children as] raw materials for social consumption" (p. 325) became the operational metaphor of that era. The voices of dissent were lost in the scramble of schools to emulate business practices and adopt scientific management as the new gospel of education. Benjamin Gruenberg (1912) argued the folly of yielding to the arrogance of big business and accepting their criteria of efficiency without questioning whether manufacturing processes and education processes are analogous and whether adopting an ideology and technology that prevail in the factory apply equally well in schools (p. 90). The efficiency movement that began with scientific management has had a pervasive influence on the way schools are hierarchically organized and administered. The emphasis or overemphasis (Callahan, 1962) placed on financial and business management aspects of managing the educational enterprise including budget development, budget administration, accounting, cost effectiveness analysis, public relations, annual reports, and other accouterments associated with the corporate practices eclipsed the importance of making decisions on the basis of the needs of children and pedagogical value.

Comparing of Total Quality Management and Scientific Management

Corporate executives and other reformers envisioned public schools operating on similar premises and possessing the same efficiencies as private corporations and championed the adoption of corporate management ideology and practices. Deming's (1982, 1986) principles that compose Total Quality Management focus on using statistical methods, quality control, and customer satisfaction as the means to increase corporate success. These innovative approaches found a receptive audience among a broad spectrum of advocates for school restructuring who borrowed different organizational, management, and leadership theories and structural models from the private sector (Schlechty, 1990). The strong desire to emulate private sector practices led to their routine transfer to public schools. Many of these practices, like TQM, had their roots in classical organizational theory.

Recent events, characterized by increased competition and economic decline, created the circumstances for increased involvement of business in reforming education. To many observers, American industry and schools found themselves in similar circumstances. Both were accused of inefficiency, producing inferior products, not listening to their respective customers, and incapable of correcting fundamental weaknesses. In this milieu, key reform advocates comprising corporate, political, education and interest groups articulated their new expectations for public schools, prescribed modern business management approaches that held promise, and actively campaigned to transform schools.

One technique that was widely adopted by a disparate cross section of businesses (Walton, 1990) and prescribed by the corporate sector to remedy the ills of public schools is known as Total Quality Management or TQM. Deming's (1982, 1986) approach, like Taylor's scientific management, is rooted in engineering and statistics. The fourteen points that sum up the TQM method focus on achieving quality by triangulating the output (product/student), the manner in which the customer (purchaser/parent) reacts to it, and the support services provided (product guarantee/competent graduate). The TQM approach suggests that attention to the dynamic interaction among these key elements will increase efficiency, quality, and corporate profitability. Disorganized and inconsistent manufacturing processes tend to increase the variability in products and decrease customer satisfaction. The TQM approach uses rigorous data collection techniques, statistical programs, and analytical procedures to discover, classify, understand, and ameliorate the causes of variation and improve product quality through systems thinking, constant monitoring, and continuous improvement. The use of scientific methods is intended to apply statistical controls, rather than intuition, in the regulation of manufacturing processes.

The TQM method has been portrayed as a drastic move beyond the current notion of school administration by liberating educators from the constraints of entrenched bureaucracies, facilitating teacher empowerment, stressing the personal motivation of workers to perform at high levels, and engage in systems thinking (Betts, 1992; Bonstingl, 1992).

A close examination of TQM indicates that it is very similar to Taylor's failed notion of scientific management in its use of metaphor, reliance on scientific method, distinction between workers and managers, and dependence on hierarchy and authority to succeed. For example, the metaphor of the "enlightened corporation" (Szjtjan, 1992) may provide some insight into basic philosophy. It alludes to production oriented goals including efficiency, quality, constant monitoring, continuous improvement, and competition. The business metaphor used by TQM, school-as-factory or school-as-enlightened-corporation (Capper & Jamison, 1993, p. 26), tends to accentuate the corporate and economic purposes of improving schools and its management dimension. The idea of the enlightened corporation is indistinguishable from that of a machine bureaucracy or Ellwood Cubberly's metaphor of the school-as-factory. It, like scientific management, places exclusive and inappropriate emphasis on the school organization rather than encompassing children and their learning described by Fullan, (1993) as the moral purposes of schooling. Thus linking these business metaphors and goals with educational processes may be both inappropriate and imprudent as was the case with the uncritical adoption of scientific management earlier in the century.

A comparison of the principles of scientific management and Deming's fourteen points encompassed in the Total Quality Management approach may clarify the similarities between these two approaches (see Figure 1). In several instances, the redundancy among several of TQM's points required their being combined in common cells in the analytic framework. In other instances, implementing TQM in established industries suggest that fundamental patterns of coordination continue including reliance on hierarchies, supervision, and communication continue. Although the form may have been altered, the underlying function remains. The application of scientific management and TQM in

FIGURE 1
A Comparison of Basic Assumptions of Scientific Management[1] and Total Quality Management (TQM)[2] and their Bureaucratic Application to American Public Schools

	Principals of Scientific Management	TQM's 14 Points	Bureaucratic Application to Schools
1	Creation of a hierarchal management structure with graded levels of authority.	Top management supervisors must direct the efforts of workers in implementing TQM.	Bureaucratic structure with levels of administrative control: Superintendent, Central Office Personnel, Principals, Assistant Principals, Teachers and Students.
2	Scientific measurement of task performance to assess efficiency and productivity.	Statistical analysis of production facilities worker-based inspection to increase efficiency and productivity.	Student performance on standardized tests.
3	Establish shared goals (unity of ends) that guide the efforts of management and workers in the organization.	Constancy of purpose based goals focus the organization's purpose and improves production and service.	A fundamental assumption that administrators and teachers work towards meeting the best interest of the children.
4	Develop a scientific structure for work.	Department and units facilitate production by systematically removing barriers to communication and collaboration which reduce competition, limit shared goals, and inhibit problem solving.	Graded schools assume that lower levels of academic work prepare students for the next level in ascending order. Greater articulation, may enhance student success.
5	Divide labor according to task and expertise needed to successfully complete assigned work.	TQM assumes a division of labor by maintaining corporate structures based on specific task and worker expertise.	Management, teachers and staff are divided by level (elementary, middle school, secondary and by grade), by management areas (principal, assistant principal), and areas of expertise (English, history, math teachers, etc.).
6	Determine an effective span of control for the supervision of work.	TQM assumes supervisors are most effective working with small production teams.	State mandated pupil teacher ratios and students counts prescribe the number of assistant principals and counselors.
7	Establish a formal chain of command.	Corporations suing TQM approach maintain hierarchal and production team structures with explicit requirements that problems be solved at the lowest level before being referred up.	Teachers and support staff are required to discuss problems with their principal before bringing it to the attention of supervisors.

[1] Adapted from Massie, J. L. (1965). Management theory. In J. G. March (Ed.), *Handbook of Argomization*. Chicago: Rand McNally, 405.

Total Quality Management

A Comparison of Basic Assumptions of Scientific Management and Total Quality Management (TQM) and their Bureaucratic Application to American Public Schools

	Principals of Scientific Management	TQM's 14 Points	Bureaucratic Application to Schools
8	Promulgate clear rules and regulations to guide behavior.	The supervisor's tasks consists of helping workers understand common goals, expectations, and production strategies.	Teacher handbooks; contractual conditions of work; school handbooks, operational memoranda, and informal norms of conduct set expectations and guide behavior.
9	Establish and maintain worker discipline and accountability.	Company-wide agreement on the tenets of TQM will help remove fear and enhance worker productivity and quality. Worker discipliner is focused on quality not quotas which, in turn, drives accountability.	Students and teachers are expected to conduct themselves according to formal rules and regulations and informal norms of behavior of society and the profession.
10	Recruit new employees based on their demonstrated ability, technical skills, and knowledge, and provide training as needed.	Hire competent, motivated workers, then train them to do their jobs properly.	Teachers and administrators are required to hold professional credentials and licenses to practice before being employed. Additional training is required for re-certification.
11	Define the single best way of performing specific tasks.	Establish optimum production strategies and constantly improve them to reduce waste and improve quality. Barriers to good performance must be removed.	Prescribed strategies insist that one best and acceptable way of schooling will improve the quality of outcomes.
12	Establish systematic management practices for planning work based on scientific data.	Corporations should plan and systematically seek out best quality suppliers to improve produce quality.	Cost-effective analysis; long term planning; annual schedules.
13	Workers acceptance of "piece work" is necessary to ensure successful implementation of scientific management and slogans of efficiency emphasize commonality among workers and the organization.	Workers are expected to adopt a new philosophy to ensure the implementation of TQM. It makes mistakes and poor workmanship unacceptable. Workers establish their own slogans to indicate commitment.	School districts mandate programs which require changes in philosophy and are accompanied by slogans emphasizing efficiency and effectiveness.
14	The organization and the worker have a common economic interest in efficient production.	Workers benefit from efficient production and high quality products in the form of continued employment.	Schools and teachers benefit from quality instruction in the form of strong public support.

[1] Adapted from Massie, J. L. (1965). Management theory. In J. G. March (Ed.), *Handbook of Argomization*. Chicago: Rand McNally, 405.
[2] Adapted from Hunt, V. D. (1992). *Quality in America: How to implement a competitive quality program*. Homewood, IL: Technology Research Corporation.

schools remains remarkably similar.

While TQM speaks to the issue of participatory decision making, those processes fail to challenge the deep structures of the school hierarchy or administrator control. In the TQM equation, there is a distinct separation of top management from bottom management and a heavy dependence on top level administrators in making it work. This deliberate distinction between management and workers compromises the notion of empowerment and reinforces the status quo rather than being the means of emancipating educators. This need for administrative oversight is reminiscent of the management versus labor orientation of classical organizational theory embraced by American industry at the turn of the century. During this era, scientific management fostered the development of a machine bureaucracy which also needed concentrated hierarchical control and tight regulation. This approach depended upon worker acceptance of the notion of piece work and the commitment of managers to implement the key principles. TQM does not appear to be substantively different either in its manipulation of workers or in management's reserving ultimate control in the implementation.

The standardization of factory production systems using reliable scientific methods is the cornerstone of TQM. Collecting quantitative data, employing robust statistical methods, and analyzing the results are directed towards identifying and solving production related problems. Their use in conjunction with systems thinking, constant monitoring, and continuous improvement ensures consistency and product quality. TQM advocates suggest that an education system can be similarly controlled if administrators and teachers gather statistical data, analyze it, and apply findings to identify and resolve problems to respond to parents and the community. The strict reliance on quantitative methods, to the exclusion of other qualitative ways of knowing about organizational and educational problems suggests that it is primarily concerned with a narrow set of quality and production issues.

It is evident that some reform advocates have given inadequate attention to the inherent contradictions that exist among the disparate business philosophies transferred to schools and the consequences of concurrent implementation. For example, undertaking school decentralization requires strong central office administrator directives (Firestone & Wilson, 1985; McLaughlin, 1887). The idea of professionalism advanced in the second wave of reform and its emphasis on empowerment of teachers conflicts with the notion of choice which stresses the empowerment of parents through choice. Both conflict with the empowerment of administrators and perhaps teachers involved in authentic site-based managed schools. While other similar contradictions remain, these serve to illustrate that each of these approaches reflects a fundamentally different assumption of who should control schools. Many aspects of the TQM approach are praiseworthy such as employing a systems perspective in understanding the interrelationships among internal components and external agencies which impact educational outcomes; applying data collection techniques to better understand problems and focus solutions; advancing the notion of employee participation in decision making processes, and regarding change as a process rather than as a terminal activity. Although these elements may be used constructively, they may also be "used as tools of domination, control and coercion" (Capper & Jamison, 1993, p. 30). Their use in pursuit of narrowly defined private sector goals without regard for teachers or broad-based social wellbeing, is a gross distortion of the potential of TQM and the purpose of American schools. Chester Barnard (1938) observed that corporations could increase their success by designing structures, policies, and processes that found common ground with regard to the interests of the organization and workers. Whether, as Capper & Jamison (1993) note, TQM is "the next great hope for the salvation of both business and public education" (p. 26) or a recent manifestation of Taylor's concept of scientific management will depend not only on the goals to be achieved but on how it is implemented (Kaufman & Hirumi, 1992).

The Noncritical Adoption of Business Ideology

The work of Callahan (1962), Tyack and Hansot (1982), Beck and Murphy (1990) and other noted historians have recorded the transfer of business ideologies and management practices to public schools at the beginning of the twentieth century and commented on the extraordinary similarity of those events unfolding during the reform movement of the 1980s. During this earlier period of reform, the nation's education system was being challenged by strong public demands for school improvement. Administrators were unable to find viable solutions to problems facing schools and were also highly vulnerable to the resolve of school boards (Callahan, 1962) to transfer private sector management practices to school governance. Tyack (1974), however, provides another, pragmatic view of why school administrators conceded to adopt the principles of scientific management. Progressive educators saw an opportunity in allying themselves with the corporate sector and accepting the precepts of scientific management as a powerful means through which they could extricate schools from local political control. Thus, their ostensible capitulation to private sector ideology in adopting private sector management techniques to make schools "run as efficient as corporations" (Timar & Kirp, 1988, p. 77) was consistent with their overarching interest in wresting the control of education from politicians and shifting it to professional administrators. Linking with powerful business interests gave school administrators greater control over their schools.

Although school administrators succeeded in separating schools from the overt political spoils system, the return on this long term investment in business perspectives, values, and scientific management, however, wasn't greater efficiency but creating well entrenched school bureaucracies. After fifty years, American industry and schools recognized that the wholesale adoption of the principles of scientific management to business operations and their export to public schools was a mistake (NASSP, 1988). During the 1970s and 1980s innovative American corporations began to extricate themselves from its rigid principles, and moved to institutionalize approaches that drew upon the combined strengths of systems thinking, data collection and analysis and worker participation. Scientific management advanced similar notions. In its implementation, however, administrators placed greater emphasis on control than on balancing the interests of the organization and workers.

The tendency to look beyond education for solutions can be seen in the move towards adopting business ideology and practices. As a consequence, a full range of market-based strategies (choice), TQM (efficiency, product quality), and decentralization (site based management and empowerment) (Murphy, 1991) were bequeathed to public schools. Recent experiences with TQM in both industry and education indicate that powerful administrator biases towards retaining control may distort Deming's intent of merging quantitative techniques with solid humanistic approaches. This same problem accompanied efforts to implement scientific management earlier in the century.

A Poststructuralist Critique of TQM

The search for understanding human behavior in formal organizations during the Modern period (1920-1970) was dominated by scientific methods which guided research in the natural sciences. This tradition insisted that human behavior be studied with detachment, examined objectivity, demanded that theories be tested quantitatively, and believed that the ultimate goal of research was to produce mathematical proofs. It was believed that patterns of behavior could be discovered only through use of controlled studies and the application of stringent procedures and rules of evidence. Research using different methods of disciplined inquiry and rules of evidence were criticized and dismissed as unscientific and anecdotal. The Modernist perspective emphasized logic and believed that human behavior, like plants and animals, could be systematically classified or structured using taxonomies. Structuralists, who embraced this modernist position, organized theories of human behavior into orderly compartments such as scientific management, bureaucratic theory, and social systems theory. This approach had a pervasive impact on understanding human behavior in school organizations and on administrative practices. The rigid delimitations of quantitative methods of traditional science restricted the scope of research and thus limited understanding the human behavior in organizations.

Studying behavior in context, however, required different subjective ways of knowing. The work of Carl Rogers (1963), James Bryant Conant (1964), Thomas Barr Greenfield (1974), and Arthur Blumberg (1988) argued persuasively that phenomenological, subjective, and intuitive ways of knowing were valid for studying human behavior in school contexts. Blumberg (1988) suggested that researchers should "break out of the straitjacket of logical positivism" (Owens, 1995, p. 4) and expand their ways of knowing. Greenfield (1974) lay the groundwork for this important theoretical development in education by advancing two key points. First, because organizations are socially constructed realities, the driving forces (shared values, assumptions, and beliefs) of the people who inhabit them must be understood. Second, understanding events are constrained by subjective interpretations. Thus, as Greenfield (1974) noted, research methods employed in social science research, which fundamentally differ from those of the natural sciences, are uniquely appropriate to studying human behavior in school contexts.

In the postmodern and poststructural period a growing number of researchers questioned the application of traditional scientific methods in understanding human behavior. This discourse raised awareness that the values, beliefs, and assumptions of those who have power in organizations eclipse the nature and direction of discussions with and about those who do not. Thus, the agenda of those in power is to use formal and informal mechanisms to influence the behavior of others to behave in acceptable ways that reinforce their exclusive position in organizational hierarchies. Aryris and Schön (1974), noted that discrepancies between what we say we do and what we actually do are common in organizations. This perspective helps to explain the obvious discrepancies between the principles of scientific management advocated by Taylor during the early part of the twentieth century and their implementation by administrators. Taylor, his associates, and prominent corporate executives articulated the importance of worker participation and acceptance of his principles and believed that the economic interest of workers and industry were compatible. The implementation of these principles in manufacturing settings, however, indicated that management control far outweighed other more humanistic considerations.

Another "modern" management approach, TQM, also articulates that worker participation is indispensable to improving efficiency and product quality. In practice, however, there is strong evidence that in its application in school settings the goals of management and the need for centralized control diminishes the interests of teachers and school constituency groups. A close examination of the warp and weft of scientific management and Total Quality Management indicate that they are cut from the same ideological cloth that emphasizes efficiency and management control. Although TQM may be cloaked in humanist language, this method is neither postmodern nor poststructuralist but a popular attempt to repackage Taylors principles of scientific management.

References

American Association of Colleges of teacher Education. (1988). School Leadership preparation: A preface to action. Washington, DC: Author.

Argyris, C., & Schön, D. (1974). Theory into practice: Increasing professional effectiveness. San Francisco: Jossey-Bass.

Association for Supervision and Curriculum Development. (1986). School reform policy: A call for reason. Alexandria VA: Author.

Bacharach, S. (Ed.) (1990). Education reform: Making sense of it all. Boston: Allyn and Bacon.

Barnard, C. (1938). The functions of the executive. Cambridge, MA: Harvard University Press.

Beare, H. (1989, September). Educational administration in the 1990s. Paper presented at the national conference of the Australian Council for Educational Administration, University of New England, Amandale, New South Wales.

Beck, L., & Murphy, J. 1990). Understanding the principalship: A metaphorical analysis of from 1920-1990. Nashville, TN: National Center for Educational Leadership, Peabody College, Vanderbilt University.

Bell, D. (1976). The coming of the post-industrial society. New York: Basic Books.

Betts, F. (1992). How systems thinking applies to education. Educational Leadership, 50 (3), 38-41.

Björk, L. (1995). Substance and symbolism in the education commission reports. In R. Ginsberg & D. Plank (1995). Commissions, reports, reforms, and educational policy (pp. 133-149). Westport, CN:

Praeger.

Björk, L. (1993). New directions for principal preparation programs. Education Issues, 3 (2), 23-37.

Blumberg, A. (1988). School administration as craft: Foundations of practice. Boston: Allyn and Bacon.

Bobbitt, J. (1913). The supervision of city schools. Chicago: University of Chicago Press.

Bonstingl, J. (1992). The quality revolution in education. Educational Leadership, 50 (3), 4-9.

Borman, K., Castenelli, L,. & Gallegher, K. (1993). Business involvement in school reform: The rise of the business roundtable. In C. Marshall (Ed.), The new politics of race and gender (pp. 69-84). London: Falmer Press.

Boyd, W. (1988). Policy analysis, educational policy, and management: Through a looking glass darkly? In N. Boyan (Ed.), Handbook of research on educational administration (pp. 501-524). New York: Longman.

Boyer, E. (1983). High school. New York: Carnegie Foundation for the Advancement of Teaching.

Bracey, G. (1991). Why can't schools be like we were? Phi Delta Kappan, 73 (2), 104-117.

Bracey, G. (1993). The media's myth of school failure. Inter Ed, 1.

Brogan, D. (1962). The American character. New York: Time Paperback, 137.

Boorstin, D. (1975). Democracy and its discontents. New York: Vintage Books.

Boyer, E. (1983). High school. New York: Carnegie Foundation for the Advancement of Teaching.

Boyer, E. (1991). Ready to learn. Princeton, NJ: Carnegie Foundation for the Advancement of Learning.

Callahan, R. E. (1962). Education and the cult of efficiency. Chicago: University of Chicago Press.

Campbell, R., Fleming, T., Newell, L., & J. Bennion. (1987). A history of thought and practice in educational administration. New York: Teachers College Press.

Capper, C., & Jamison, M. (1993). Let the buyer beware: Total quality management and educational research and practice. Educational Researcher, 22 (8), 25-30.

Carnevale, A. (1992, August). Anthony Carnavale on the role of schools in the new economy. The School Administrator, 49 (7), 30-32.

Carnegie Council for Adolescent Development. (1989). Turning points. Washington, DC: Author.

Carnegie Foundation for the Advancement of Teaching. (1986). A nation prepared: Teachers for the twenty-first century. New York: Author.

Carnegie Foundation for the Advancement of Teaching. (1988). Report card on school reform: The teachers speak. Princeton, NJ: Author.

Cibulka, J., & Derlin, R. (1992, April). State leadership for education restructuring: A comparison of two state policy systems. Paper presented at the Annual Meeting of the American Educational Research Association, San Francisco.

Committee for Economic Development. (1985). Investing in our children. New York: Author.

Committee for Economic Development. (1987). Children in need. New York: Author.

Commission on Minority Participation in American Life. (1988). One third of a nation. Washington, DC: American Council on Education/ Education Commission of the States.

Commission on Policy for Racial Justice of the Joint Center for Political Studies. (1989). Visions for a better way: A black appraisal of public schooling. Washington, DC: Joint Policy Center for Political Studies.

Commission on Precollege Education in Mathematics, Science, and Technology. (1983). Educating America for the 21st century. Washington, DC: National science Foundation.

Conant, J. (1964). Modes of thought: My encounters with science and education. New York: Trident Press Book.

Cremin, L. (1989). Popular education and its discontents. New York: Harper & Row.

Cuban, L. (1993). The lure of reform and its pitiful history. Phi Delta Kappan, 75 (3), 182-185.

Cuban, L. (1992). The corporate myth of reforming public schools. Phi Delta Kappan, 72 (4), 264-71.

Cuban, L. (1990). Four stories about national goals for American education. Phi Delta Kappan, 72 (4), 264-271.

Cubberly, E. (1916). Public school administration. Boston: Houghton Mifflin.

Deming, W. E. (1986). Out of the crisis. Cambridge, MA: Massachusetts Institute of Technology, Center for Advanced Engineering Study.

Deming, W. E. (1982). Quality productivity and competitive position. Cambridge, MA: Massachusetts Institute of Technology, Center for Advanced Engineering Study.

Doyle, D. (1991). America 2000. Phi Delta Kappan, 73 (3), 185-191.

U.S. Department of Education. (1993). Education and states and nations: Indicators comparing U.S. states with OECD countries in 1988. Washington, DC: Author.

Education Commission of the States, Task Force on Education for Economic Growth. (1983). Action for excellence: A comprehensive plan to improve our nation's schools. Washington, D.C.: Education Commission of the States.

Fireston, W. A., Fuhrman, S., & Kirst, M. W. (1990). An overview of educational reform since 1983. In J. Murphy (Ed.), The reform of American public education during the 1980s: Perspectives and cases. Berkeley: McCutchan.

Firestone, W., & Wilson, B. (1985). Management and organizational outcomes: The effects of approach and environment in schools. Philadelphia: Research for Better Schools, Inc.

Fowler, F. (1985, November, 6). Why reforms go awry. Education Week, 5 (10), 24, 17.

Fox, J. (1993). The wrong whipping boy. Phi Delta Kappan, 75 (2), 118-119.

Fullan, M. (1993). Change forces: Probing the depths of education al reform. London, The Falmer Press.

George Washington University. (1991). Got to learn to earn. Washington, DC: Author.

Guthrie, J., & Reed, P. (1991). Educational administration and policy: Effective leadership for American education. Boston: Allyn & Bacon.

Greenfield, T. (1975). Theory about organizations: A new perspective and its implications for schools. In G. Hughes (Ed.), Administering education: International challenge. London: Athlone.

Gruenberg, B. (1912). Some economic obstacles to educational progress. American Teacher, 1.

Hansen, M. (1991). Educational administration and organizational behavior, (3rd ed.). Boston: Allyn & Bacon.

Hayes, M. (1992). Incrementalism and public policy. New York: Longman.

Henderson, H. (1977). A new economics. In D. Vermilye (Ed.), Work and education. San Francisco: Jossey-Bass.

Holmes Group. (1986). Tomorrow's teachers. East Lansing, MI: Author.

Howe, H. (1991). America 2000: A bumpy ride on four trains. Phi Delta Kappan, 73 (3), 192-203.

Hoy, W., & Miskel, C. (1991). Education Administration: Theory, research, practice. New York: McGraw-Hill.

Hudson Institute. (1988). Workforce 2000. Washington, DC: Author.

Jaeger, R. (1992). World class standards, choice, and privatization: Weak measurement serving presumptive policy. Phi Delta Kappan, 74 (2), 118-128.

Kanter, R. M. (1983). The change masters: Innovation and entrepreneurship in the American corporation. New York: Simon and Schuster.

Kaplan, G. (1992). Images of education: The mass media's version of America's schools. Washington, DC: Institute for educational leadership.

Katz, M. (1971). Class, bureaucracy, and schools. New York: Praeger.

Kaufman, R., & Hirumi, A. (1992). Ten steps to TQM plus 5. Educational Leadership, 50 (3), 33-34.

Kearns, D. L. (1988a). A business perspective on American schooling. Education Week, 7 (30), 566.

Kearns, D. L. (1988b), An education recovery plan for America. Phi Delta Kappan, 69 (8), 565-570.

Koppich, J. E., & J. W. Guthrie. (1993). Examining contemporary education-reform efforts in the United States. In H. Beare & W. Boyd (Eds.), Restructuring schools: An international perspective on the movement to transform control and performance of schools (pp. 12-29). Washington, D.C: The Falmer Press.

Lane, J., & Epps, E. (Eds.). (1992). Restructuring the school: Problems and prospects. Berkeley, CA: McCutcheon.

Lindbloom, C. (1977). Politics and Markets: The world's political-economic systems. New York: Basic Books.

Maccoby, M. (1989, December). Looking for leadership now. Paper presented at the National Center for Educational Leadership conference. Harvard University, Cambridge MA.

Mazzoni, T. (1995). State policy-making and school reform: Influences and influentials. In J. Scribner & D. Layton (Eds.), The study of educational politics (pp. 53-73). Washington, DC: Taylor & Francis.

McGuire, K. (1990). Business involvement in the 1990s In D. Mitchell & M. Goertz (Eds.), Education politics for the new century. London: Falmer Press.

McLaughlin, M. (1987). Learning from experience: Lessons from policy implementation. Educational Evaluation and Policy Analysis, 9 (2), 171-178.

Mitchel, B. (1990). Children, youth and educational leadership. In B. Mitchell & L. Cunningham (Eds.), Educational leadership in changing contexts of families, communities, and schools. Chicago: The University of Press of Chicago.

Mishel, L., & R. Texeira. (1991). Some economists challenge the view that schools hurt competitiveness. Education Week, 11 (12), 1.

Murphy, J. (1991). Restructuring schools: Capturing and assessing the phenomenon. New York: Teachers College Press.

Murphy, J. (1990). Educational reform of the 1980s: A comprehensive analysis. In J. Murphy (Ed.), Educational reform of the 1980s: Perspectives and cases (pp. 3-56). Berkeley, CA: McCutchan Publishing Corporation.

Murphy, J., Hallinger, P., & Mesa, R. P. (1985). School effectiveness: Checking progress and assumption sand developing a role for state and federal government. Teachers College Record, 86 (4), 615-641.

National Center for Education and the Economy. (1990). America's choice: High skills or low wages. Rochester, NY: National Center for Education and the Economy.

National Commission on Children. (1991). Beyond rhetoric: A new American agenda for children and families. Washington, DC: Author.

National Commission on Excellence in Education. (1983). A nation at risk. Washington, DC: U.S. Department of Education.

National Commission on Excellence in Educational Administration. (1987). Leaders for tomorrow schools. Tempe, Az: University Council for Education Administration.

United States Department of Education. (1993). National

excellence: A case for developing America's talent. Washington, DC: Author.

National Governors' Association. (1986). Time for results: The governors' 1991 report on education. Washington, DC: National Governors' Association.

National Governors' Association. (1989). Results in education. Washington, DC: Author.

National Policy Board for Educational Administration. (1989). Improving the preparation of school administrators: An agenda for reform. Charlottesville, VA: Author.

National Science Board. (1983). Educating Americans for the 21st century. Washington, DC: National Science Board, National Science Foundation.

Nelson, D. (1980). Frederick W. Taylor and the rise of the rise of scientific management. Madison, WI: University of Wisconsin Press.

Odden, A. (1992). Education policy implementation. Albany: SUNY Press.

Owens, R. (1995). Organizational behavior in education. Boston: Allyn & Bacon.

Perry, N. J. (1988). The education crisis: What business can do. Fortune, 70-75.

Peters, T., & R. Waterman. (1982). In search of excellence: Lessons from America's best run companies. New York: Harper & Row.

Peterson, P. (1985). Did the education commissions say anything? Education and Urban Society, 17 (2), 126-144.

Plank, D., & R. Ginsberg. (1990). Catch the wave: Reform commissions and school reform. In J. Murphy (Ed.), The educational reform movement of the 1980s: Perspectives and cases. Berkeley, CA: McCutcheon Publishing Corporation.

Quality Education for Minorities Project. (1990). Education that works: An action plan for the education of minorities. Cambridge, MA: Massachusetts Institute of Technology.

Reich, R. (1990). The work of nations: Preparing ourselves for 21st century capitalism. New York: Alfred A. Knopf.

Reich, R. (1983). The next American frontier. New York: Times Books.

Rogers, C. (1963, Fall). Toward a science of the person. Journal of Humanistic Psychology, 137, 645.

Schlechty, P. (1990). Schools for the twenty-first century:

Leadership imperatives for educational reform. San Francisco: Jossey-Bass.

Spring, J. (1986). The American school 1642-1985. New York: Longman.

Snyder, D. (1984). The strategic context of education in America 1985-1995. Washington, DC: National Education Association.

Sykes, G., & Elmore, R. (1989). Making schools manageable. In J. Hannaway & R. L. Crowson (Eds.), The politics of reforming school administration. New York: Falmer Press, 77-94.

Sztjan, P. (1992). A matter of metaphors: Education as a handmade process. Educational Leadership, 50 (3), 35-37.

Taylor, F. (1911). Shop management. New York: Harper & Bros.

Thomas, C., & Hrebenar, R. (1991). Nationalizing of interest groups and lobbying in the states. In A. Cigler & B. Loomis (Eds.), Interest group politics (3rd ed.). Washington, DC: CQ Press.

Timar, T., & Kirp, D. (1988). State efforts to reform schools: Treading between a regulatory swamp and an English garden. Education Evaluation and Policy Analysis, 10 (2), 75-88.

Twentieth Century Task Force on Federal Educational Policy. (1983). Making the grade. New York: Twentieth Century Fund.

Tyack, D. (1974). One best system. Cambridge, MA: Harvard University Press.

Tyack, D., & Hansot, E. (1982). Managers of virtue: Public school leadership in America, 1920-1989. New York: Basic Books.

Underwood, J. (1990). State legislative responses to educational reform literature. In P. W. Thurston & L.S. Lotto (Eds.), Recent advances in educational administration (Vol. A) (pp. 139-178). Greenwich, CT: JAI Press.

United States Department of Education. (1993). TI. Washington, DC: Author.

United States Department of Education. (1991). TI. Washington, DC: Author.

Walton, M. (1990). Deming's management at work. New York: Putnam.

Peters, T., & Waterman, R. (1982). In search of excellence: Lessons from America's best-run companies. New York: Harper & Row Publishers.

Weisman, J. (1991, November 13). Some economists challenge the view that schools hurt competitiveness. Education Week, p 1.

Wirth, A. (1992). Education and work in the year 2000. San

Francisco: Jossey-Bass Publishers.

Chapter 9

THE QUALITY PRINCIPAL

Dennis W. VanBerkum
Moorhead State University

Today, more than any other time in history, our schools are under close scrutiny. Studies attempt to measure everything. Some studies find problems, some try to solve problems, and some even deny that there are any problems. However, almost every study agrees that a quality school relates to the quality of its leader, the principal.

The role of a quality principal has taken many forms during our recent history. Cuban (1988) writes that the principal is a pivotal role to school success. It is a position that influences and makes a difference in schools. Often, the demands of managing a well run school have taken priority over instructional improvement with many principals in more recent times. To be a successful principal, the public perceived the principal as the one: in control; operating a school where little controversy and conflict exists; and procedures who creates for a safe secure environment. Instruction is controlled by prescribed teaching methods for all teachers. However, the current organization of school does not facilitate this process; prompting Block (1991) to state: "One of the failings of our democracy is that our organizations, in this case schools, continue to be managed in an autocratic and top-down way despite our espoused belief in the fundamental value of individuals and their right to create paths of their own choosing." (p. xiii) Power over others drives the corporation (schools) to produce specific results and fails to recognize the human component within schools.

Recent criticism of school management can be heard from students, parents, and business. They view schools as controlling and insensitive to their needs. Further, they claim the power and the control a principal has limits growth of the school and its mission. Tanner (1986) offers that "too much has been made of casting the school principal as a managerial rather than educational leader." Bennis and Nanus (1985) distinguish between management and leadership. Their distinction has clear implications for principals in today's effective schools. They define management as a means "to bring about, to accomplish, to have charge of or responsibility for, to conduct." Conversely, leadership is defined as "influencing, guiding in direction, course, action, opinion." Put in educational terms, management is related to efficiency, and leadership to effectiveness. Quality management principles are forcing the principalship to be viewed as a different process, one where the principal seems to have gone full circle from the concept of the principal being the master teacher back to the concept of the principal being the instructional leader.

Development of the Principalship

The principalship, as we view it today, is in a constant evolution. The position evolved from the appointment of head teachers, to teaching principals, to full-time principals, to that of executive of a administrative staff, faculty, and student body. A lack of documentation does not allow one to fully understand the development of the position; however, as the complexity of the school organization grew so did the responsibilities of the principal. In the early years of the principalship, governing school boards determined that there was a need for someone to be in charge of the school. The first principals were called head teachers in charge of the school, but spending most of their time on instructional programs.

About the middle of the 19th century, formal records indicate that this position emerged as a routine administrative position where principals became managers of bureaucratic functions (Kimbrough & Burkett, 1990). Much of the design of the principalship was impacted by the industrial revolution in business. Early principalships were viewed as custodians of schools where the organizational concepts of scientific management governed schools. Institutionally, the organization was viewed as a triangular structure where the principal sat on top of the apex and teachers were the base. Communication was one-way. Faculty meetings were formal. Information was shared by the principal with the teachers or parents. The principal was recognized as the authority leader and had legal responsibilities for decisions. Teachers were viewed as incapable of making decisions or accepting responsibilities for the decision making (English & Hill, 1990).

During the 20th century, the principalship grew in administrative responsibility as changes in educational philosophies moved from a traditional subject center curriculum to one with a child-centered focus. The effective schools movement in the late 1970s impacted school operations, placing further emphasis on the role of the principal as leader. Edmonds (1979) researched schools in an attempt to define the components that were "effective." Specific student outcomes (i.e., test scores and other observable behavior) were used for assessing effectiveness. His research, and the subsequent research with others, outlined the basic components of an effective school. Their number one priority was leadership of the school. The effective principal was viewed as integral to the school's academic success, instructional leadership and day to day operations.

According to Sashkin and Huddle (1986), these effective school principals demonstrate five nomothetic behaviors:

> They establish a safe and secure physical setting within which the educational process is to occur;
> They have and communicate high expectations of students and teachers;
> They emphasize basic skill instruction and time-on-task;
> They develop clear instructional objectives; and
> They establish school-level goals and create incentives for learning.

Smith and Andrews (1989) expand these behaviors into the following traits of effective principals. Effective principals: (a) identify staff who require direct and intensive supervision/remediation, (b) reassign individuals who require new skills, (c) provide inservice needs for staff, (d) provide opportunities to develop skills and expertise, (e) extend the school's influence through focused communication, (f) provide constructive feedback; evaluate performance, (g) provide others with opportunities to explore new methods, (h) provide recognition for individuals who exhibit low profiles, (i) model behaviors for colleagues, (j) promote staff morale, support and instructional leadership, (k) provide specific details and insights regarding teacher performance, and (l) assist teachers to master changes in existing classroom practice (p. 90).

English and Hill (1989) maintain an effective school is one where the principal teaches and persuades teachers to accept the principal's personal vision. Teacher initiatives are supported or sanctioned if they are consonant with the principal's vision. Communication is a one-way process. Feedback is requested of teachers to be used in conjunction with the principal's vision. Little interaction exists between the principal and teachers. Thus, effective schools become "managerially tight and culturally loose" (Sergiovanni, 1991, p. 49). Emphasis was on "the principal for school success. The principal was identified as:

> According to Snyder (1986), instructional leadership that built school success was to be done in three phases. The first phase is the planning stage: (a) school wide goal setting, (b) team action planning, and (c) individual planning. The second phase is developing: (a) clinical supervision, (b) staff development, (c) curriculum development, (d) performance management, and (e) resource management. The third phase is achieving and assessing: (a) replanning, (b) school effectiveness, (c) performance outcomes for staff, students, and teams, and (d) mastery learning. The principal was held accountable for the effectiveness of the school.

Sergiovanni (1991) summarizes this best by concluding that the effective principal is an:

> instructional leader who holds strong views about instruction and exhibit strong and highly visible managerial skills to ensure that all features of the model are properly aligned. They practice close supervision and monitor carefully what teachers do. They provide direct help to teachers to facilitate the model's implementation. (p. 96)

The Movement Past Effective Principals

In 1980, Deming developed 14 points in quality management. These points were translated to educational purposes (Stu-Runyan & Heart, 1992) and represent a new approach to school operations causing the effective schools movement to be questioned. Gradually, the effective schools movement has given way to the quality schools movement of the 1990s and a new view of the principalship.

In quality schools, the principal's position of leadership changes from a traditional leader who controls by power to one who develops a supportive climate where others are empowered. Cunningham and Gresso (1993) offer that:

> If empowerment occurs individuals become more fully aware of their unique abilities, how those abilities can help the organization, and how they complement and interfere with the skills of others within the organization. Organizations are improved the more individuals learn about their own nature. Thus, the key to organizational effectiveness is learning how to use individual differences to the fullest. This is the exact reverse of trying to force all individuals to follow the same set of roles, rules, and regulations in order to try to make them interchangeable. (p. 205)

Quality principals orchestrate this process. Organizational goals become those of all persons in the organization and everyone participates in the future vision of the school. Interpersonal skills become important in leadership styles creating linkages with people for the purpose of motivating teachers to become self-actualizers. Key to the quality principal is the importance of establishing goals all educators can agree upon. This new philosophy in the management of schools moves from "boss management" to "lead management" (Glasser, 1990) where all members of the group cooperate to implement the commonly agreed upon goals (Richardson, Flannigan, & Lane, 1992).

English and Hill (1989) suggest this represents a restructured school where the principal is linked to the cabinet established in the effective school by means of teams of teachers who are linked to learners and parents. However, the term linked takes on a new meaning. Two-way communication exists for issues and proposals on a vertical axis and job-like communication on a horizontal axis for consultation. Much collaboration is used where decisions are made at the implementation level. Principals and others have a clear understanding of decisions to be made alone, decisions that require advanced advice, and decisions that are corporate. Leadership by the principal is viewed as a transforming process, creating opportunities for others to lead.

Sergiovanni (1991) offers that this concept is a "new and broadening definition of effectiveness" (p. 76). He calls these schools "successful schools" that were viewed by Goodlad (1983) as more comprehensive and expansive and more consistent with the high quality schooling that most Americans want for their children. English and Hill (1989) suggest that schools have gone through a conceptual change base from the earlier custodial schools that fostered scientific management to the effective school that fosters effective school research to a restructured school that is based upon Theory Z. Principals have become facilitators of process and implementation.

In these schools, the principal, as in effective schools, has a clear view of the process of schooling, teaching, and learning. In addition, he/she elicits from others clarity, consensus, and commitment to the school's common purposes and values. Leadership styles may vary. The style is less important than what the principal stands for, believes in, and communicates to others. Thus, schools become less managerially tight and more culturally appropriate. To avoid confusion at this point, the image of "quality" is to be emphasized rather than restricted. Success is offered as a broadening of the term effective. Quality is intended to broaden the term success.

Curran (1983) suggests that the identity of quality principals is predicated on the attributes of a quality school: (a) active leadership by the principal, (b) a positive school climate, (c) workable discipline policies and procedures, (d) teachers who have high expectations for students, (e) parents who are involved in the educational process, (f) productive methods of evaluating the curriculum, (g) efficient methods of evaluating teacher performance, (h) consequential methods of developing and evaluating student growth, (i) a realistic philosophy of education, (j) an extensive and adequate student activities' program, and (k) significant student services.

The quality school is a purposeful organization whose members seek, through common efforts, to achieve established goals. School systems are composed of people, and people will determine whether the system succeeds or stagnates, serves its clients effectively or squanders its limited resources. Therefore, the operation of a quality school now requires the coordination of several members of a leadership team. The success of a school is dependent upon the quality of leadership provided by the principal, combined with the competency and cooperation of all stake holders in the school.

The principal's role is seen as operative in a variety of the school initiatives. Priority initiatives are based upon an identifiable vision which is expressed and modeled by the principal through personal actions. Teachers' initiatives are supported or sanctioned if they are consonant with this vision. In promoting teachers' efforts, principals provide essential resources and limit unnecessary intrusion by outsiders. Further, they are supportive by maintaining school-wide discipline. Finally, they serve a vital role promoting community support while fostering teacher autonomy.

A quality principal must have a vision of what he/she wants the school to become. The principal must also have a plan for the staff to work toward that vision. The quality principal must also have a personal knowledge base in learning, teaching, organizing work groups, and organizing people. This person must have skills to help the group work toward a common goal. These items must be combined with a very strong commitment to help the staff and students work toward improving schooling. The attribute that separates the quality principal from the ineffective principal is a personal sense of mission. This mission must be communicated continuously to the staff, students, and parents in a variety of forms.

The quality principal also must possess prerequisites in the cognitive, effective, and behavioral areas. Snyder and Anderson (1987) list these requisites in the effective area: (a) Openness to the ideas, influences, and recommendations from staff, parents and students, (b) A sense that one can and must guide collaborative activities, (c) Motivation to alter the school's learning norms, (d) Openness to ideas for altering the organizational structure, and (e) Motivation to share leadership responsibilities with selected staff members. Prerequisites in the behavioral area include: (a) Ability to listen to and value the ideas of others, (b) Ability to create a work climate that will motivate staff members, (c) Ability to provide counsel to individuals or groups, (d) Ability to provide leadership or group problem-solving meetings, and (e) Ability to listen to the public and to involve them productively in school improvement tasks.

Flannigan and Richardson (1992) suggest these actions are political activities where the principal exercises influence others. This political influence is seen as a means of achieving both individual and group goals associated with the school. School is seen as " a stage for marketing the political agenda" (p. 9). Successful maneuvering empowers staff members within the school. A principal's personal authority and powers are in turn derived through the perceptions of those subordinates under one's charge. Empowerment becomes a means to further develop quality schools.

However, a paradox of empowerment exists similar to a self-fulfilling prophecy much like McGregor's idea that managers regard people as either X (needing control), or Y (motivated). If principals view teachers and students as needing control and impose limits on student power, they create a dependency that requires an X style of classroom management. Principals who view teachers and students as motivated (style Y) will encourage classrooms structured so that students reach agreements on shared responsibilities. As the principal moves from one who leads by directives is depended upon, to one who becomes a facilitator of the learning process, he/she could be viewed as indecisive and lacking control. This forces the principal to exercise power to maintain control of the school. A careful balance of techniques is needed for one to be successful as a principal in a quality school.

Block (1991) suggests this view is not a set of techniques one chooses. If we believe that control of the school is the principal's domain, we will not look to empower teachers and students. Empowerment seeks to shift the responsibility and control to those who do the "core work of the organization" (p. xv). For example, classrooms need to move from conventional ways of conducting education that supports conventional politics to one that supports individual thought and expression. Teachers learn to model responsibility and self-respect while they develop a strong sense of their own competence and independence whether it be circumstance or substance. The principal becomes a facilitator of the process.

Brennan and Brennan (1988) suggest this will not be an easy task. Ethical and legal mandates will require that the principal not align with any particular group. In meeting the requirements of law, principals must weigh actions that negate meeting absolute interpretation of law in favor of compliance to statutes while considering ethical limits of enforcement. That is, a degree of discretion in enforcement would demand considering individual circumstances while still maintaining order and support within the school setting.

Seldin (1988) supports this position by first considering the welfare of students or dignity of staff members as it applies, while maintaining confidentiality of communications with them. Principals must model appropriate behaviors while addressing the limits imposed by ethical considerations with circumstances of acts brought before them for resolution. This requires that a school clearly state its beliefs about students, its mission, and its vision for student learning. In doing so, the principal must create a situation conducive to learning where empowerment is viewed as a logical progression of individual development for all in the school (Van Berkum, in print).

Harden (1988) places the focus of the principal's attention upon the welfare of the community. To him, ethics dictate that the family unit is the primary concern, while the school's function serves as an extension of the family unit in promoting the development of the child. The role of the state, and consequently that of the school as an extension of the family, is to promote: social, moral and civil development of the child through the school as an intermediate. Parents are assumed to have the best interests of the child in mind and it is the duty of the school to supply appropriate discipline, special education, and counseling services as necessary to maintain equity and harmony within an academic community.

Finally, it is the role of the principal to assure that this balance is implemented. Promoting "ethical excellence" within a school setting often involves a revitalization of the status quo. This excellence is assured by providing positive criticism in the evaluation of teacher performances, even at the risk of conflict. Evaluations should be accomplished in an equitable manner, in a competitive atmosphere. Accountability is fostered by promoting technical support and exhibiting fair play in interpersonal disputes (Doggett, 1988).

Calabrese (1988) suggests the principal facilitates the belief that schools can improve existing practices on the basis of establishing and applying standards of performance. Although principals accept the views

of others, they have a moral obligation to guard against bias in promoting school climate. They establish curricular priorities, perfect instructional delivery, and maximize limited resources to accomplish these ends. Calabrese identifies guidelines to insure progress in promoting positive school climate.
1. Develop vision consistent with sound education philosophies;
2. Apply strong moral leadership;
3. Condemn discrimination;
4. View effective teaching as a duty;
5. Build community;
6. Balance the rights of all groups;
7. Recognize that rights issues are not always popular;
8. Base decisions on what is right;
9. Make moral courage an integral part of your role;
10. Communicate ethical behavior, integrity & moral action.

The Characteristics of the Quality Principal

The National Association of Elementary School Principals (NAESP, 1986) identified four basic characteristics for the success of K-8 principals. Successful elementary principals had knowledge about child growth and development, teaching and learning, general educational knowledge, and school climate. These characteristics were expressed in a set of performance dimensions and behaviors. The leadership proficiencies include leadership, communication skills, and group processing skills. Supervisory proficiencies include leading curriculum improvement, instructional improvement, performance, and evaluation. Administrative proficiencies include organizational arrangements, fiscal management, and political awareness. From this process an administrator inventory was developed (NAESP, 1991) to measure the performance domains of creativity, decisiveness, educational values, group leadership, human relations competence, instructional leadership/supervision, and judgment.

In 1975, the National Association of Secondary School Principals (NASSP) with cooperation with the American Psychological Association (APS), developed an Assessment Center Project to improve the selection process for entry-level elementary and secondary building administrators. The project identified a set of 12 generic leadership skills necessary for successful school administrators: leadership, problem analysis, organizational ability, judgment, sensitivity, educational values, personal motivation, written communication, oral communication, range of interest, decisiveness, and stress tolerance (Hersey, 1987).

King (1988) incorporated these skills in to a Reasoned Action

Leadership model which combines the knowledge and personal skills needed to be successful with respective contents. Van Berkum (1994) refined the model using the Internal Administrative Relationships model developed by Getzels and Guba suggesting that the two act in concert with one another. The knowledge base identifies a cognitive component derived from the eight <u>Skills for Successful School Administration</u> developed by Hoyle et al (1990). This knowledge base consists of six broad areas: (a) Theory and Practice of Administration, (b) Legal, Political, and Ethical Foundations of Education, (c) Supervision and Staff Development, (d) Statistics, Research, Analysis, and Writing, (e) Educational Foundations, Curriculum, and Instruction; and (f) Fiscal Responsibility.

The personal dimension focus was organized into three areas: (a) The idiographic or personal characteristics of educational values, personal motivation, range of interests, and sensitivity, (b) The role-related responses of decisiveness, judgment, organizational ability, and problem analysis and (c) The action responses of leadership, stress tolerance, oral communication, and written communication. These skills have been expanded to include other skills such as delegation, planning, implementing, and developing, through a series of support activities.

Currently, 21 performance domains have been identified by the National Commission for the Principalship (Thomson, 1993). These domains were developed integrating the outcomes of two processes: induction and task driven and deductive and theory driven. The resulting list was then juried and arranged in four broad themes:

I. Functional Themes address "the organizational process and techniques by which the mission of the school is achieved. They provide for the educational program to be realized and allow the institution to function." The domains within this theme are: leadership, information collection, problem analysis, judgment, organizational oversight, implementation, and delegation.

II. Programmatic themes "focus on the scope and framework of the educational program. They reflect the core technology of schools, instruction, and the related supporting services, developmental activities, and resource base." The specific domains are: instruction and the learning environment, curriculum design, student guidance and development, staff development, measurement and evaluation, and resource allocation.

III. Interpersonal themes "recognize the significance of interpersonal connections in schools. They acknowledge the critical value of human relationships to the satisfaction of personal and professional goals, and to the achievement of organizational purpose." The specific domains are: motivating others, interpersonal sensitivity, oral and nonverbal expression, and written expression.

IV. Contextual themes "reflect the world of ideas and forces within which the school operates. They explore the intellectual, ethical, cultural, economic, political, and governmental influences upon schools, including traditional and emerging perspectives." The specific domain are: philosophy and cultural values, legal and regulatory applications, policy and political influences, and public relations (Contents).

The Leadership Role

Leadership is viewed as the ultimate necessity for any successful organization, by forging organizational goals, assisting the group with personal goals, setting and clearly defining objectives, and cooperatively working toward attainment of organizational and personal goals and objectives. The principal is responsible for leading and managing everything that transpires in a school as it works to become a quality school. Therefore, leadership takes on new meaning. Snyder and Anderson (1986) believe that principals must have particular attributes to run a quality school: (a) A clear vision of possibilities, (b) Social engineering skills, (c) A broad knowledge base, (d) Unshakable commitment, and (e) A personal sense of mission.

A closer view of leadership as defined by the national administrative associations reflects a change in the concept of leadership. The National Association of Elementary School Principals (1986) suggests:

> Principals who are proficient in leadership tend to share many traits in common. They are characterized by eagerness to improve; while disinterested in change for its own sake, they are never satisfied with the status quo. They are open to new ideas, grateful for constructive criticism, avid to learn. (p. 5)

The NASSP's Principal Assessment Center defines leadership as:

> The ability to get others involved in solving problems, and the ability to recognize when the group requires direction, to interact

with the group effectively, and to guide them to the accomplishment of a task. (Hersey, 1987, p. 3)

The National Policy Board For Educational Administration defines leadership as:

> Providing purpose and direction for individuals and groups; sharing school culture and values; facilitating the development of a shared strategic vision of the school; formulating goals and planning change efforts with staff and setting priorities for one's school in the context of community and district priorities and staff needs. (Thompson, 1993, p. 1-3)

If one collectively reviews these definitions of leadership, the traditional leadership role found in effective schools moves toward focusing more on a facilitative role for quality schools. Berman (1971) defines the facilitator as an individual who intervenes and enables another individual to perform a new task, perform a task more efficiently, or ease burdens imposed on another person that would inhibit task completion. This assistance is provided by being knowledgeable and demonstrating intuition regarding issues associated with a select discipline. Other characteristics of a facilitator include: integrity, defined as consistency in dealing with other persons regarding information sharing and other communications and a climate of mutual trust, which is established among individuals who support compassion for others.

Adams and Baily (1989) describe traits that delineate the more competent principals. Using a semantic differential scale to identify patterns of exhibited behavior, these authors outline a continuum of observable characteristics. These include the ranges include:

```
Stability      <——> Activity
Intention      <——> Distinction
Accountability <——> Efficacy
Regularity     <——> Variability
Intervention   <——> Facilitation
Control        <——> Empowerment
Holism         <——> Desegregation (p. 68).
```

This construct serves as a useful reference when considering the breadth of issues that could come to bear when dealing with a variety of settings, personalities, and events, where performances are compared. No pattern is judged as ideal. Often actions are weighed in view of the situations

The Quality Principal

encountered. This device also serves to illustrate the complexity of examining climate issues. A degree of stability would be sacrificed when one perceives the need to promote an action.

For Tewel (1989) the principal's role should entail "collaborative supervision" (p. 76). That is, planning and decision making should embrace management practices that involve and motivate teachers to resolve problems that directly effect them. Implementation of these practices, whether through the aid of assistant principals or departmental chairpersons, can be accomplished by cooperative goal setting, definition of performance standards, monitoring of performance and the addressing of safe topics first.

The hesitation on the part of many principals is experienced when they feel the reduction of decision making prerogatives. They must resist the tendency to intervene in the process when their influence is not necessary. The degree of success collaborative teams achieve is determined by: the commitment of staff in addressing issues, full problem definition within the realm that team members have direct control, the setting of attainable goals, the stressing of more than short term initiatives, the development of meaningful assessment criteria to measure the impact of innovation, sufficient training in innovative practices, and freedom from unnecessary interventions on the part of higher officials. Finally, it is crucial that the quality principal stress the direct benefits that accrue to participants and allow the participants an opportunity to adjust the process to meet demands of the setting.

Clauser (1985) identified three potential roles for the competent facilitator: (a) the catalyst displaces inactivity of a group, communicating current conditions and what conditions could or should be; (b) the solution giver determines when and how to direct action toward chosen goals; and (c) the process helper helps the group recognize and define problems, diagnose, set objectives, acquire resources, select solutions, adapt, implement, and evaluate results. In doing so, Clauser identified steps that facilitators must take in order to accomplish their ends:

1. identify populations;
2. perform a needs assessment;
3. clarify roles and analyze tasks;
4. build relationships;
5. establish goals, objectives and priorities;
6. assess the status of resources and adjust plans;
7. design changes for the target;
8. design the staff development program;
9. establish appropriate linkages and diffuse information;

10. implement and stabilize the plan; and
11. evaluate the results of actions taken (p. 11).

Further, all facilitation should accomplish several key objectives. These are:

1. Fulfill organizational goals;
2. Make use of other people in fulfilling these goals;
3. Meet humanitarian aspects of the job; and
4. Build organizational mechanisms for innovation, change and development (p. 21).

This is not intended to infer that all issues in a quality school are delegated to groups. By attempting to determine what kinds of tasks are best accomplished by whom and when, reoccurring patterns can be identified. A quality principal exercises leadership to legitimize whether a change is to be taken seriously and serves to support teachers. Involvement on the part of principals not only better equips principals to advise teachers but also imparts important messages. Quality principals more often than not, involve others to assist them with interventions. They utilize a face to face mode of communication. Quality principals do not allow themselves to be consumed with second order priorities.

An area often neglected when one considers facilitation of change is that of second change facilitators (SCF) (Clauser, 1985). It is recognized that not all of the facilitator role is performed by the principal. This individual may assume a parallel role, or an ancillary role, promoting the initiatives of the primary facilitator (change agent). Further, the SCF may be as active or more so than the principal! The style of the quality principal may be examined in terms of which kinds of second change agents serve him most compatibly and effectively. The location of this second facilitator in the organization is seen as crucial with reference to the style exhibited by the principal and in turn the principal's effectiveness

Characteristics observed most frequently for the SCF are:

1. The SCF initiates actions nearly equal to that of the principal;
2. The principal makes more simple interventions, those which are briefer or less involved than the SCF. The SCF's actions are longer, or consist of multiple actions;
3. Targets of the SCF parallel those of the principal;
4. The SCF makes fewer support and organizational interventions, provides more of the formal training, provides more actual

consultation and reinforcement, provides equal degrees of monitoring and evaluation, has less extended communication with contacts and makes half as many responses to their concerns;
5. The medium of delivery for the SCF is the same but is less interactive;
6. The SCF spends half as much time in the office and three times as much time in the classroom; and
7. If the SCF is an assistant principal, that person may intervene more often, and there is more of a division of labor (Clauser, 1985, p. 21).

Hall et al. (1982) identified three styles of facilitation that principals commonly exhibit. His analysis was based upon the frequency of incidents associated with kinds of intervention strategies employed. The three styles are defined as: 1) the initiator, one who makes a few simple incident interventions; 2) the manager, one who frequently monitors progress and makes short reports of findings to individuals or groups; and 3) the responder, one who exhibits more of a laissez faire attitude toward teachers, initiates few incident interventions, and aims interventions primarily at students.

Hall et al. (1982) concluded that "the most desirable style is not known despite the mass of research addressing this issue. For each style there appears to be a benefit and a risk. There appears to be a predominance of characteristics which would suggest an identifiable style on the part of the principal, but a blend of characteristics from various styles may be more frequently observed" (p. 28). Further, they suggested that initiators who exhibited a more aggressive style were best left with more discretion and approached less often by central staff. Responders who acted primarily on centrally dictated policy functioned best when central staff worked closely with them. Finally, managers who concentrated on local internal policies-yet were self-starters, could adapt well when provided sufficient understandings so that they could proceed on their own.

Pavan (1991) studied facilitator styles using the Change Facilitator Style Questionnaire (CFSQ) developed by Hall and others. Profiles of principal behaviors were taken by teachers influenced by these principals. Teachers reported the effectiveness of principals in influencing their actions. Principals then responded in a manner that would theoretically assist teachers in selected kinds of problem solving tasks. These principals were found to have performed better as perceived by teachers and observers when they exhibited a given style appropriate to school settings and the associated compatibility of staff.

Summary

The quality principal is seen a operative in many situations and therefore is required to possess many different traits. Some of these traits seem to contradict each other. Research tells quality principals to be forceful and dynamic leaders but also to enable rather than direct activities. The quality principal can distinguish between the two. A quality principal must also be able to: (a) decide who will participate in innovative school projects, (b) control behavior and image, (c) exercise personal judgment with discretion. (d) manage events, (e) create proper discipline, (f) control the climate of the school, (g) consult effectively with others, (h) seek the advice of staff members on important issues, (i) listen to teachers' problems and ideas, (j) establish structures within which participation can be fostered, (k) disperse decision-making authority and encourage its use, (l) be flexible, and (m) fulfill expectations of teacher autonomy. Quality principals must be authoritative but humanistic.

The quality principal today must be a person who can wear many hats and is not afraid to take one off to put another on. He/she must be involved in every aspect of the school, appropriately involved in pertinent issues and delegating responsibilities to those closest to the decisions. If the principal is an instructional leader and becomes more skilled at organizing teachers to work toward specific goals, the school can become more effective. Therefore schools can reach the levels of learning that society expects.

The principal must work to improve human relations in his/her school and community. The principal must be an enabler and enable teachers to concentrate on teaching. Teachers must do the same and allow students to concentrate on learning. The quality principal must strive to help teachers and students solve problems; look out for their personal welfare such as doing them personal favors, stay after school to help with extra work, and provide necessary services (Duttweiler & Hord, 1987).

The quality principal supports a climate in which the staff has a high level of satisfaction with their work. He/she also encourages a strong sense of participation and control over important educational decisions and activities in the school. The quality principal accomplishes this by: (a) using a participatory style of leadership, (b) exhibiting an open, professional, and collegial style that fosters joint discussion, evaluation, and improvement, and (c) working with others in order to integrate the perspectives and incentives of those he or she would persuade (Duttweiler & Hord, 1987).

Trust and honesty are a important in dealing with people. A principal may need to be very direct at times. Therefore, he/she must have the ability to persuade or influence others through a number of possible means: gaining and sustaining attention and interest in group situations, using information or arguments, modeling the behaviors expected, or being direct in specifying what others will do. The quality principal is also sensitive to the ideas and opinions of others but also behaves to ensure an understanding of the feelings and verbalizations of others.

Effective communication is essential for any leader, and the school principal is no exception. This communication must be between groups and individuals. The principal must be able to communicate in a variety of ways. A principal does not have to be a great speaker to be successful but must be able to communicate to different groups. The quality principal must develop the ability to make oral presentations to large groups, small groups and individuals. This is vital for the success of students, teachers, and the school. In addition, he/she must be able to communicate to others clearly in writing.

Studies show the quality school has a principal who expects high standards of performance from teachers and students and models this behavior. The quality principal is one who earns the respect of his/her teachers, students, and community and can bring about change.

Conclusion

To paraphrase Walt Disney: You can build the most wonderful place in the world but it takes people to make it work. It is true that quality principals can have a great vision for a school and a definite plan to reach that vision but it takes staff, parents, and students, who are aware of and behind the vision, to make it work. The quality principal must be a person of diverse qualities with may attributes sometimes contradicting one another. Quality principals should have: the ability to perceive the needs, concerns, and personal problems of others; skill in resolving conflicts; tact in dealing with persons from differing backgrounds; ability to deal with people concerning emotional issues; and the ability of knowing what information to communicate and to whom (Hersey, 1987). This explains partly the ability to deal with so many people successfully. This person is assertive, yet patient. He/she communicates in a variety of forms to groups or individuals. The quality principal sees that things are done right and does the right things.

Sergiovanni (1991) issues a challenge to quality principals. A basic level of competence in leadership is needed to get extraordinary commitment and performance. Sustained commitment and performance require an approach to leadership that connects people to work for moral reasons. It is this reasoning that will bond people together for common purposes, values, and norms. Quality principals are able to obtain the extraordinary!

Thomas Peters said "quality involves living the message of the possibility of perfection and infinite improvement, living it day in and day out, decade by decade." The quality principal is one who is committed to quality. This person leads by a clear vision. He/she makes a difference. The qualities of leadership are many. Quality principals possess the necessary knowledge to be successful. They empower others to be successful. They treat others with mutual respect, fairness, and integrity. They bring out the best in others and honor diversity. They encourage innovation, remain open to new ideas, and shun complacency. The quality principal blends power and influence to create a vision for schools and work to make it reality.

References

Adams, W. F., & Baily, G. D. (1989). Principal leadership behaviors: Making a choice. NASSP Bulletin, 73, 86-91.

Bennis, W. (1989). Why leaders can't lead. San Francisco, CA: Jossey Bass

Bennis, W., & Nanus, B. (1985). Leaders. New York: Harper & Roe.

Berman, L. M. (1971). Supervision, staff development and leadership. Columbus: Charles E. Merrill Publishing Company.

Block, P. (1991). The empowered manager: Positive political skills at work. San Francisco, CA: Jossey-Bass Inc.

Blumberg, A. & Greenfield. (1986). The effective principal: Perspectives on school leadership (2nd). Boston: Allyn & Bacon.

Brennan, A., & Brennan, R. J. (1988). The principal, the ethics and special education decisions. NASSP Bulletin, 72 (512), 16-19.

Calabrese, R. (1988). Ethical leadership: A prerequisite for effective schools. NASSP Bulletin, 72 (512), 1-4.

Clauser, T. G. (1985). The principal as a change facilitator (Bulletin No. 1753). Baton Rouge: Louisiana State Department of Education. (ERIC Document Reproduction Service No ED 262471)

Cuban, L. (1988). The managerial imperative and the practice of leadership in schools. Albany: State University of New York Press.

Cunningham, W. G. (1991). Empowerment: Vitalizing personal energy In W. G. Cunningham & D. Gresso, Cultural leadership (pp. 208-213). Needham Heights, MA: Allyn & Bacon.

Cunningham, W. G., & Gresso, D. W. (1993). Cultural Leadership. Needham Heights, MA: Allyn & Bacon.

Curran, T. (1983, October). Characteristics of the effective school—a starting point for self-evaluation. NASSP Bulletin, 67 (465), 71-73.

Deming, W. E. (1989, July). Foundations for management of quality in the Western world. A paper presented at the meeting of the Institute of Management Sciences in Osaka, Japan.

Doggett, M. (1988). Ethical excellence for school based administration. NASSP Bulletin, 72 (512), 6-8.

Duttweiler, F. C., & Hord, S. (1987). Dimensions of effective leadership. Austin: BEDL.

English, F. W., & Hill, J. C. (1989). Restructuring: The principal and curriculum change. Reston, VA: The National Association of Secondary School Principals.

Edmonds, R. (1979). Some schools work and more can. Social Policies, 9 (2), 28-32.

Flannigan, J. L., & Richardson, M. D. (1992). A view from the office: The politics of the school principalship. A paper presented at the 46th Annual Summer Conference of National Council of Professors of Education Administration (NCPEA). Terre Haute: Indiana State University, 8-13.

Goodlad, J. I. (1984). A place called school: Prospect for the future. New York: McGraw-Hill.

Hall, G. E. (1988). Development of a framework and measure for assessing principal change facilitator style. (ERIC Document Reproduction Service No. ED 336401)

Hall G. E., Rutherford W. L., & Hord, S. M., & Huling L. L. (1984). Educational Leadership, 41 (5), 222-229.

Hall, G. E., Rutherford, W., & Griffin, T. (1982). Three change facilitator styles: Some indicators and proposed framework. (ERIC Document Reproduction Service No. ED 220961)

Harden, D. G. (1988). The principals ethical responsibility and parents right to know. NASSP Bulletin, 72, 12-14.

Hersey, P. W. (1987). How NASSP helps identify, develop superior principals. Reston, VA: NASSP.

Hoyle, J. R., English, F. W., & Steffy, B. E. (1990), Skills for successful school leaders (2nd ed.). Arlington, VA: American Association of School Administrators.

Kimbrough, R. B., & Burkett, C. W. (1990). The principalship: Concepts and practices. Englewood Cliffs: Prentice Hall.

King, D. (1988). Reasoned action leadership: A knowledge-based model for the preparation of school administrators. National Forum of Educational Administration and Supervision Journal, 5 (3), 25-35.

McCurdy, J. (1983). The role of the principal in effective schools: Problems and solutions. Reston, VA: American Association of School Administrators, 22.

Murray, T., & Roehr, E. (1983, May). An open letter to principals from teachers. Educational Digest, 36-37.

National Association of Elementary School Principals. (1986). Elementary and middle schools proficiencies for school principals: Kindergarten through eighth grade. Alexandria, VA. Author.

National Association of Elementary School Principals. (1991, December). Administrator diagnostic inventory. Paper presented at the meeting of Leadership in Educational Administration, Washington, D.C.

Oliva, P. F. (1984). Supervision for today's schools. New York: Longman.

Pavan, B. N. (1991, April). Principal change facilitator styles and the implementation of instructional support teams. Paper presented at the Annual Meeting of the American Educational Research Association, Chicago. (ERIC Document Reproduction Service No. ED 339138)

Sashkin, M. (1988). The visionary principal: School leadership for the next century. Education and Urban Society, 20 (3), 239-249.

Sashkin, M., & Huddle, G. (1986). Recruit top principals. The School Administrator, 45 (2).

Sergiovanni, T. J. (1991). The principalship: A reflective practice perspective (2nd ed.). Boston: Allyn and Bacon.

Seldin, C. A. (1988). Ethics, evaluation and the school principal. NASSP Bulletin, (72). 9-11.

Shoemaker, J., & Fraser, H. W. (1981). What principals can do: Some implications from studies of effective schooling. Phi Delta Kappan, 63 (3), 178-182.

Smith, W. F., & Andrews, R. L. (1989). Instructional leadership: How principals make a difference. Alexandria, VA: Association for Supervision & Curriculum Development.

Snyder, R. J., & Anderson, R. H. (1987). What principals can learn from corporate management. Principal, 66 (4), 22-26.

Snyder, S. (1986). Creating a positive school atmosphere—the principals responsibility. NASSP Bulletin, 70 (493), 89-91.

Silver, P. F. (1983). Educational administration: Theoretical perspectives on practice and research. New York: Harper & Row.

Stu-Runyan, Y., & Hart, S. J. (1992). Management manifesto. Executive Educator, 14 (1), 23-26.

Tanner, D., & Tanner, L. N. (1980). Curriculum development: Theory into practice. New York: MacMillian.

Tewel, K. J. (1989). Collaborative supervision—Theory into practice. NASSP Bulletin, 73 (516), 74-83.

Thomson, S.D. (1993). Principals for our changing schools: Knowledge and skill base. Fairfax, VA: National Policy Board for Educational Administration.

Weller, L. D. (1985). The principal: Catalyst for promoting effective schooling. Action in Teacher Education, 7 (3), 7-12.

Van Berkum, D. W. (1994). The personal skill development of the aspiring principal integrated into principal preparation. The Journal of School Leadership, 4 (1), 52-68.

Van Berkum, D. W. (1995). The classroom with the empowered student. In M. D. Richardson, K. E. Lane, & J. L. Flannigan (Eds.), School Empowerment (pp. 277-290). Lancaster, PA: Technomics.

Chapter 10

CASE STUDIES OF TWO SCHOOLS: A LOOK AT THE STAGES OF PROGRESS TOWARD TOTAL QUALITY MANAGEMENT

Garth Petrie & Gordon Friberg
Georgia Southern University and University of Montana

The two schools discussed here have in no way climbed to the top rung in their efforts to become a Total Quality Management (TQM) school. Both schools represent excellent efforts and strong progress in their attempts to make their teaching—learning environments and indeed their decision making structures the best possible for their students. It is always important to keep in mind that TQM, collaborative decision making, and teacher empowerment are "journeys rather than destinations per se." Deming, himself, suggests it takes a decade or more to get to the ultimate position in TQM and David Scott in his doctoral study of teacher empowerment speaks of the "journey of empowerment."

The two schools described here are; a rural elementary-middle school located in a state with strongly mandated reform from the state legislature and an urban high school from a state where little encouragement for reform is noticeable. Both schools have been working for three or more years toward restructuring under site based management and TQM programs. The concept of a "journey" is very real for both schools. It is worthy of note that while both have had their share of set backs, both are ever progressing toward the goal of improving student achievement. The elementary school houses approximately four hundred (400) students in grades K-8, while the high school deals with approximately fourteen hundred (1400) students in grades 9-12.

Elementary/Middle School

This school is located in a rural area of the mid-south and has approximately four hundred (400) students in grades K-8. Forty-nine percent (49%) of the student body come from low socioeconomic status, based on the number of free and reduced lunches provided. Nine percent (9%) of the students are black, two percent (2%) are Asiatic or Native American and the remaining (89%) are Caucasians. The school building is located in a town of less than one thousand (1,000) inhabitants. The majority of the students come from the surrounding farming community. Most students are bussed to school and the community itself could be considered rather closely knit, with most families having three and four generations rooted in the community.

Approximately twenty-five (25) certified staff, a single administrator, a full time secretary/bookkeeper and seven (7) teacher aides are responsible for the basic instructional program and the major restructuring efforts. The school staff volunteered to be a trial school for the state's mandated reform program in 1990, and a new principal was hired to serve as a leader for the effort. The staff, for the first time, was directly involved in the selection of the building administrator. For the first time in the history of the seven building school system, a woman was selected as a building administrator.

It is worthy of note, that there was considerable debate between school boards and central office personnel, the state department of education and local school councils about the interpretation of several of the reform laws which hampered many schools in their efforts to actually capitalize upon the opportunities to change their schools for the better. However, the local superintendent, with the wisdom of experience and a concerned dedication for the students in his charge, was able to guide both the board and the central office staff through the treacherous waters of major change in a way that afforded the local school staff and administration the freedom and security to begin the journey toward the ideal TQM school.

Deming: "Adopt the new philosophy." As applied to schools: "School leaders must adopt and fully support the new philosophy of continuous improvement through greater empowerment of teams." As applied to business: ". . . leaders must adopt and fully support the new philosophy of continuous improvement through the empowerment of front-line workers" (Bonstingl, 1992). Unlike many schools around them, this school chose to begin the process of change with deep saturation of all staff in the concepts and ideas of basic change and the vagaries of the change process itself. This effort involved the contracting of a long range consultant for consistency and continuity, as well as a wide variety of other shorter term individuals to direct: a diversity of workshops, lock-ins and excursions to insure that each and every staff member, council member and other interested parties were well versed and thoroughly prepared to participate in the entire process. The first six months were devoted to the formation of a massive personnel development program with a continued effort spanning a four year period. One of the most enduring effects of the staff development program was the nomination of several faculty members to a variety of state, district, and national committee assignments. Surprisingly, or perhaps not so surprisingly, those staff members who had never been involved in such things became highly motivated, actively participative, and strongly contributing members of the restructuring efforts in the school, within the other schools of the district, and in the state and regional structures established to encourage and assist the reform efforts. The motivation gained from these liaisons was invaluable.

Deming: "Institute programs of training." As applied to schools: "School leaders must institute programs of training for new employees unfamiliar with the specific culture and expectations of the school. Effective training programs show new teachers how to set goals, how to teach effectively, and how to asses the quality of their work with students. Teachers must also institute programs in which students learn how to set learning goals, how to be more effective in their school work and how to assess the quality of their own work" (Bonstingl, 1992).

To say that extra time was needed and expended by the staff would be an understatement, but to say that the staff needed to be coerced to expend the extra time would be a falsehood of huge proportions. The staff eagerly committed to the project primarily out of a sense of dedication to the children in their school and partially because they wanted to be the first and best school in the county. (To say that sense of pride did not have its effect on the other schools in the system would be missing an important point. However, each of the other schools, some of which accepted the challenge and others that did not, was left to deal with individual school issues and concerns.)

The second step involved basic organizational changes in the operation of the decision making process of the school. The two basic changes that occurred were structured under state mandates handed down by the legislature. However, the way the process was developed was purely through the ingenious ideas of the staff and administration. The two changes involved the selection of a school council and the restructuring of committees within the school. The processes used were, to some extent, mandated by the state, but the unique flavors that added to the success of these changes were the creative outcomes of group commitment and involvement in the total process. Two of the ideas were: concern with how to select parents who would be contributing and concerned for all students' welfare in this school, and how to get maximum commitment/ involvement from all staff members within the school.

Deming: "Institute leadership." As applied to education: "School leadership consists of working with teachers, parents, students, and members of the community as coach and mentor so that the organizational context in which all students' growth and improvement is valued and encouraged can be maximized by teachers and students, parents, and community members who support the common effort. Leading is helping, not threatening or punishing." As applied to business: "Leading consists of working with others as coach and mentor so that the organizational context in which improvement is valued and encouraged can be maximized by front-line workers" (Bonstingl, 1992).

The solutions themselves were quite simple, once the basic concerns were identified. Identification of solutions was slow forthcoming as new structures, new expectations and new untried decision-making processes were being used. The basic concern identified was that all participants had to believe that processes used and decisions reached were fair and appeared fair to everyone. This proved to be an astute recognition; all communities have their factions and fairness is an essential ingredient, if one eventually hopes to gain the support of the entire community and staff. The solution to the selection process was to have all candidates for any position on the council put into writing a statement of why they desired to serve, what they hoped to accomplish, and that they would accept the position if elected. The solution to the committee assignment process was to have each staff member identify and rank the two or three committees on which they would most like to serve. The council with administrative recommendations then made assignments from those choices.

The solutions worked well, perhaps partially because so many were actively involved in identifying and adopting the solution, and because all believed that they had been treated fairly. It should be noted that after six (6) elections of parent representatives to the council, not a single poor choice has been made and that all staff members continue to be satisfied with their committee assignments in the system.

Deming: "Drive out fear." As applied to education: "Fear is counterproductive in school as it is in the workplace. Fear is counterproductive, especially in the long term. Fear is destructive of the school culture and everything good that is intended to take place within it. Fear breeds distrust, cynicism, divisiveness, apathy, and disaffection, all of which lead to declines in productivity. Institutional changes must reflect shared power, shared responsibilities, and shared rewards" (Bonstingl, 1992).

The third step in the process was twofold; to continue and strengthen the staff development efforts of both the council and the school staff in their respective responsibilities. A major decision for staff development lay in deciding to remain either strictly within the state mandate of the moment or expand beyond the mandates and simultaneously develop a variety of programs that would involve every student and teacher in the school. In spite of the consultant's recommendations to the contrary, staff members unanimously agreed to work for all students simultaneously. A portion of the state's mandates at the time required the formation of a non-graded primary program in each school, housing grades K-3. Rather than have personnel who were already motivated and committed delay their participation in the TQM process, the faculty undertook development of a team teaching program involving teachers at all grade levels. Multi-grade level teams of students in the fourth and fifth grades were formed, and block scheduling with an integrated curriculum in the middle school was developed. In this manner each staff member was actively included in the restructuring effort. The School Council made a decision to begin an intensive development program for themselves that would allow members to become knowledgeable and skilled in team-building and decision making.

Deming: "Break down barriers between staff areas." As applied to schools: "Teacher and student productivity is enhanced when departments combine talents to create more integrated opportunities for learning and discovery. Create cross-departmental and multi-level quality teams to break down role and status barriers to productivity. Productivity is enhanced when departments view themselves as partners in progress and work to maximize their potentials" (Bonstingl, 1992).

While the staff development was taking place, which for the first time was designed by the staff and council members in cooperative/ collaborative settings, (a definite change from the old method where the supervisor makes one plan for all staff approach), the council was directly involved in identifying and employing consultants and selecting other identified means of training. The council was simultaneously undergoing an in-depth development of its own. The council was developing collaborative/team cohesiveness and establishing operational procedures/

by-laws by which they could successfully lead the school. The inservice training was based on the use of an outside consultant who served as much as a moderator as anything else. The initial activities consisted mainly of trust building exercises, team-building exercises, and the development of a mission statement for the council. Later sessions were concerned with the development of by-laws and procedures for dealing with council business.

Deming: "Institute a vigorous program of education and retraining." As applied to schools: "All of the school's people benefit from encouragement to enrich their education by exploring ideas and interests beyond the boundaries of their professional and personal worlds. Company management and the entire workforce require continuous learning programs if the company is to be on the leading edge and maximize customer satisfaction. Administrators, teachers, and students require continuous learning programs if the school is to be on the leading edge and maximize customer satisfaction" (Bonstingl, 1992).

The Mission Statement developed and accepted by the council proved to be invaluable to all parties in the school. It stated that the school existed for the benefit and service of all children and that all decisions made in the school would consider children and their welfare first. It turned out that the wording expressed the basic philosophy of the principal who had recently been hired, but rather than create problems this fact apparently made it easier to institutionalize as the working attitude for the whole school.

Deming: "Create constancy of purpose for improvement of product and service." As applied to schools: "Schools must focus on helping students to maximize their own potentials through continuous improvement of teachers' and students' work together. Maximization of test scores and assessment symbols is less important than the progress inherent in the continuous learning process of each student " (Bonstingl, 1992).

The decision making system became a multiple-approach method based upon issues of time constraints, types of decisions being made, and severity of issues. It turned out that all policy matters were made on a consensus basis when time played a lesser role. Decisions having less flexibility in time and having some controversy, such as selection of personnel, were decisions voted upon by the council as a whole. Decisions that were urgent and demanded immediate action were arbitrarily made by the administrator/principal. The council chair/principal made every attempt to call the type of decision needed prior to the introduction of an issue. All arbitrary decisions were explained to the council so that they were continually informed. These processes of decision making proved to be workable in providing efficient and effective management of the school.

A second decision was made for the council to work through the committee structure with as many decisions as possible. That process also proved effective. The committees, in reality, became the decision makers for the school: the council directed assignments, committees, and accepted or redirected decisions made by the committees. The results were often slow but staff morale, motivation and pride in accomplishments were enhanced through this process. Too, the policies of the school became staff policies, written, tested, and presented for approval to the council so they were easily incorporated into the culture of the school.

Deming: "End the practice of doing business on price tag alone." As applied to schools: "Build relationships of trust and collaboration within the school, and between school and the community. Everyone's roles as supplier and customer must be recognized and honored. Work together whenever possible to maximize the potentials of students, teachers, administrators, and the community " (Bonstingl, 1992).

With the emphasis placed on the student as the basis for all decision making, several changes began to take place within the instructional program of the school. Testing became a daily event with emphasis placed upon formative rather than summative purposes. Peer tutoring and cooperative learning began to replace the old idea of competitiveness between students. Team learning began to change the attitudes of the students toward more cooperation rather than competition within the learning environment. However, that cooperative spirit did not carry over to the inter-school relationships of athletics, club competitions and academic tournaments. In fact, the school became fiercely competitive at both the county and state level.

Deming: "Cease dependence on mass inspection." As applied to education: " Reliance on tests as a major means of assessment of student production is inherently wasteful and often neither reliable nor authentic. It is too late at the end of the unit to assess students' progress if the goal is to maximize their productivity. Tests and other indicators of student learning should be given as diagnostic and prescriptive instruments throughout the learning process. Learning is best shown by students' performance, applying information and skills to real-life challenges. Students must be taught how to assess their own work and progress if they are to take ownership of their own educational processes " (Bonstingl, 1992).

As success began to come their way, the spirit of cooperation within the school and community started to meld. Parents began seeing the results of what had been, up to that point, strange happenings with the pay-off carrying into home life of the students. Attendance began to improve with many parents commenting that even when ill, their children refused to stay home. Children became more and more enamored with "their school." The students became fierce defenders of their school, their teachers and what was happening, whenever questions or issues arose.

Deming: "Eliminate numerical quotas." As applied to education: "Assignments and tests that focus attention on numerical or letter symbols of learning and production often do not fully reflect the quality of student progress and performance. When the grade becomes the bottom-line product, short-term gains replace student investment in long-term learning, and this may prove counter-productive in the long run." As applied to business: "Quotas are numerical symbols that do not reflect the quality of the productive process, the integrity and health of the system, or long-term indicators of successes and failures. In fact, "hitting the numbers' as a short-term bottom-line solution to worker or company challenges is often useless or counterproductive in the long run" (Bonstingl, 1992).

Benefits of the new approach to decision making and processing at the school are numerous. Not only did the staff begin viewing the entire school as important, a change from the previous view of "only my class or my grade needs to be considered," the children themselves began forming new attitudes and taking pride in their school. Staff members began seeking ways of contributing to the effort, as exemplified by the cafeteria manager who found ways to do special things for students and faculty. The cafeteria manager became one of the most loved members of the entire staff. Student discipline improved for practically all faculty and staff. Community support for school programs and activities increased. Most importantly, student achievement increased dramatically, with fourth grade scores jumping fifteen (15) points and eighth grade scores consistently improving four to five points; enough improvement to net the school recognition for the reward portion of the state's reform act.

Deming: "Eliminate slogans, exhortations, and targets for the workforce." As applied to education: "Teachers, students, administrators, families, and community members may collectively arrive at slogans and exhortations to improve their work together, as long as power, responsibility, and rewards are equitably distributed. When educational goals are not met, fix the system instead of fixing blame on individuals." As applied to business: "Workers who are in charge of their own production will create slogans, exhortations, and targets that are more meaningful than those imposed from above, as long as power, responsibility, and rewards are equitably distributed" (Bonstingl, 1992).

When putting down the events in a major restructuring effort, it all appears so easy to accomplish, when in fact each of the steps detailed above involve much agonizing, loss of extra time, intense soul searching and more than just a few tears and angry confrontations among the staff and sometimes between the staff and assorted members of the community. For example, middle school staff had come to expect that they would have planning time when they desired it. As the school shifted to all members of the staff receiving equal amounts of planning time (which forced the middle school to make several adjustments), unhappiness arose. When the Council decided that not every Tom, Dick, and Harry could have keys to the school to come and go as they pleased, there were some irate citizens in the community, though most were not parents. (The school had moved into a new building by the end of the first year of operation as a restructured school.) The Council and staff were unanimous in the decisions to limit and control the abuse of "their new school."

Deming: "Improve constantly and forever the system of production and service." As applied to schools: "School administrators must create and maintain the context in which teachers are empowered to make continuous progress in the quality of their learning and other aspects of personal development, while they learn valuable lessons from (temporary) failures" (Bonstingl, 1992).

Staff, too, were beginning to wear thin in patience by the end of the first year with two staff members showing up as either unwilling, unable, or both to make the necessary changes to accommodate a TQM school. One of these was a male teacher who could not control students and the other was a female who desired influence and control but who was unwilling to put forth the effort to hold such a role. In the case of the former, early retirement was taken. In the case of the latter, complications with central office personnel arose which eventually affected and retarded the progress of the entire school; a strong indication of the complex nature of community politics and interrelationships over which the school, as an institution, has little or no control albeit it does exert some influence within the community setting.

Deming: "Take action to accomplish the transformation." As applied to school: "School personnel at all levels (including students) must put this new philosophy into action so it becomes embedded into the deep structure and culture of the school. Teachers and students alone cannot put the plan into effect. Constant top-level dedication to full implementation must be supported by a critical mass of school and community people to implement the plan and make it stick" (Bonstingl, 1992).

Two issues will be used to illustrate the lack of control; first is the lack of control over staffing the school. While local schools are gaining some influence over hiring, they, unlike business and industry, have little to say about the removal, assignment and/or reassignment of existing staff. They are expected to live with and exert influence; changing an individual who may be too lazy, too incapacitated, or too contrary to make needed changes for the benefit of children, is difficult. The same is not true of business or industry where dismissals or reassignments are relatively routine or commonplace. This very limitation presents another set of issues or hurdles for educational institutions. Though not impossible to overcome, new strategies and techniques will have to be developed, if entire staffs are expected to develop TQM systems in effective and efficient ways.

The council by this time had grown into a true team that had built a strong level of trust between its six council members. The trust level was built to such an extent that the rule of annual elections, a decision mandated by the state, became a burden. The loss of continuity was perceived as very damaging. Concern over this loss of continuity caused the council to devise a plan to limit such losses. Members on the council were allowed to serve legally for more than one year if reelected. The strategy for dealing with the problem was accomplished by having one teacher and one parent go off the council each year by choice, thus allowing two new members to join the council annually. It became necessary for all members of the council to help educate the community and the faculty of the necessity for such continuity. Needless to say, the strategy worked well and the gains with continuity in place began to have almost immediate payoffs. For one, the administrator was not saddled with a need to spend inordinate amounts of time training a totally new council each year. Second, there was not a need to "reinvent the wheel" of policies and by-laws that was so time consuming. Many schools operating under the same mandate failed to anticipate the enormity of this problem. Even today, many schools are spending a major portion of their time developing council member knowledge, skills, and cohesiveness so that the business of the school can be conducted. (In the authors' opinions the lack of continuity is a fatal flaw.)

The same trust level that existed among the council permeated the relationships between the council and the staff, as well. This fact was due to three major factors: the desire and willingness of the staff to become involved in the process and their willingness to cooperate almost completely in all aspects of the school; the development and appointment of several staff members into the leadership roles; the expenditure of energy, compassion; and the leadership role and ability of the principal of the school. The phenomena of these three factors cannot be over stated because, as the leadership function goes, so goes the effectiveness of the team's achievement. Nowhere is this more important, than in the educational setting where, unlike industry and business, leadership is, many times of short duration. This situation is particularly acute when compared to Japanese settings where the whole culture is bounded by the ideology of loyalty to the employees by the management and of loyalty to the company by the employees. The United State's educational system is almost the antithesis of the Japanese TQM model because to rise and to have credibility in an existing organization, it is mandated that one be mobile. Unless we become aware of the need for continuity and longevity, the opportunity to develop TQM may never become viable. TQM, as an entity that exists in other cultures and fields in the United States, may not develop in education. In point of fact, the principal in this school, for a variety of reasons discussed later in the chapter, finally left her position and the resultant leadership shift brought the program to its knees.

The developing leadership realized they could not accomplish the ultimate change needed to reach a fully functioning educational program unless they were able to involve the entire community. To undertake such an arduous task they identified two factors they believed were hindrances and concerns of the community. The first was that the community did not feel they were truly a part of the schooling program. Second, there was a real lack of communication between the school and the community. To deal with these issues, a program was designed to involve as many community members as possible. A few of the more successful activities included a reemphasized volunteer program: a parent involvement program, and a shadow-your- child program in which numerous parents became more highly aware of the school's concern for the education of their children. The second activity involved the establishment of Mondays as the day when the school would communicate with all parents. (A parent could be assured that if they did not hear from the school on that day, their child had miscued.) Key communicators were also developed as buffers against the often exaggerated rumors that are always amply evident in all communities and perhaps even more in small, rural ones.

The successes of the two approaches to increase community involvement were somewhat mixed. The programs were successful enough in that parents became increasingly involved in the education of their children. The Key Communicator Program succeeded in not only helping the school avoid and/or deal with some seriously damaging "tall tales" circulating in the community, but also helped the council avoid some divisive decisions.

Returning to a comment made earlier in this study concerning the value of leadership continuity, it bears repeating that a key component of success in many educational endeavors, especially in Site Based Decision Making (SBDM) and TQM, is the continuity of the leadership. It is sad to say that the district office became divided over the leadership of the school and about the very success of the endeavor and began to sabotage the principal, due primarily to an assistant superintendent's actions. These actions lead to the principal of the school accepting another position, in another district. The "fall-out" of that action created an unbelievable dissolution of leadership, which in the end literally sabotaged the progress made up to that point in the school. The new principal was interim for two or three months, and the selection of a new principal proved to be disastrous to further TQM growth, due to a widely differing philosophy and educational emphasis on program and structural paradigms.

While the school is regrouping and attempting to regain its desire to do good work, much of the spirit of the school has dissipated. Jealousies that had existed, "Yes Johnny even in the best of times jealousy exists," came to the forefront and the "in-group and out-group" differences contained in the former program drove some rather serious wedges between formerly cooperative staff and parents. In essence, if the school is to pick up and move forward, leadership will need to play a much more active role; including the leadership of the superintendent, the principal, the council, and faculty. Perhaps this proves that in a search for excellence, whether it be TQM, SBDM or some other plan, there must be strong and consistent leadership.

High School

This high school is located in a middle sized urban area in the Northwestern United States and has approximately fourteen hundred (1400) students in grades 9-12. Ninety-eight percent (98%) are Caucasian with the remainder made up of Eastern Asian and Native American students. Twenty-five percent (25%) of the students, based on system statistics come from lower socioeconomic homes. The school building is located in a suburban setting with two other similar sized high schools and one K-12 school completing the high school district. Nearly twenty-five percent (25%) of the student body of this school come from the immediate vicinity of the school itself with the other seventy-five percent (75%) being bussed or driving from a small adjoining rural area.

Approximately ninety-five (95) faculty, three administrators and several secretaries and clerks comprise the basic instructional unit for the school. Only the faculty and building administrators are currently involved with the restructuring efforts. In this state where practically no mandates for restructuring exist, the faculty led the way by expressing dissatisfaction with the status quo. More than three years ago they established a core group to study and recommend ways of restructuring the school. The initial restructuring activity was the establishment of a faculty study group whose first recommendation dealt with scheduling. The faculty agreed to go to an eight (8) period schedule on a rotational basis (four periods every other day). Once the plan was agreed upon by the faculty, they approached the central administration to gain the required approval. Much of the sales pitch to convince the board to allow the experiment was that the move would save the board approximately $150,000 in faculty salaries, a rather unusual commitment for faculty members who are unionized. Needless to say, the acceptance was easily acquired after that. (As an aside, the union accepted the proposal from the faculty because of their unanimous stand. To date, no repercussions have arisen.)

It should be noted that during this time-period the high school district was merged with the local elementary district forming a new K-12 district approximately four times the size of the former 9-12 district. This unification caused the normal series of distractions and realignment problems with the one caveat that the disparity between the elementary and high school teacher salary schedules was as much as $5,000.00. Attempts to resolve the issues brought on a threatened teacher strike, which could have delayed the opening of the school year, and did cause some deep rifts within the district itself.

A new superintendent was employed for the newly formed school district. While permission was given for the restructuring efforts at the high school, little formal support or encouragement was given to these efforts. Faculty and school administrators were left to their own devices in identifying, preparing and implementing any changes and improvements. In defense of the central administration, the overwhelming task of merging two systems, restructuring the two seven (7) member boards, and settling wage disputes, not to mention the many other issues, were enough for any organization to deal with at any one time. The void of support was certainly understandable. The point to be made, however is that once the faculty reached a high level of readiness for change, it is better to move forward than to wait for all things to be correctly aligned. It seems apparent to the authors that had a hiatus of one semester or a year passed without movement, the impetus for change could definitely have been impaired or lost, and, while some type change would have developed in other ways, the current change is taking place in a constructive and positive way.

Deming: "Adopt the new philosophy." As applied to schools: "School leaders must adopt and fully support the new philosophy of continuous improvement through greater empowerment of teams." As applied to business: "Company leaders must adopt and fully support the new philosophy of continuous improvement through the empowerment of front-line workers" (Bonstingl, 1992).

The high school attempted to deal with their commitment to improving the situation for their students by appointing a committee of all departmental chairs and the local administration to study and recommend a structure that would aid them in their quest for excellence. Fifteen months passed with little or no progress being made. A growing sense of frustration permeated the entire school. During that time, central administration did provide building administrators with some inservice training on the concept of SBDM. The faculty did some work on their philosophy for the school. Little other progress was reported.

Deming: "Institute programs of training." As applied to schools: "School leaders must institute programs of training for new employees unfamiliar with the specific culture and expectations of the school. Effective training programs show new teachers how to set goals, how to teach effectively, and how to asses the quality of their work with students. Teachers must also institute programs in which students learn how to set learning goals, how to be more effective in their school work and how to assess the quality of their own work" (Bonstingl, 1992).

Though the appointed directory group of twenty (20) members did much soul searching and agonizing over many issues the school faced, the sheer time demands began to wear them down. While the committee was dedicated, motivated, and eager to accomplish the ideal of a better system, they (the committee) alone could not find enough hours in the day to "do it all." It was at this point that the school principal and the chairman of the study committee decided to find an outside consultant to guide the committee through a personnel development program designed for change. At the same time, the principal was asked by the central administration to provide a mission statement with specific goals and objectives. These two decisions reignited the desire for more involvement and more effort being expended in the development of an improved school.

Deming: "Institute a vigorous program of education and retraining." As applied to schools: "All of the school's people benefit from encouragement to enrich their education by exploring ideas and interests beyond the boundaries of their professional and personal worlds. Company management and the entire workforce require continuous learning programs if the company is to be on the leading edge and maximize customer satisfaction. Administrators, teachers, and students require continuous learning programs if the school is to be on the leading edge and maximize customer satisfaction" (Bonstingl, 1992).

First a strategy for identifying and establishing a mission and goals statement for the school was developed. While that effort was under way, the personnel development phase of the program was started by the faculty and administration joining together for in-depth study and decision making strategy sessions. It was decided at those meetings that to be truly restructured the old rules needed to be disearoled and all become involved in finding solutions for the needed improvements. This process is actually on-going with many rules being questioned and changed, but students still have very little input.

Deming: "Create constancy of purpose for improvement of product and service." As applied to schools: "Schools must focus on helping students to maximize their own potentials through continuous improvement of teachers' and students' work together. Maximization of test scores and assessment symbols is less important than the progress inherent in the continuous learning process of each student" (Bonstingl, 1992).

The basic decisions included the establishment of a thirteen (13) member council. The council's consisted of ten (10) teachers; one administrator, either the principal or her designee; one parent elected by other parents; and one classified staff member selected by classified constituents. Student representation was organized by establishing a cadre of students serving as an advisory, non-voting unit. The second basic decision was to involve all faculty and administration in a comprehensive committee structure that would do the yeomen's share of the work. This organization provided that the majority of the decision making be done at the "grass roots level." In reality the total staff did become deeply involved in committees and areas of their own choosing; the resultant outcomes were both important and gratifying. The new council was allowed the freedom to concentrate on leadership tasks that would guide the entire effort. The third decision directed the establishment of a complete set of by-laws, the hope to prevent many of the frustrations new organizations have in initial stages of their development.

Deming: "Institute leadership." As applied to education: "School leadership consists of working with teachers, parents, students, and members of the community as coach and mentor so that the organizational context in which all students' growth and improvement is valued and encouraged can be maximized by teachers and students, parents, and community members who support the common effort. Leading is helping, not threatening or punishing." As applied to business: "Leading consists of working with others as coach and mentor so that the organizational context in which improvement is valued and encouraged can be maximized by front-line workers" (Bonstingl, 1992).

A timeline was established for the implementation of all goals that was, to say the least, ambitious and a little scary. The timetable was adhered to despite a human tragedy: the untimely death of the chairman who had labored so hard and diligently to bring about the change. Regardless, elections were held, the committee assignments made, and a transition team worked to establish a working committee structure for the school and its divergent communities/populations.

The insecurities of the faculty played a considerable role in the make-up of the council with its ten member faculty majority. While it was the faculty who had identified the need, engineered the permission for restructuring, and brought about the series of events causing the change to be implemented, the faculty were less courageous in allowing all stake holders equal participation in the new structure. While demanding its own empowerment, the faculty was brought face to face with the realization that other groups were also stakeholders in the "preparation of students for the uncertain world of the twenty-first century;" a realization harder to accept. A final decision was formulated whereby a compromise was formed and a token set of parents and classified staff allowed to help with decisions. This was an agonizing decision made by the faculty with students allowed only non-voting status.

Deming: "Drive out fear." As applied to education: "Fear is counterproductive in school as it is in the workplace. Fear is counterproductive, especially in the long term. Fear is destructive of the school culture and everything good that is intended to take place within it. Fear breeds distrust, cynicism, divisiveness, apathy, and disaffection, all of which lead to declines in productivity. Institutional changes must reflect shared power, shared responsibilities, and shared rewards" (Bonstingl, 1992).

The process of establishing the role of the school building administrator was an even more agonizing one. In the beginning, the faculty believed the administrator should only give them enough guidance to keep them from violating current board policy, state laws, and regulations. However, after much deliberation, the faculty decided that the building administrator could have the added input of equal voting rights and the task of controlling the agenda as a shared responsibility with the council chair. It was also decided that at no time would the administrator become the chair of the council. The committee chair position was specifically identified and reserved for one of the faculty members on the council. While no team building exercises have been initiated thus far, it is evident that such plans will need to be made if real advancement is to be garnered.

In spite of the deep concerns evident in the plan for restructuring, some basic issues have been identified and addressed. The concept of fairness was identified as a major issue in selection of council members. Methods that would be considered fair by each constituency were adopted as processes for selection. A second key ingredient for the success of restructuring was also identified; that of communicating and breaking down the old departmental barriers and at the same time vastly improving the communication both within the school and between the school and the community. The technique for addressing these two issues was quite creative. The plan was designed to accomplish both at once. The ten faculty members were selected "at large" and their constituents assigned at random. Faculty representatives were required to come together in newly formed groups and communicate and plan for many of the functions of the school. This plan is achieving a measure of success even as this is being written.

Deming: "Break down barriers between staff areas." As applied to schools: "Teacher and student productivity is enhanced when departments combine talents to create more integrated opportunities for learning and discovery. Create cross-departmental and multi-level quality teams to break down role and status barriers to productivity. Productivity is enhanced when departments view themselves as partners in progress and work to maximize their potentials" (Bonstingl, 1992).

This faculty, much like the aforementioned elementary faculty, also chose to make massive and far reaching changes impacting all faculty and students of the school. The restructuring movement involved everyone. It capitalized on the interest, motivation, and enthusiasm of the majority of a large and diverse faculty. The primary goal was the integration of various disciplines in broad curricular projects that crossed traditional discipline lines. It appears that enough faculty members see this as a major break through, that major emphasis will be placed on these efforts very soon. Certainly, the new emphasis on staff involvement in professional development will bring a new approach to the inservice efforts of the entire school and perhaps the entire school system. It is certain that the faculty of this school has developed a sense of pride and ownership through their restructuring efforts. The formation of a cooperative spirit embracing and enveloping innovation and experimentation with restructuring is most refreshing.

The continued work with the consultant on a long range basis holds promise in that the credibility of a consultant with no stake in the outcome appears much more palatable than similar efforts from those with inside or vested interests. When developing leadership and team skills, the use of a consultant appears to work best.

The role of the high school principal, though basically different from the elementary school principalship, served a real purpose in the early stages of this restructuring effort. The high school principal, approaching retirement, was more laissez faire, more accommodating, and more accepting of faculty demands for power. Under different circumstances, the relinquishing of power might have created a different scenario. Differences between the elementary faculty and the secondary faculty might have prevented a strong, driving leader from enjoying the same success as experienced in the high school setting. In fact, little is known about the success of people with differing leadership styles in elementary versus high school restructuring and TQM. The administrative team concept in the high school brought some unique factors to the change process. It becomes crucial that the team be able to refine its own goals and speak with a singular voice. Any dissension may be magnified in large faculties and schisms can easily spring up. It is not enough to appear unified. The administrative team must be unified. This is no place for power plays and dissension.

Benefits of the new restructuring efforts in the high school are numerous. Improvements in faculty morale are perhaps the greatest gain. The faculty members have begun seeing themselves as innovators; leaders in efforts to improve secondary education. The faculty have found themselves as "out-front" educators. The pride, they see themselves well ahead of the other schools in the system, though slow to reach full bloom, has begun mobilizing more and more staff. A second benefit is the empowerment of individual staff members. Both situational leaders, such as department chairs and regular faculty, have begun to "stretch their wings" through empowerment. Traditional power investments that were once associated with stronger departments are beginning to shift to the total faculty.

Deming: "Take action to accomplish the transformation." As applied to school: "School personnel at all levels (including students) must put this new philosophy into action so it becomes embedded into the deep structure and culture of the school. Teachers and students alone cannot put the plan into effect. Constant top-level dedication to full implementation must be supported by a critical mass of school and community people to implement the plan and make it stick" (Bonstingl, 1992).

It is easy to see that growth towards a solid TQM program is taking place in this three plus (3+) year experience with change. It remains to be seen how much growth is forthcoming. The reader is reminded that Deming himself cautions that full implementation of the TQM ideas takes a decade or more to accomplish.

Chapter 11

ACHIEVING QUALITY SCHOOLS THROUGH TECHNOLOGY CHANGE

S. John Gooden and Randall L. Carlson
University of North Carolina–Charlotte and Georgia Southern University

As Deming's Fourteen Points provide the basis for change in American industry—a change that had occurred in Japanese industry decades earlier—many educators look to Deming's philosophy as a basis to provide quality in American (National Leadership Network Studies Group, 1993). The American educational system has been hit with an unrelenting barrage of criticism from all corners—some well deserved, some undeserved. But regardless, there is a lack of confidence in the American educational system that began in the early 1980s and continues even now. We have the opportunity to change perceptions and to impart increased quality into our educational system. This opportunity comes about because our system is facing massive change whether we want it or not. The change is the new technology that surrounds, even inundates us. If we choose to manage the coming change with a look towards improving system quality, then we will provide the products of this system, our children, with better tools which will afford them opportunity for success in life. Deming's 14 points can be applied to the current opportunities that changing technology provides. Highlighted are eight areas in which Deming's philosophical perspective can impact: technology leadership, technology planning, technology integration in the curriculum, student accountability and assessment, staff development, fear of technology, and financing technology.

Technology Leadership
   Deming's Point 7: Institute Leadership. School leaders must

become technology leaders. They must articulate and model the technological mission, vision, values, and beliefs of their school and district. This role includes much more than locating funding for hardware or software or planning technology staff development activities. The technology leader must drive the technology plan by providing opportunities for teachers and students to achieve the plan's goals and objectives. The leader should demonstrate an excitement and interest in technology while modeling the behavior expected from teachers and students.

The leader must realize that her/his role in technology growth is different from the leadership provided by the technology team. Although the technology leader is ultimately responsible for technology development and implementation, the technology team is compose of formal and informal members of the school community. At the heart of the formal team is the technology committee which is composed of the technology leader, technology specialist, media specialist, and other representatives of the various school constituencies. Formal team members usually have decision making authority for planning and financing technology. The informal team, on the other hand, can be internal and external members of the community — administrators, teachers, parents, and students - who are knowledgeable and sought out for technology support. Informal team members influence the system's ability to change through acceptance and integration of new ideas and policies into the system.

Technology Planning

Deming's Point 1. Create constancy of purpose for improvement of product and service. Quality problems face us both in the short and long terms. Short term problems can bleed off most of our energy and resources leaving little as a resultant. The school system that follows every new technological fad trying to raise test scores faces almost sure failure due to lack of planning and dedication. When first learning to fly, flight instructors impress upon students the need to keep focused on the horizon. Doing that allows the leader to see changes in the big picture and keeps her/him from overcontrolling by focusing in too close. In the same manner, we have to keep from focusing on short term scores— student achievement, students/computer ratio, classrooms with a computer—and other helpful statistics that are frequently over interpreted and overmanaged.

What can we do, then, to apply this point? First, we must systematically plan for technology growth. The plan must include:

- training for teachers and administrators in the use of technology
- shaping of attitudes for all stakeholders
- time sequencing of equipment, services, and training
- planning for equipment replacement as technical capabilities improve
- teaching and learning strategies for each implementation phase.

Next, we must insure that we pay attention to current research in technology use and education. Failure to do this will almost surely provide us technology that is outdated prior to implementation with no plan to follow-on with updates. Certainly, if the current rate of change for technology keeps up, we will never implement a "cutting edge system". What we will do, however, is be able to manage the technology system currency and plan for update and expansion. Finally, we need to resolve to continually improve the quality of the educational experience that we provide to our students. Only when this is accomplished will our constituency place the faith in us that will allow us to move forward.

Deming's Point 2. Adopt a new philosophy. That new philosophy has to expect quality from all levels of the organization. We can no longer afford to focus simply on quantity. For too long, educators have measured if students filled up the measuring pitcher—not what the pitcher was filled with. Teachers and administrators must take the lead in modeling this new philosophy for students. Technology provides a tool to improve quality at all levels, but the improvement is only as good as those responsible for the change. They must demand quality from themselves. They must usher out the old standards and usher in the new quality standards:

- Accuracy. Technology provides the tools to improve accuracy in various skill areas. Students should never have a spelling or a simple mathematics error. More complex operations (i.e. grammar, word usage, formula structures) should have few errors and those errors should become fewer as the accuracy and usability of support applications (grammar checkers, thesauri, spreadsheets) continue to improve.
- Innovation. Technology provides us the tools to gain access to new data. Gone are the times when every child in the class reports on the volcano because it is the only example of radical landmass change reported in the reference book. Through the use of the worldwide web (WWW), the student has access to a virtually limitless source of information. We cannot afford to tolerate excuses based on lack of data.

Deming's Point 9. Break down barriers between departments. The planning process has to be inclusive, but more importantly it needs to be exhaustive. A new spirit of cooperation and selflessness must be engendered so that existing walls can be broken down allowing planners to see the new possibilities for the organization. The new organization may include existing units and may create new or modified components. Technology will allow new and more productive organizational schemes, but not if constrained by the old structure. One must think in terms of:

• Interdisciplinary organization. This is enabled by new and future technologies focusing on real world integration tasks.
• Intersite organization. Advancing technology allows for rapid storage and retrieval of all types of data and communication. Sharing of information and ideas can be facilitated by a new structure. Imagine the increased effectiveness that may occur if conventional departments are not constrained to routinely sharing ideas within the "school."

Deming's Point 14. The transformation is everybody's job. Get everyone to work planning for new technology. Everyone connected with the school is a stakeholder. Form action groups to help guide the process. These groups may include administrators, teachers, students, staff, community leaders, and business leaders.

Integration of Technology Into the Curriculum

Deming's Point 2: Adopt a new philosophy. In the quest for "never-ending quality," technology leaders must envision and advocate the role that technology will play in the curriculum. To achieve quality using technology, the curriculum must actively engage students in the acquisition of knowledge and skills. As a first step towards technology integration, leaders must understand that there are different ways to approach technology in the classroom. Teachers using technology to enhance or present information in new and exciting ways, teaching about technology in separate courses in the curriculum, and viewing technology as "tool" that empowers students to take charge of their learning are all models of how teachers and students may use technology in the classroom (Bailey, 1996). Technology as an empowerment tool is the model that would best achieve quality; however, there should be a place in the curriculum for each approach. The technology leader must adopt a philosophy that encourages teachers to model the use of technology and encourage interested students to enroll in technology courses, meanwhile working to achieve the ultimate goal of empowering students by teaching them to use technology tools.

Deming's Point 8: Driving out fear. To achieve the goal of quality

Achieving Quality Schools

through technology integration, technology leaders must try to remove any reason teachers might have for not using the technology. One way to achieve this is by insuring teachers that they will have the necessary technology support when needed. In the most ideal situation, support should be provided by a trained technology specialist or media specialist. If total technology integration is the goal, schools must have the faculty to provide on-going technical support. Having these individuals available to staff will help diffuse the anxiety about the technology.

Students are another valuable resource that should be used to provide technology support. Schools should identify a team of students who will provide technical support as a service to the school community. These students could assist with the staffing of the various labs and act as on-call troubleshooters for students and teachers. Once students participating in this program develop a reputation as being knowledgeable and skilled, teachers will be less apprehensive about calling them for assistance.

Deming's Point 9: Breaking down the barriers among staff areas. When thinking about curriculum, the technology leader must understand that the technology integration can diminish curricular isolation. Schools might not be ready to change their structure and organization, but technology will allow teachers to use a more interdisciplinary approach to learning. For instance, besides corresponding with students in France via e-mail, students can study French history, culture, and current political and social issues at their desktops via the Internet. Technology leaders must understand that the current information revolution is changing how we access, utilize and think about information. If they don't make every effort to break down the barriers that hamper technology integration, their students will become seriously disadvantaged.

Student Accountability and Assessment

Deming's Point 3. Cease dependence on inspection to insure quality. Technology allows us to do two things:

- Raise the quality of our inspections
- Raise the quality of our products.

Too often we have chosen the former as our goal. We can become very sophisticated in deciding who passes, by how much they pass, and do it with increased surety that our judgment is correct. Our testing has enabled us to reliably predict who will succeed at the next level. Our energies, however, should be focused instead on using technology to help increase achievement, not diagnose failure. We need to reduce the non-productive time that we spend on assessment of student learning and increase the time applied to learning activities. Technology helps in two ways:

- enabling the establishment of new, student-centered learning paradigms and
- reducing reliance on continuous mass testing and increasing reliance on sophisticated, controlled sampling of student achievement.

Deming's Point 5. Improve constantly and forever every activity in the company to increase quality and productivity. Technology tools allow school leaders to focus on systematic analysis of root causes of problems and to institute solutions to those problems, instead of looking at symptoms. When viewed in this way, school leaders may concentrate on using the tools available to them to analyze and find solutions to systemic problems.

Deming's Point 11. Eliminate numerical quotas. Technology tools allow us to predict with surprising accuracy the effect of various instructional interventions. We are able to manage toward a set of achievement figures which would be the measured goal for the school year. Deming, however, warns against managing toward that "bottom line" or standardized test score, instead encouraging leaders to guide their organization toward more complex performance measures. The challenge for technology leaders is to encourage the development and use of complex measurement schemes that assess broad, multidimensional behaviors.

Deming's Point 14. The transformation is everybody's job. New technologies allow everyone to provide data to assess student performance. Consistent with new assessment paradigms is the need to fully involve every member of the organization in the assessment. Expanding communication and data management technologies allow not only the new measurement schemes, but also provides the means to input and analyze the data to successfully interpret complex performance.

Staff Development

Deming's Point 6: Institute training on the job. Technology leaders must realize that technology is not commonplace for most teachers. Unlike their students who were raised with video games, most teachers lack knowledge about technology and have a low comfort level with electronic media. Moreover, they lack the ability and skills necessary to effectively integrate technology into instruction. Therefore, schools must develop a systematic staff development training program that addresses the needs of the whole faculty, while also meeting the needs of the individual teacher. Staff development training must be continuous, and faculty must be key players in program development and implementation.

A planning committee composed of volunteers representing various constituencies should be established. The committee should begin its work by surveying the faculty and curriculum to determine needs. Once the data is analyzed, the findings should be reported to the faculty in an effort to continually include faculty in the planning of staff development programs.

Some points the committee should take into consideration when planning a staff development program are format, time, and location. When developing a program, the committee must keep in mind that "one size doesn't fit all." The one-to-one format might be better than small or large group activities. It might be better to have staff development activities on designated days rather than after-school or on weekends. Faculty might be more receptive to staff development activities if they are held in the building's computer lab rather than at the central office, local college, or some other off-campus teaching site. Activities might include sending a group to visit schools where technology is integrated, sending a group to a technology conference with the understanding that they will share their experiences with their colleagues, having a group of teachers do in-house workshops for those interested in learning about a particular piece of software, offer a staff development course on integrating the technology in the classroom offered by outside consultant, or have software vendors visit the school to demonstrate programs.

Although every program should include strategies for evaluation, the process should be informal and non-threatening. The technology leader should evaluate the success of technology integration by listening to faculty and students, observing what is happening, and checking use of equipment and facilities. This sort of feedback will provide the leader with good information as to the success of the staff development program. Full integration will come slowly, teacher by teacher, and class by class, but it will come.

Deming's Point 13: Institute a vigorous program of education and retraining. Schools, like business and industry, will have to institute their own program of technology training for teachers who are just entering the profession. Many new teachers have minimal knowledge of the technology because most colleges of education provide limited exposure. Although colleges of education have been often referred to as the "cash cow," they lack the necessary funding, infrastructure, hardware, and software to properly train teachers in instructional technology. Moreover, the average professor lacks the technology knowledge and skills and is unable to model technology integration for their students. Therefore, to achieve quality, school districts must assume that new teachers come with a blank slate and must be prepared to train them so that they will acquire the necessary knowledge and skills. Besides creating formal in-service training sessions for new teachers, schools might create mentoring relationships by pairing seasoned teachers who have a strong commitment to the integration of instructional technology with neophyte teachers.

Deming's Point 12: Remove barriers that rob people of pride of workmanship. Achieving the "A" on a paper or teaching an outstanding lesson are examples of achieving pride or quality workmanship for students and teachers. To remove the barriers that rob teachers and students of the satisfaction of achieving quality in the area of instructional technology should be of the utmost importance to school leaders.

Dated and incompatible hardware and software, lack of funding, inability to access technology because there is not enough available equipment or poor infrastructure, lack of support in the building and district, and lack of quality staff development activities are all examples of barriers. Teachers and students want quality hardware and software that is compatible, readily available, and works seamlessly. They want and need to be able to accomplish tasks with little or no difficulty and want immediate support so that their problems are handled with minimal delay. If these barriers are not removed, teachers and students become discouraged and avoid using technology.

Fear of Technology

Deming's Point 8. Drive out fear. Technology leaders must encourage all constituents students, teachers, and administrators, to become risk takers by using the technology tools in a non-threatening environment. Constituents who are not willing to take a risk will never be able to take advantage of technology's power. Leaders have to reward the constituents who take those risks and who do occasionally fail. If negative rewards are observed, the group likely will not take advantage of the bonuses of technology, even though those bonuses are potentially great. Technology use is baffling to all users at times. This feeling is potentially intense among adults, especially those in positions of power, who are used to being correct all of the time. The technology leader must convince teachers, administrators and staff that they will not always be correct and provide an encouraging, supportive environment that is attuned to psychosocial needs of the user.

Deming's Point 9. Break down barriers among personnel. Technology leaders must use the new technologies to establish an atmosphere of cooperation and collaboration among the organization's personnel. These new communication methods provide ample opportunities to work together. These methods must encourage the personnel to be inclusive instead of exclusive. Many new technologies tend to encourage exclusion and isolation, so this area is one that must be continually monitored and resolved.

Deming's Point 10. Eliminate slogans, exhortations, and targets. These exhortations tend to create adversarial relationships among constituent groups. They imply that problems are the result of lack of skill, concern, or care by those groups and that if workers would only try harder they can fix the problem. Frequently in school situations, the problem is not under the control of the constituent groups. The real problem is the lack of the correct tools to accomplish the task. Technology offers the tools to improve productivity of the groups without having to resort to counterproductive blaming behaviors. Technology can help groups work more efficiently and effectively, thus providing a real solution to the problem.

Deming's Point 11. Eliminate numerical quotas and goals. Stable systems produce whatever the system will produce (Deming, 1986). Attempting to increase the productivity of these systems provides frustration to all involved. One of the most frequently heard goals in schools is "We will increase our SAT scores to the state average." This is a sure way to frustrate all school constituents: teachers, students, parents, administrators, the community... . The list goes on. Without a plan to change something within the system, the system will continue to produce SAT averages within a narrow band with some variation. Changing the system by adding new technology to it allows the system production to change as well.

Financing Technology

Deming Point 2: Adopt the new philosophy. Enabling acquisition of technology is a matter of the utmost importance—certainly on a par with leadership, planning and technology integration. Therefore, how technology is financed must be a major part of your school's technology plan. The plan must not only reflect the district's commitment to technology, it must outline efforts to raise funds and identify possible funding sources. Writing grants for funds from federal, state, local and private agencies; and soliciting funds from local businesses are just some of the ways schools can raise technology dollars. Investigating special programs offered by companies (i.e., telephone and software) may prove helpful because they might have special programs designed to improve the infrastructure and access schools have to technology.

The technology leader should look for creative solutions to finance technology. For instance, most school districts want to buy the technology outright without looking at other financing strategies. Leasing or purchasing computer hardware and software on installment plans from a third party vendor are two financing options that are often overlooked by schools. The National School Boards Association (1989) outlines the following as the advantages of leasing and installment plans:

- immediate use of hardware and software;
- no large initial cash outlay;
- transfer of title at outset of contract, so school district ownership is guaranteed;
- option to buy out contract early; and
- preferential low interest rate available to government agencies (p. 24).

Your ultimate goal is to achieve quality which means putting your customers on the cutting edge. Schools without funds to finance technology will be able to provide state-of-the-art technology for their students and, if they do proactive negotiation, they might even get the vendor to provide regular upgrades and replace equipment.

Summary

Deming's Point 14: The transformation is everybody's job. As schools deal with the challenges of the informational revolution, they must utilize Deming's principles to insure that all members of the school community are engaged in the quest for quality. To achieve change, technology leaders, as the unifying force, must establish and become advocates for the "purpose" which undergirds the "new philosophy" that includes the vision, mission, values, and beliefs. The technology leaders must insure access and productivity by "breaking down barriers" and "driving out fear" of technology. They must realize that achieving quality can only be accomplished by schools reconsidering how students learn and teachers teach. Therefore, schools must adopt new paradigms of teaching and learning, and develop different methods of evaluation which includes conceptualizing the role that technology tools will play. Technology in-service training should be on-going, and new and creative staff development models adopted. Finally, schools should adopt "a vigorous program of education and training" as part of the induction for new faculty to insure that they develop technology knowledge and skills.

References

Bailey, G. D. (1996). Technology leadership: Ten essential buttons for understanding technology integration in the 21st century. Educational Considerations, 23 (2), 2-6

Deming, W. E. (1986). Out of the crisis. Cambridge, MA: MIT Center for Advanced Engineering Study.

National Leadership Network Study Group on Restructuring Schools. (1993). Toward quality in education: The leader's odyssey. Washington, DC: U.S. Department of Education.

National School Boards Association. (1989). On Line: Financing strategies for educational technology. Alexandria, VA: Author.

CHAPTER 12

STATISTICAL PROCESS CONTROL IN EDUCATION: UTILIZING TQM TO MAINTAIN CURRICULUM ALIGNMENT

Donald V. Cairns and Roberta D. Evans

During the late 1980s and into the early 1990s the application and usage of Dr. W. Edward Deming's fourteen principles of management received a great deal of attention in the field of business and industry. Only recently have attempts been made to use and to apply Dr. Deming's manifesto to the field of education (Bonstingel, 1992). By utilizing statistical process control, Deming's fifth principle "constant improvement of product and service," can be applied to maintaining and improving a well-defined school curriculum. However, this requires that "Total Quality Management" (TQM) or "Statistical Process Control" (SPC) be viewed and utilized as was originally intended, not as a new recipe for a quick fix of educational problems. When combined with what is currently known about leadership skills, organizational behavior, and the effective schools correlates, a powerful set of dynamics may be set into motion in those schools desiring to utilize such methods. Consequently, prior to embarking upon such a program of improvement, the school leader needs to understand how the effective school correlates, curriculum alignment, and statistical process control come together as an integrated system for school improvement. However, before offering any general discussion of school improvement, the meaning of Deming's fifth principle of constant improvement must be explained.

Constant Improvement Defined

School organizations desiring to build a culture around Dr. Deming's fifth principle, "dedication to constant improvement," must have a staff dedicated to continuous improvement in themselves (skills) and the betterment of the school through resolution of organizational problems, or attainment of commonly agreed upon goals. This demands that an atmosphere conducive to life-long learning and self-improvement be fostered and encouraged by the administrative leadership in a district. School leaders must be able to create systems that empower employees to solve organizational problems through the use of data. As a result, staff development programs, peer coaching policies, and staff collegiality are encouraged in the workplace. While it is at times difficult to determine precisely what Dr. Deming means in his fourteen points, he is emphasizing the very important social and cultural aspects that have long been recognized from the Hawthorne studies. That is to say that the social side of the school is as important as the technical side of the organization in achieving the educational mission. Improvement programs involve taking some risk, in combination with a willingness to learn from failures, in order to gain insights into problems in the school organization. Constant improvement efforts require leaders at the building site level to be capable of maximizing on the strengths inherent in loosely coupled systems (Weick, 1982). Only in this manner will educational leaders be able to move forward into the areas of the effective schools correlates.

Effective Schools Background

During the last half of the 1960s and the first half of the 1970s, several educational reform reports appeared, focusing upon the question, Do schools make a difference?

One factor that appears to make a difference is the aligned curriculum (Caplan & O'Rourke, 1988; Hathaway, et al., 1985; Miller, Choen & Sayre, 1985; Niedermeyer & Yelon, 1981). Brookover contends (in Crowell, 1986) that, "an effective school reflects an aligned curriculum." Although an aligned curriculum is posited as a fundamental issue, there is little practical research available upon the subject (Caplan & O'Rourke, 1988).

That an aligned curriculum is becoming increasingly important to school administrators and educational policy makers is of little doubt. Policy makers at all levels are demanding that student outcomes (as evidenced by higher test scores on standardized tests) improve in proportion to higher operating costs and concomitant increases in state and local taxes. Such demands to demonstrate improved levels of student achievement generate pressure upon the practitioner of educational administration, to produce test scores which probably reflect the local schools' levels of effectiveness.

Such an emphasis upon testing stresses the importance of curriculum to school improvement efforts, simply because a misaligned curriculum will generate widely-differing results on standardized achievement tests, thereby obfuscating any school improvement efforts. However, what is meant by proper alignment in curriculum requires clarification.

Aligned Curriculum Defined

English (1987) defines the aligned curriculum as the degree of congruency between the written curriculum (work performed) in the school setting and the tested curriculum (work measured). This may be further described as the degree to which the locally defined curriculum matches or deviates from any particular standardized test as a measurement of student progress or achievement. It assumes that alignment is the degree of congruency between: (a) what the teacher teaches, (b) what the test provides in the form of objectives, and (c) what the standardized test measures. This model is premised upon the belief that the teacher is the foundation upon which the real school curriculum is based. This is due to the fact that it is what the teacher does behind the closed door that determines what the true curriculum is or is note. In the absence of wide-range adoption of alternative assessment practices, many districts must contend with standardized tests as the public measure of a quality school. Currently, few procedures exist that provide practical guidelines for the alignment of the curriculum. English (1987) writes about "frontloading" or backloading" a curriculum in relation to a commonly standardized test, but this concept is still poorly understood.

Frontloading and Backloading a Curriculum

If the curriculum and the instructional objectives are adopted from a statewide test, the process is referred to as frontloading. In contrast, backloading is the traditional method of (a) adopting a text and then (b) adopting or using a statewide test, hoping that the test measures what is taught. While these processes will produce a curriculum with a high degree of congruence, it does not begin to reflect the taught curriculum. Additionally, Lortie (1975); Liberman & Miller, (1984); and Cairns (1990) have pointed out that principals of most schools spend little time in direct observation of the teaching - learning process. This lack of direct attention to the instructional process makes a well coordinated curriculum even more important to the maintenance of an aligned curriculum.

An alternative model, which builds upon concepts of curriculum mapping as conceptually defined by English (1987), needs to be made available to the working administrator. In English's model, a team of district teachers and administrators are required to map out those essential learning skills (elements) that are deemed most important to the teaching staff. The mapping exercise requires the teaching staff to decide on (a) the amount of instruction, (b) amount of application, (c) skills required to attain mastery, (d) whether adequate materials are available, and (e) if adequate preparation is accessible to the teaching staff. This mapping, according to English, "was initiated to deal with discrepancies between what might be in a curriculum guide and what teachers actually decided to teach" (p. 211). The major intent, therefore, is to define the curriculum through the mapping process. While this process is lengthy and time consuming, it produces an extremely functional and consistent curriculum. Furthermore, it fosters the professional collegiality of administrators and the teaching staff in making decisions on such critical issues as scope and sequence and assessment. After the mapping exercise has been completed, then and only then is the standardized test selected based on congruency of test objectives to the newly defined curriculum.

When the steps outlined herein are followed, it is possible to assess the degree of curriculum triangulation, or congruency through SPC or statistical process control. This is especially important after a school district has completed a mapping exercise and selected the appropriate standardized test. Maintenance of the aligned curriculum is as important as the mapping exercise.

Preventing Misalignment

Consistent with Deming's change for leaders to "manage the system," principals as instructional leaders need to ensure that misalignment will not creep back into the mapped curriculum and that the newly-defined curriculum will be constantly improved. Misalignment can only be prevented by utilizing curriculum mapping (English, 1987) and SPC processes as espoused by Dr. Deming's fifth principle (Walton, 1986). This is particularly important given the enormity of monitoring today's school curricula. In most school districts, curricular revisions and their related mapping activities occur, by subject area, every five to six years. Thus, it is critical to recognize the important role that any valid and reliable standardized testing program may play in keeping a school district's curriculum on track, during and after the selection of the standardized test and mapping activities have taken place. What normally is overlooked in such tasks is the role that a standardized test may play in the development of total quality management concepts and statistical process control measures. This is important to those working in the school environment where outside technical assistance is often difficult to obtain.

If the final product of curriculum mapping is not constantly monitored or improved through the use of statistical measures, the results of standardized tests will not be appropriately utilized. This allows for misalignment to be evidenced in a relatively short period of time due to a variety of reasons: 1) the movement of personnel into and out of a school system, 2) a new textbook adoption, or 3) a combination of other factors. That is to say that, as a school changes teaching personnel, the curriculum has been altered to the degree of personnel change. Teachers teach what they value and enjoy, not necessarily what the curriculum map indicates should be taught. This "egg carton structure" (Lottie, 1975) or loosely-coupled system found in the majority of the schools (Weick, 1976, 1979, 1982) contributes to schools operating in a fractured manner, which in turn accelerates curriculum misalignment. Consequently, the isolated organizational structure of schools contribute significantly to their lack of effective curricular cohesion.

The fact that schools are structurally loose makes them vulnerable to all types of well meaning but ill-conceived reforms which may actually diminish performance on a standardized test. What may ultimately transpire is that those schools that consistently fail to know how the defined curriculum is performing lend additional weight to the argument for a "national standardized test." Rather, local school administrators need to utilize whatever standardized tests best match the local district's curriculum as determined through statistical process control.

Standardized Test Utilized

It must be recognized that the use of a standardized test is only one method available to instructional leaders planning an assessment of a school's curriculum. Any school anticipating such an assessment must avail themselves of alternative forms of assessment in conjunction with a standardized test. While the utilization of a standardized test may not be the single most meaningful measure of a school's curriculum, it does offer useful indices of misalignment. Administrators must understand and utilize them as long as they are "the public test" of school effectiveness. Other models, such as performance based assessment, portfolios, and a district's own criterion referenced tests will someday supplant the current sad reality of a single-dimensional measure of student assessment. But until that day arrives, a standardized test does serve a useful, though somewhat limited, function.

Within any system, variations of performance may be traced to one of two causes: a) random variation, and b) common causes of variation

(Walton, 1986; Bostingel, 1992). Using the model proposed by Deming (Walton, 1986), any district—regardless of size—may adequately locate areas of weakness within its curriculum, subsequently identifying whether a variation from the established norm is due to random variation or common cause of variation.

Random variation results from true variance in the performance of any selected population of students. In the case of a school, this means that, while all students are capable of learning, not all students will perform at the same level, on the same test, on any given day. Some naturally occurring variation in performance will, in fact, occur.

Common causes of variation, however, are due to some of the issues discussed above: 1) the change in instructional personnel, 2) a change in test, or 3) a shift in standardized test selection. If the cause of variation is due to any of the above mentioned items or to some other cause, then only through the use of statistical control process, in combination with curriculum mapping, will the variation in the application of the defined curriculum be identified. The causes of misalignment must be identified and rooted out. This can only be accomplished collegially, utilizing basic descriptive statistics that exist within any highly reliable and valid standardized test. This is the heart of the statistical control process for curriculum management.

Basic Descriptive Statistics

Total quality management, or TQM, concepts offer many data gathering techniques which are useful, both for solving organizational problems and in eliminating the common causes of variation in school outcomes. One of these tools is the control chart (Walton, 1987; Bostingel, 1992) that sets upper control limits and lower control limits as guiding parameters for the organization. This model is represented in Figure 1.

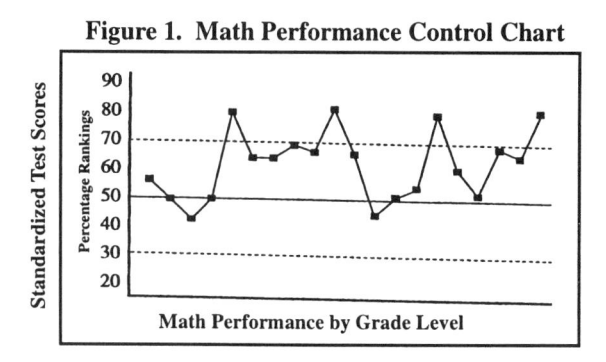

Figure 1. Math Performance Control Chart

Adapted from: Walton, M. (1986). The Deming management method. New York, NY: Perigree Books.

The control chart model is predicated upon the assumption that any mapped curriculum, in conjunction with the proper text and standardized test, is suitable for statistical processes that will "establish upper control limits and lower control limits."

Utilizing basic descriptive statistics, the control chart process formulates boundaries that accomplish two necessary tasks: 1) mandates that curriculum alignment be completed as discussed, and 2) sets boundaries to which the principal and staff need to react.

Upper control and lower control limits are set by establishing boundaries from which variation is not allowed. While TQM requires that the upper control limits are to be calculated, the example used here will be set artificially. This is due to the fact that in an industrial application, the SPC control chart calculates the degree of allowable variations on the quality of the "raw processing material," and schools are unlikely to gain control of the total rearing of the nation's children.

For the purpose of maintaining the quality of the curriculum and the degree of success or failure of that curriculum, the upper and lower control limits of the standardized measures may be defined artificially, rather than calculated from a mathematical formula.

This process takes several steps:

1. Data is gathered over a period of 3-5 years on the established mean for a particular content or subject area, within the same successive classes or grade level. Based on the mean performance of the classes (grade levels), each range is established and fed into the formula as follows:

    a. From the normal curve, a quality control standard of $\pm$ .25 of one standard deviation from the national mean, is established (see figure 2) as the local boundaries for two thirds of the districts school population.
    b. The scores are easily obtained from most standardized tests, either from the test booklet or from the publisher, in the form of **standard Z scores**. Standard scores are easily understood as they represent the same scores as a standard deviation that a particular raw score is above or below the mean. It measures the distance that an individual varies from the group mean. Whatever the standard score is, it mirrors the standard deviation. These limits establish the ranges of allowable variation from the mean and are used to begin the process to identify which areas within the curriculum need attention.

When an area has been identified as needing attention, teams of professionals in the school determine whether the variation is due to random variation or common cause of variations. This requires further investigation into probable causes based upon the following three simple decision rules.

Decision Rules for Alignment

Three decision rules are applied against these locally-bounded norms, as measured against locally reported standardized test results. These rules are applied to the two thirds of the school population that normally fall between -1 standard deviation from the norm and +1 standard deviation from the norm. The process as outlined here requires that 2/3 of the school population will not vary more than ± .25 from the national mean on a standardized test. Using ± .25 of a standard deviation as the local guide, the following rules are applied.

1. When the district norm is above the bound norm (+.25), program improvement is <u>not</u> required, and staff should be aware of "what is new in the literature." Any attempts at curriculum revision should be approached with much caution so as not to create curriculum misalignment.

2. When the difference between the current and the previous instructional year is between ± .25 of a standard deviation, then program improvement is <u>not</u> required. Performance is to be continually monitored, so that all remains well in the program. Teachers and principals should be alert for any potential problems.

3. When the district standard score falls below -.25 of a standard deviation, program improvement must be undertaken. Problems must be identified and alternative solutions examined for potential implementation according to team established priority schedules.

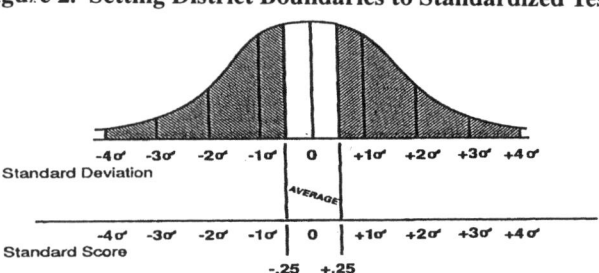

Figure 2. Setting District Boundaries to Standardized Test

Adapted from: Barrett, S. (n.d.). Unpublished film slides. Springfield, OR 97477. Springfield School District No. 19. 525 Mill Street.

When the boundaries are below the lower control limits of ±.25 of a standard deviation, district personnel must investigate to determine whether the problems are resulting from <u>common cause of variation</u> or random variation.

Frequently the variance will result from curriculum misalignment due to some type of artificial problem (i.e., a shift in text, personnel, etc.). If the basis of variance from the predetermined boundaries is due to random variance, the staff may continue to administer the mapped curriculum as in the past. Random variance is a naturally occurring deviation from the norm and outside the sphere of administrative or staff influence. It is important to recognize that curriculum revisions take time. Therefore, priorities must be set in accordance with the district or state adoption cycle, as this makes a difficult process more manageable.

One of the advantages of implementing SPC is that an available target norm may be set (the national mean) and no attempts are made to rewrite the entire local curriculum each time a problem arises. Additionally, schools cease trying to force everyone above the mean on a standardized test, which is not possible for any length of time on a nationally norm-referenced test. Instead, the curriculum is constantly under review after the mapping process has occurred, therefore building upon what the teaching staff have determined is or is not important to classroom instruction. The standardized test, therefore, becomes more of a diagnostic tool and less of a measure (artificially constructed) of any one school's success or failure. Further, when a planned review of the curriculum is built around the state or district curriculum revision cycle, the problem of rewriting an entire district's curriculum is avoided. As outlined, the process discussed above is well within the capabilities of most school administrators, even within the smallest of schools.

For small rural schools, the pressure to have all students climb above the 50th percentile on a standardized test, which is itself an unrealistic expectation, has been reduced significantly. The process is defensible, manageable, and highly functional.

Where to Begin

Any principal or superintendent who wants to utilize statistical process control in order to maintain an aligned curriculum, needs to generate a staff development program that trains the leadership in all of Dr. Deming's fourteen principles. Only after the leadership is fully trained in this manner, and not just the statistical aspects of school improvement, can the school or district train the teaching staff in those same principles. It should be noted that such training should precede efforts to utilize statistical process control. Any school district or school site which attempts to initiate statistical process control measures without the other aspects of Dr. Deming's fourteen principles is in danger of having a valuable organizational tool fail. The major reason would be related to a failure to understand the change literature and what it says about individual and organizational change processes.

Both organizational and individual change processes must be initiated within the bounds of the leader, follower, and situational triad that has been covered in depth in the leadership literature (Hersey & Blanchard, 1977, 1982, 1988, 1993; Hall & Hord, 1987). True organizational change arrives when the organizational leaders accurately assesses the organizational culture, maturity level, skills, and inherent readiness for change prior to embarking upon a change endeavor. A failure to accurately assess any one of the elements mentioned above, in relation to the leader's style, background, skill level and ability to direct the change process, will only lead to failure.

After the work of training and mentoring a staff has been completed, the next task is to utilize statistical process control in a manner that is both non-threatening and functional. An example of how SPC may be utilized prior to a curriculum application, might be to simply chart out some chronic problems within the organization prior to seeking solutions; i.e.: student tardiness, or absenteeism. In this manner, confidence is gained, the staff polishes a new skill, and the change process becomes less threatening. What is accomplished is a carefully structured sequence of events that takes the members of the school organization through all the levels of CBAM (Hall & Hord, 1987).

In order for SPC or any of Dr. Deming's fourteen points to be successfully incorporated into the nation's public schools, a good grasp of planned change, how organizations work, and how situational leadership fit together is essential.

Conclusion

While the effective schools research maintains that an aligned curriculum is an organizational characteristic found in association with those schools deemed to be effective, empirical research on curriculum alignment is lacking. The process outlined herein builds upon the TQM model, as applied to the teaching staff, empowering them to formulate solutions to curricular weaknesses. More importantly, the utilization of SPC builds upon what is currently known about leadership theory, organizational behavior, and integrates specific aspects of TQM to improve and strengthen the school organization itself. Commonly held beliefs

about each school's mission become the foundation of continuous renewal.
In summary, the process for maximizing the information available from standardized tests may be outlined as follows:

1. Collect and analyze data from the tests over a three year period.
2. Develop local standards based upon all students achieving within statistical norms derived from the national (state) mean.
3. Involve all the appropriate stakeholders in developing solutions to curricular problems.
4. Implement collaboratively developed staff and administrative procedures to assess standardized test data.
5. Analyze both the process and results for effectiveness and meaningfulness and adjust as necessary.
6. Seek public support for multi-dimensional assessment of students and curricula.

Statistical control process is a tool available to many school administrator in the nation. It does require some basic understanding of statistics, but more importantly, it mandates that school administrators utilize the tools currently available. These tools augment the best practices of TQM and what has been known about human motivation, leadership theory, and organizational theory.

References

Airasian, P. W. (1985). The ninth mental measurements yearbook, Volume I. Buros Institute of Mental Measurements. Lincoln, NE: University of Nebraska.

Alaska State Department of Education. (1981). The governor's task force on effective schooling. Administrative Order #64. Jeneau: Author.

Barrett, S. (n.d.). Unpublished film slides. Springfield, OR 97477. Springfield School District No. 19. 525 Mill Street.

Bostingel, J. (1992). Schools of quality: An introduction to total quality management in education. Alexandria, VA. Association for Supervision and Curriculum Development.

Cairns, D. V. (1990). Differences in organizational structure between selected elementary and secondary schools in Washington State. Doctoral Dissertation, Washington State University.

Caplan, M. K., & O'Rourke, T. J. (1988). Improving student achievement on standardized tests: One approach. NASSP Bulletin, 72 (505), 54-58.

Cooperman, S., & Bloom, J. (1985). Getting the most from the New Jersey HSPT: A practical guide to resolving curriculum design and delivery problems. Farmington, MA. Center for Teaching and Learning Mathematics. (ERIC Document Reproduction Service No. ED 278-713)

Crowell, R. (1986). Curriculum alignment. Washington, D. C.: U. S. Department of Education, Office of Research and Improvement. (ERIC Document Reproduction Service No. ED 280-874)

English, F. (1987). Curriculum management for schools, colleges, and business. Springfield, IL: Charles C. Thomas.

Firestone, W. A., & Herriott, R. E. (1982). Prescriptions for effective elementary schools don't fit secondary schools. Educational Leadership, 40 (3), 51-53.

Fortune, J. C., & Cromack, T. R. (1987). Test critiques, Volume III. Test Corporation of America. Blackberg, VA: Virginia Polytechnic Institute and State University.

Fry, E. (1980). Test review: Metropolitan achievement tests. The Reading Teacher, 34 (2), 196-201.

Getzels, J. W. (1958). Administration as a social process. In A. Halprin (Ed.), Administrative theory in education (pp. 140-165). Chicago: Midwest Administrative Center.

Hall, G., & Hord, S. (1987). Change in schools: Facilitating the process. Albany, New York: State University of New York Press.

Hanson, E. M. (1985). Educational administration and organizational behavior. Boston, MA: Allyn and Bacon.

Hathaway, W. (1985). A regional and local item response theory based on a test item bank system. (ERIC Document Reproduction Service No. ED 284-883)

Henson, K. T., & Saterfiel, T. H. (1985). State mandated accountability programs: Are they educationally sound? NASSP Bulletin, 69 (477), 23-27.

Hersey, P., & Blanchard, K. (1977). Management of organizational behavior: Utilizing human resources (2nd ed.). Englewood Cliffs, NJ: Prentice-Hall.

Hersey, P., & Blanchard, K. (1982). Management of organizational behavior: Utilizing human resources (3rd ed.). Englewood Cliffs, NJ: Prentice-Hall.

Hersey, P., & Blanchard, K. (1988). Management of organizational behavior: Utilizing human resources (4th ed.). Englewood Cliffs, NJ: Prentice-Hall.

Hersey, P., & Blanchard, K. (1993). Management of organizational behavior: Utilizing human resources (6th ed.). Englewood Cliffs, NJ: Prentice-Hall.

Hertel, E. H. (1978). Metropolitan Achievement Tests (5th ed.). In The Ninth Mental Measurements Yearbook (pp. 959-968). Lincoln, NE: University of Nebraska.

Liberman, A., & Miller, L. (Eds.). (1984). Teachers, their world, and their work: Implications for school. Alexandria, VA: Association for Supervision and Curriculum Development.

Lezotte, L. W., & Bancroft, B. A. (1986). School improvement based upon effective schools research. Outcomes, A Quarterly Journal of the Network for Outcome Based Schools, 6 (1), 13-17.

Lortie, D. (1975). School teacher. Chicago: University of Chicago Press.

Mann, D. (1986). Testimony given is support of H. B. 747. Outcomes, 6 (1), 10.

Mehrens, W. A. (1984). National tests and local curriculum: Match or mismatch? Educational Measurement: Issues and Practices, 3 (3), 9-15.

Miller, S. L., Cohen, S. R., & Sayre, K. A. (1985). Significant achievement gains using the effective school model. Educational Leadership, 42 (6), 38-43.

Nidermeyer, F., & Yelon, S. (1981). Los Angeles aligns instruction with essential learning skills. Educational Leadership, 618-620.

Oregon State Department of Education. (1985). Curriculum alignment with the essential learning skills. Salem, OR.

Spady, G. W., & Marx, G. (1984). Excellence in our schools: Making it happen. Arlington, VA: AASA.

Walton, M. (1986). The Deming management method. New York: Perigree Books.

Weick, K. E. (1976). Educational organizations as loosely coupled systems. Administrative Science Quarterly, 21, 1-19.

Weick, K. E. (1979). The social psychology of organizing (2nd ed.). Reading, MA: Addison-Wesley Publishing Company.

Weick, K. E. (1982). Administering education in loosely coupled systems. Phi Delta Kappan, 63 (10), 673-676.

Chapter 13

TOTAL QUALITY MANAGEMENT AND THE CLASSROOM TEACHER

Connie Ruhl-Smith
Western Michigan University

> Young people who grow up believing that, despite their best efforts, they are incapable of achieving quality results in their schoolwork, begin to see themselves as having little inherent quality. (Bonstingl, 1992, p. 5)

As is evidenced by the epigraph above, schools as we know them today are under attack by parents, students, researchers, politicians and even educators. This attack is not necessarily unjustified when examining reports published by commissions, blue ribbon panels, census bureaus and other interested investigators. In fact, "common . . . is the conclusion that school performance and quality are severely inadequate to meet the needs of modern society" (Branson, 1987, p. 15). When we examine the statistics of student drop-outs, we see that the schools and classrooms are inadequate to meet the needs of many students. The problem is not realizing the need for change in the schools and classrooms; the problem lies in identifying strategies for effective change.

"We have been tinkering with education and nibbling around the edges of true change" (Kaufman, 1992, p. 153). Consequently, educators have been asked to change repeatedly over the years; often these changes are made without being considered analytically and without valid research to support such change initiatives. In fact, some school and classroom reform initiatives occur and recur with little improvement; offering no proof that such reforms will work any better the second (or third) time around. As poignantly stated by Charles Silberman, reform returns because there is no tendency for policymakers "to think seriously about educational purposes" (1972, p. 10). Schools are granted some freedom in decision-making "but the all-important purposes of education remain the property of legislators, who turn them into 'standards' and hammer them home through assessment" (Holt, 1993, p. 386).

But still, education does not seem to be able to significantly deliver on its promises (Clark & Astuto, 1994). Superintendents, administrators, and teachers blame the learners and their parents. Many believe that we have reached the point where spending more time and money in an attempt to do better what we are presently doing will only prove disappointing but increasingly less cost effective (Branson, 1987; Perelman, 1989; Perelman, 1990). As stated by Schlechty and Cole (1992):

> If it turns out that our schools are doing what we want them to do, but are not achieving what we want them to achieve, it may be because we want them to do the wrong things. (p. 48)

A focus on quick-fixers, final products and short-term goals has not been successful to this point in education. As is noted by Clark and Astuto (1994):

> The language of education reform is still dominated by the harshness of bureaucracy, control, competition and intervention. It is a discouraging language of distrust and inspection. The current education reform movement is. . . destructive to the human spirit. (p. 520)

What educators must instead focus upon is "a fundamental change in a [school's] culture" (Holt, 1993, p. 384). This change can be initiated only through a comprehensive reevaluation and reexamination of the purposes, goals, outcomes, and structures of schooling. One such framework for accomplishing a task of this magnitude can be found in the work of W. Edwards Deming and others, who have struggled to bring forth the notion of total quality and the practices of Total Quality Management (TQM) for professionals in both the for-profit and not-for-profit arenas.

Understanding Deming

W. Edwards Deming was born in 1900 and grew up in an industrialized society operated under the basic philosophies of Frederick Taylor and the followers of scientific management. Deming began working at Western Electric's Hawthorne Plant, where he observed other workers, mostly females, completing mundane tasks in a repetitive, machine-like manner. At the Hawthorne Plant workers were paid in a piecework fashion, based exclusively upon the number of items produced which could pass inspection. Hence, quality of work or workmanship was not an internal issue. Workers were not required, or even expected, to think. Deming quickly saw the banality of such organizational actions.

Dr. Deming, under the mentorship of Walter Shewhart of Bell Laboratories, progressively perceived a need for worker involvement in improving production; and thus, improving overall quality. Shewhart developed many procedures to help ensure increasingly higher levels of quality in production—these procedures were shared with Deming. Deming's ideas proved useful during war-time production but seemed to fall on deaf ears in America after World War II, when production again became the motivating factor in industry.

Deming was given the opportunity to travel to Europe and Japan to assist in various phases of the war recovery effort. In Japan, he was encouraged to share his quality control information; gradually the Japanese accepted and integrated Dr. Deming's theories of quality and production. At the heart of the production line, as Deming so powerfully stated, was the consumer (Walton, 1986). The Japanese listened, believed and acted upon Deming's suggestions regarding quality and consumer satisfaction.

It was not until 1980 that America rediscovered W. Edwards Deming. During a television documentary, Deming discussed how he had assisted Japanese industry in a rebirth of competence. American industry could do the same, in Deming's view, but American management had to do more than simply replicate Japanese methodologies (Walton, 1986). Deming believed strongly that people had "to work smarter, not harder" (Walton, 1986, p. 19).

In conjunction with this view of smarter organizational behavior, came Deming's charge for management involvement and support of quality production. As explained by Deming, many problems attributed to the work force are ingrained in the system—thus, a management problem (Deming, 1986). In fact, Deming chided the system for causing 85% of the problems that occur in organizational life. Concomitantly, Deming noted that workers created only 15% of all such problems (Walton, 1986, p. 94). Dr. Deming also believed that management, in search of instant success, frequently attempted to copy programs and processes from other organizations. These managers often failed to question the why or the how of such successes, thus setting the system and the workers up for further failure and blame. Managers, he believed, were also remiss for discouraging teamwork in the organization and failing to break down the barriers that interfered with such teamwork; again, leaving those with little or no control struggling with obstacles created by the system itself (Deming, 1986). Healthy organizations "realize that they have to define and achieve total quality" (Kaufman, 1992, p. 149). This quest for quality is accomplished through management-worker collaboration and a persistent focus on continuous improvement. As Kaufman (1992) so clearly states:

> ... there must be continuous input in what organizations use, do, process, and deliver. If you are not consistently improving, you are falling behind. (p. 149)

This redefinition of organizational behavior and need for systemic change was and is the essence of Deming's approach to total quality management.

Total Quality Management in Education

Although the philosophy of TQM is rooted in the world of business, many leaders in education are beginning to adopt this as an appropriate operational philosophy as well. TQM offers a systematic approach to examining the entire organization. Unlike other reform efforts, the theories and beliefs behind TQM offer education and educators a way to holistically transform their manner of conducting business. This redesign, though, is based upon "a solid theory and vision" (Brandt, 1992, p. 31)—it is ongoing and never complete.

Unlike many other reform movements, there is not one best way for TQM to be accomplished. There are, though, fundamental tenets that help to steer the organization in a proper direction; primarily, the organization's work processes must be viewed as a single system (Rhodes, 1992). In order for this to occur, all aspects of effective organizational functioning—the inputs and processes and the outputs and outcomes (Kaufman & Zahn, 1993)—are considered with customer satisfaction in mind. Since TQM is a "people process," everyone must attempt to work together to deliver total quality (Kaufman, 1992, p. 152).

With the emphasis on change, both in the system and the processes, TQM offers the tools and procedures to initiate needed organizational change. Only those programs, though, "that meet are not meeting the needs, wants, and expectations of the school's customers" (Texas Education Agency, 1992, p. 1) should be examined. None of this will occur quickly or without a great deal of effort and education. To think that to accomplish quality satisfaction on the part of customers is simplistic in nature is both a false and misleading impression. Ample time must be permitted for all members of the organization to be educated in and develop an understanding of the principles and concepts of TQM. Then the

Total Quality Management and the Classroom Teacher   225

employees must be given the necessary time to begin incorporating these systematic approaches into the day-to-day activities of the classrooms or school. As is stated by Leigh (1993):

> It will take from five to ten years before the principles of TQM become a permanent part of the fabric of an organization. (p. 86)

Time, effort and cooperation by all are important, but even more important is a thorough understanding of Deming's 14 points which he believes to be the basis for transformation of organizations (Deming, 1986). As stated by Deming:

> Adoption and action on the 14 points . . . formed the basis for lessons for top management in Japan in 1950 and subsequent years. (1986, p. 23)

It is Deming's belief that these 14 points can be successfully applied in any size organization or to a division within any organization (i.e., a school or a classroom). These 14 points (Deming, 1986), with a brief explanation as to how they could or should be applied to schools (Bonstingl, 1992; Schmoker & Wilson, 1993), are as follows:

1. <u>Create constancy of purpose for improvement of product and service</u>. The primary purpose for educators should be a focus on academic achievement and assisting students to maximize their true potential. This can only come about when students and teachers work together to develop a continuous learning process designed to benefit each and every student.
2. <u>Adopt a new philosophy</u>. Conventional school management cannot persist. All school leaders must adopt the new philosophy and encourage and support teacher and student empowerment.
3. <u>Cease dependence on mass inspection</u>. Reliance on standardized tests as the major determiner of student performance is inherently wasteful and does little to encourage the student to work toward improvement. Students need to be taught how to monitor and assess their own work with tests being used solely in a diagnostic and prescriptive nature. Methods of assessing authentic learning must be identified.
4. <u>End the practice of awarding business on the basis of price tag alone</u>. It is better to work hard to build a relationship of trust and collaboration in order to build quality than to always look for the lowest price tag.

5. <u>Improve constantly and forever the systems of production and service</u>. "Improvement of the process includes better allocation of human effort" (Deming, 1986, p. 51). Teachers must be empowered to work collaboratively to improve the processes that affect outcomes and results. This process must be on-going.
6. <u>Institute training</u>. On-going education and in-service for both new and experienced teachers must be provided, so that continual educational improvement can occur. Students must also receive training on how to establish effective goals and how to assess the quality of their own work.
7. <u>Institute leadership</u>. A leader removes the barriers that prevent employees (teachers and students) from doing quality work. School leadership requires working collectively with teachers, students, parents, and community members to enhance student growth and to improve the processes that allow such quality work to occur.
8. <u>Drive out fear</u>. "No one can put in his best performance unless he feels secure" (Deming, 1986, p. 59). Unless people feel secure in the workplace (i.e., schools), they are not going to risk working together, doing new things and trying new ideas. Change will not occur without trust and "trust is a much better motivator than fear" (Gabor, 1990, p. 22).
9. <u>Break down barriers between staff areas</u>. When different departments begin working together as teams, the entire school will benefit. The weaknesses of some can and will be enhanced by the strengths of others. This also enhances communication throughout the entire institution.
10. <u>Eliminate slogans, exhortations, and targets for the workplace</u>. Such slogans or targets, especially those set by management (administration), can often create fear leading to resentment. Accomplishment of such targets or slogans may occur without actually improving quality. Realistic targets may be set cooperatively as a way of working toward actual improvement.
11. <u>Eliminate numerical quotes and targets for the workforce</u>. There is nothing inherently wrong with setting a numerical goals as a target for improvement or achievement, but this target must be employee-determined. For students, when the grade becomes more important than working toward quality, this may well be counterproductive to what the school is trying to achieve, as well as counterproductive to what the student can or will learn.
12. <u>Remove barriers to pride and joy of workmanship</u>. Most people, teachers and students included, want to do a good job, if they are given the opportunity. Often times, teachers and students are

hampered by systematic causes of failure. Schools must work collaboratively to remove these, so that all students and teachers who want to succeed are given the opportunity.
13. Encourage education and self-improvement. "What an organization needs is not just good people; it needs people that are improving with education" (Deming, 1986, p. 86). This requires knowledge; this new knowledge can only be gained "by exploring ideas and interests beyond the boundaries of their professional and personal worlds" (Bonstingl, 1992, p. 82). As is noted in many pieces of educational research, life-long learning is critical to overall organizational success.
14. Take action to accomplish the transformation. A comprehensive transformation like that which is being discussed is an effort only accomplished by involving all school personnel—teachers, students, administrators, central office professionals, and community members. "The emphasis on teamwork, building consensus, and using everyone's respective expertise is what makes the transformation possible" (Schmoker & Wilson, 1993, p. 16).

Simple knowledge of the aforementioned 14 principles is certainly not enough. All parties must realize that what is being discussed is a paradigm shift in education; to accomplish this we must "act on it in ways that raise achievement, self-esteem, and morale of students, employees, and management alike" (Schmoker & Wilson, 1993, p. 17). This change, one that requires fundamental alteration in the school's culture, is a way of facilitating needed improvements. The change must occur by linking theory with practice in order to make good decisions (Deming, 1986). Deming's concepts and beliefs require that workers (teachers) as well as managers (administrators) receive training in "statistical techniques so that they themselves can theorize about their own practice" (Holt, 1993, p. 385). Teachers, all of whom are responsible for the practices of their classrooms, must be given the opportunity to be educated in the theories of TQM and also be given the freedom and flexibility of initiating such theories into classroom practice. Action of this nature must be taken so as to develop quality performance in all students.

Total Quality Management in the Classroom
A school environment that encourages trust, mutual respect, and cooperation comes from the leadership of administrators and policymakers; the actual work of incorporating and encouraging quality in the classroom

comes from the teacher's work with the students. This is at the heart of the total quality movement in the school setting. In order for this to occur, the teacher must accept and develop a different notion of learning than has been accepted in the past. The student must be allowed to become in active participant, a partner in the learning process. As Fromm (1976) states:

> Instead of being passive receptacles of words and ideas, they [students] listen, they hear, and most importantly, they receive and they respond in an active, productive way. What they listen to stimulates their own thinking processes. New questions, new ideas, new perspectives arise in their minds. Their listening is an alive process. (p. 77)

Action and interaction of this nature is the essence of a total quality classroom.

As a way of discussing exactly what steps need to be taken in order for teachers to develop a total quality classroom, the PDSA Cycle or "Shewhart Cycle" will be utilized (Schmoker & Wilson, 1993; Deming, 1986). This cyclical concept was advanced by Walter Shewhart, an early associate of Deming; it was also further developed and discussed by John Dewey. The PDSA Cycle, which stands for plan, do, study, and act, is meant to be utilized for individual innovation; it is being used broadly in this work to examine the processes of implementation of total quality in the school/classroom setting.

Plan

Developing the plan for implementation of total quality in the classroom, will be the most time consuming but also one of the most important steps. In developing this plan of action, certain steps need to have occurred previously in the larger school setting. First, all members of the school environment must focus on the overarching purpose of the school, "namely the desire to improve the lives of their students" (Schmoker & Wilson, 1993, p. 24). This requires a switch from the common notion of the normal curve distribution, when evaluating students, to an acceptance of the notion that given the time, all students can perform at a quality level (Melvin, 1991). The second assumption is that this renewed philosophy has been adopted by all members of the organization, especially the administration, so that when problems within the system arise, they can be handled in an effective fashion. The third notion is that all teachers have a thorough understanding of Deming's 14 points, the theories behind total quality management, the tools for evaluating and improving the processes and methods used in the classroom, and how to help the students understand the changes that they will experience during the transformation.

After these aforementioned steps have been successfully accomplished, each teacher becomes responsible for developing a plan of achieving quality in his/her classroom. As Glasser (1993) states:

> Within the boundaries of your assignment, you figure out your own curriculum use the materials you think are best in the way you believe is most effective, use any method of teaching, . . . that you think will work, and figure out how [best] to evaluate your students so that they show you, themselves, and anyone else that they have learned. . . (p. 12)

This may be done alone, with other members of the professional community in the individual school or with practitioners in other school systems that have incorporated the total quality concept. Assistance from universities and/or teacher research centers may also be useful in seeking better methods of instruction, so as to reach all youngsters in a more effective fashion (Rankin, 1992). Continual improvement of the way the teacher does his/her job becomes a fundamental way of life; this improvement is based upon actual data or research, not hunches. This means that the teacher moves away from a dependence on such "bad" practices as lecturing, ability grouping, standardized testing, and grading on a curve (Rhodes, 1992) simply because they are more manageable or have been the way it was always done. The teacher here also establishes an alternative to the common practice of grading. Since this practice creates a situation where some students win and some lose, the practice defeats the notion of creating the joy in learning (Brandt, 1992). Using the notion of learning as a process and that learning for individual students will progress at different rates will allow us to examine each student individually. Assessment simply become a part of the on-going learning process, a way of building trust between teacher and student.

With students as the school's primary customer, the next step in our plan is to acquaint the students and the entire community with the principles and practices of Total Quality (Bonstingl, 1992). The training for the students may take several hours or several days, depending upon the age and maturity level of the student. Training in total quality management, an understanding of quality work, and the process of goal setting is imperative due to the drastic difference in the quality schools concept and schools as students know them today. The system of today seems to exert a negative effect on students. As stated by Clark and Astuto (1994):

> Not only do these structures socialize students to view work as dull and constraining, but they also rein in the natural curiosity of children and youth. For too many students, schools are not exciting, lively places that engender enthusiasm for and engagement in learning and academic pursuits. (p. 517)

It also seems to pit one student against the other, with grades being the determiner of who is more successful. This usually results in open hostility on the part of those who are less successful (Gray, 1993) and an accompanying dislike and mistrust for not only the school but the teachers within the school as well.

Because a classroom centered around total quality management is so different, the training must incorporate the most dramatic of changes. The students must understand that the traditional system of A-F grading will be eliminated. It will, instead, be replaced by forms of informal assessment that "[arise] from the normal processes of teaching and learning . . . the essential element in promoting quality" (Holt, 1993, p. 387). Students must also understand that it is acceptable to fail and that failure sometimes accompanies taking risks. Feeling of trust and support on the part of the students must exist for the above to occur. The teacher needs also to stress that the classroom is one that will "foster collegiality, cooperation, and collaboration as [he/she] and students learn and play together" (Clark & Astuto, 1994, p. 520). All of this is in an effort to help the students understand that this move toward quality is a way of helping them become a part of a true learning community; one that helps them to critically examine and assess their work on the road to continuous improvement (Bonstingl, 1993).

Do

With a plan fully developed and the training of students accomplished, a school now must put the plan into action. This should be done slowly and with patience. Students, like teachers, must be given enough time and opportunity to become acclimated to the total quality principles. As Byrnes, Cornesky and Byrnes (1992) state:

> One might have the tendency to revert to top-down management techniques because students will be constantly testing. One should expect students to. . . test one repeatedly, until they believe we are

serious about empowering them to become more responsible for their own learning. (p. 44)

An integral part of this empowerment process is the establishment of classroom rules. Both the rules and the consequences for breaking the rules must be decided upon by the teacher and students. Also important to the quality concept in the classroom is an understanding of Glasser's (1993) five basic needs: security, love, power, freedom, and fun. These needs will help determine the amount of effort students will put forth with regard to assigned work. If the work satisfies a need, the students will likely complete it in a manner that reflects quality (Glasser, 1993). Motivation to complete tasks will be tied closely to the above concept.

The movement toward continuous improvement, collaboration, respect for all and the striving toward quality and teamwork requires a different classroom climate than most students have experienced. This new and improved classroom climate must be a result of the effective leadership of the teacher (a quality teacher) and one built on trust. Through modeling, this quality teacher will demonstrate "a keen interest in learning, questioning, and respecting others and their opinions (Byrnes, Cornesky & Byrnes, 1992, p. 43). This strategy should lay the groundwork for students to show an interest in expanding their thinking and learning. All of this activity should be based on a vision. This vision must convey an image of what the school and the classroom could achieve both now and in the future (Sheive & Schoenheit, 1987). This vision is shared with the students prior to goal setting as a way of understanding what is meant to be accomplished throughout the course of the year. In affiliation with this trusting, open climate is an elimination of rigid, inflexibility rules and time-driven scheduling (Kaufman & Zahn, 1993). Quality work becomes the issue, time is given to allow the necessary effort of quality work to occur (Glasser, 1993).

As a way of recognizing their importance as the customer of the total quality classroom, students must help to establish the goals for each and every classroom. These goals must be consistently based on the vision outlined above and developed in a collaborative fashion. This action will assist them later in the year, as they are expected to establish goals for themselves as student learners. Both the student learner goals and the classroom goals must reflect student wants and needs, not merely those of the classroom teacher. This empowering process will remind the students that the class as a whole will use all resources available to help ensure student success. This process may involve varying techniques but all such techniques and methodologies will be viewed as natural and an expected aspect of helping students work toward quality. It is stated by Deming (1986) that barriers and handicaps of the system rob people of the right to feel proud of their jobs. In the classroom, the teacher must make certain that this same thing does not happen. Instead of focusing on the lack of motivation to do work, the quality teacher focuses, instead, upon the work the students are asked to do. For this reason, Glasser (1993) encourages the teacher to ask students to do work that is useful or has some connection to the real world. Motivation or the joy of learning should follow an understanding of such usefulness. With the motivation and desire to perform in a quality fashion present, students will only be able to master such a task if given the opportunity to view examples of quality work (Byrnes, Cornesky, & Byrnes, 1992). They will also take comfort in knowing that the teacher, as well as other students, are there to coach, assist, support, and offer feedback for improvement (Byrnes, Cornesky, & Byrnes, 1992.

Study and Act

At the heart of the total quality management process is the use of data upon which to base pertinent decisions in regard to organizational transformation. The same is true for the classroom setting. As Kaufman and Zahn (1993) so poignantly state:

> Decisions on what to keep and what to change must be made on the basis of valid data and analysis of results and within the context of empowering relationships. Decisions are not to be made on the basis of bias, intuition, or power but on . . . statistical performance data. (p. 12)

TQM, as a process of continuous improvement, depends upon the use of this performance data to help a teacher determine how effectively goals are being accomplished. This also requires a comprehensive examination of present teaching techniques, student accomplishments, and levels of parental involvement. All such factors become vitally important in accomplishing the task of creating total quality and customer satisfaction. Feedback, as another form of performance data, could involve completion of surveys at certain intervals throughout the school year (Byrnes, Cornesky & Byrnes, 1992). Other research could consist of student responses to new programs being initiated. Investigation and collaboration with other settings (i.e., other quality schools, other quality school districts) to determine the most effective teaching strategies could likewise be conducted. Self-measurement of individual teachers could and should be undertaken. Data regarding performance of all students within each classroom setting must also be accumulated. All information of this nature would be collected with the strict purpose of examining accomplishments and pinpointing possible problems and/or weaknesses. Again, without such identification, creation of a total quality classroom would be an impossibility.

A knowledge of statistical tools, such as control charts, Pareto charts, and flow diagrams could help with the collection and analysis of such data (Brandt, 1992). Training of faculty and staff in the use and understanding of these techniques is likewise imperative. Once the statistical data is available for investigation, the teacher or members of the teaching team must carefully analyze this information in an attempt to uncover any potential problems. If problems are identified, the teacher and/or work team (i.e., teachers from the entire school or teacher and students from a specific classroom) must begin to focus on only a few of the identified problems at one time. Causes and possible solutions must be posed with an action plan generated. At this point, the cycle begins again. Much depends on the willingness of a teacher or group of teachers to become action researchers. Without this zeal for research, continuous improvement can not happen. As this research commitment is uncovered, it must also be shared with students, so as to create the possibility of genuine team investigations.

Conclusions

As has been discussed throughout this work, TQM as a viable and effective program for the educational setting has received significant levels of support in the professional literature (Kaufman & Zahn, 1993; Glasser, 1993; Byrnes, Cornesky & Byrnes, 1992); there are others who argue against the implementation of total quality concepts primarily due to the business applications initially addressed by TQM advocates (Kohn, 1993). TQM in the classroom, and in the entire educational setting, rails against many of the pillars of educational thought (i.e., present grading systems, utilization or standardized testing to sort and label students, legislative entanglement, dogmatic domination of teachers and students, and the general acceptance of failure). Nonetheless, to ignore the powerful nature of total quality management and the techniques embedded in its processes, is much like ignoring the learning styles of students. As educational professionals ignore such issues, student performance decreases and student disinterest is exacerbated.

Change from current practice to the practice of TQM will be slow and labored. As Holt states:

> It certainly does not follow that a new philosophy of action is as readily acceptable in schools as in business, for few American businesses are embedded in social and political traditions as securely as American schools. (1993, p. 387)

Such concerns have created individual and organizational paralysis. Now is the time to cease discussion of the inability to make such change and begin to institute these needed changes on a school by school basis. As was mentioned in the introduction to this work, commissions, blue ribbon panels, census bureaus and other interested investigators have generated myriad concerns with respect to K-12 education. Many of these concerns can be eliminated only through total action. TQM provides precisely such an action plan. If our goals are truly centered on quality learning, can we continue to ignore the quality movement? Bonstingl (1993) and many others interested in TQM for education would assert that we can not ignore such powerful processes and methodologies:

> In schools of quality, teachers and students learn together, learn how to learn as they create collaborative, trusting environments in which failure is but a temporary step on the road to continuous improvement. They—along with policymakers, administrators, families, and others who support the work of the school—learn how to create true learning communities, where developing a "yearning for learning" is everyone's central focus.

Let us begin to create new schools of quality. Let us begin to allow all students the opportunity for success and satisfaction in the classroom setting. Let us begin to change the dominant educational paradigm. Let us create dangerously!

References

Bonstingl, J. J. (1992). Schools of quality: An introduction to total quality management in education. Alexandria, VA: Association for Supervision and Curriculum Management.

Bonstingl, J. J. (1993). The quality movement: What's it really about? Educational Leadership, 51 (1), 66.

Brandt, R. (1992). On Deming and school quality: A conversation with Enid Brown. Educational Leadership, 50 (3), 28-31.

Branson, R. K. (1987). Why the schools can't improve: The upper limit hypothesis. Journal of Instructional Development, 10 (4), 15-26.

Byrnes, M. A., Cornesky, R. A., & Brynes, L. W. (1992). The quality teacher: Implementing total quality in the classroom. Bunnell, FL: Cornesky and Associates.

Clark, D. L., & Astuto, T. A. (1994). Redirecting reform: Challenges to popular assumptions about teachers and students. Phi Delta Kappan, 75, 513-520.

Deming, W. E. (1986). Out of crisis. Cambridge, MA: Massachusetts Institute of Technology Press.

Fromm, E. (1976). To have or to be? New York: Harper & Row.

Gabor, A. (1990). The man who discovered quality. New York: Penguin Books.

Glasser, W. (1993). The quality school teacher. New York: Harper.

Gray, K. (1993). Why we will lose: Taylorism in America's high schools. Phi Delta Kappan, 74, 370-374.

Holt, M. (1993). The educational consequences of W. Edwards Deming. Phi Delta Kappan, 74, 382-388.

Kaufman, R., & Zahn, D. (1993). Quality management plus: The continuous improvement of education. Newbury Park, CA: Corwin Press.

Kaufman, R. (1992). The challenge of total quality management in education. International Journal of Educational Reform, 1, 149-165.

Kohn, A. (1993). Turning learning into business: Concerns about total quality. Educational Leadership, 51 (1), 58-61.

Leigh, D. (1993). Total quality management: Training module on overview of TQM. Temple, TX: Temple Junior College.

Melvin, C. A. (1991). Restructuring schools by applying Deming's management theories. Journal of Staff Development, 12 (3), 16-20.

Perelman, L. J. (1989). Closing education's technology gap. Hudson Institute Briefing Paper #111. Indianapolis, IN: Hudson Institute.

Perelman, L. J. (1990). The "acanemia" deception. Hudson Institute Briefing Paper #120. Indianapolis, IN: Hudson Institute.

Rankin, S. C. (1992). Total quality management: Implications for educational assessment. NASSP Bulletin, 76, 66-76.

Rhodes, L. A. (1992). On the road to quality. Educational Leadership, 50 (3), 76-80.

Schlechty, P. C., & Cole, R. W. (1992). Creating standard-bearer schools. Educational Leadership, 50 (3), 45-49.

Schmoker, M. J., & Wilson, R. B. (1993). Total quality education. Bloomington, IN: Phi Delta Kappa.

Sheive, L. T., & Schoenheit, M. B. (1987). Vision and the work life of educational leaders. In L. T. Sheive & M. B. Schoenheit (Eds.), Leadership: Examining the elusive (pp. 93-104). Alexandria, VA: Association for Supervision and Curriculum Development.

Texas Education Agency. (1992). Resource guide for total quality management in Texas schools. Austin, TX: Author.

Walton, M. (1986). The Deming management method. New York: Putnam.

Chapter 14

CONTINUOUS IMPROVEMENT

Patricia Lindauer and Garth Petrie
Director of Program Planning and Evaluation, Hardin County Schools, Hardin County, KY. and Georgia Southern University

Introduction

Every once in a great while momentous events occur which establish a new course, set a new direction, or revolutionize institutions to such an extent that years after the event itself, change is still being felt. Such is the impact of Kentucky's attempt to bring about continuous improvement* in its educational system.

Kentucky's Bold New Experiment

In November, 1985, Kentucky set out on a course which would eventually create a bold new experiment in education that would impact all fifty states. This adventure began with some 66 poor school districts filing a lawsuit in the Franklin County, Kentucky Circuit Court, requesting that funding, which would provide financial equity, be established. The intent of the suit was to give financial equality to all districts in Kentucky. With a favorable ruling in October, 1988, most felt the matter was settled; however, it proved to be only the beginning of a continuously changing process for the educators and children of the Commonwealth.

That following year the ruling was appealed to the Kentucky Supreme Court and the ruling of the lower court was set aside and the entire education enterprise in the state was declared inequitable. This ruling forced the Kentucky State Legislative and Executive branches of government to form a task force responsible for making recommendations on education reform to the General Assembly, thereby constructing an entire new system of common schools meant to provide a quality education to all Kentucky's children and its 176 public school districts. This new, comprehensive and revolutionary set of education laws was designed, developed, and passed by the 1990 legislature in less than one year. This new legislation became known as the Kentucky Education Reform Act (KERA).

* Historically, change in education has been considered improvement. In this chapter the authors use continuous change and continuous improvement synonymously.

In one fell stroke the 150 year history, with all its case law established during that period, was abolished. Without consulting the education community of the state, in fact, through deliberately ignoring the educational community, the state legislature designed an educational program that would change the educational face of the state and become the standard bearer for the nation, as other states began to imitate the litigation and reform pattern set in the Kentucky plan.

Today, 1996, the legislature is once again looking at the educational establishment as a place to institute more reform. As this chapter goes to press, many of the reforms hailed only six years ago as the answer to many of education's ills are being debated. In fact, some of the basic changes instituted in 1990 are being considered for the chopping block, as Kentucky continues to search for improvement in its schools.

Importance of Continuous Improvement

The importance of continuous improvement is well documented in Deming's work detailing Total Quality Management (1986). Deming expressed his belief that improvement is really a never ending process, and declares that, "it takes at least a decade" to implement the change necessary to reach a competent level of progress to insure success. Education is an even more difficult institution to demonstrate progress because it takes 12 to 14 years, depending on organizational structure, for the success to be manifested. After all, children impacted in preschool will evidence the success of the improvement only when they graduate or when they enter the work place.

Lewin's Theory of Change
Creating Chaos

Kurt Lewin and Jitehdra Singh (1951, 1990) developed a theory of change called Force Field Analysis, which provides a platform for describing Kentucky's educational changes. In his theory, Lewin stated that when opposing forces are balanced, the system (the educational institution) is frozen or stable. As one of the forces gains or loses strength the system loses its balance, thereby creating chaos; change is either allowed or forced to occur, in order to bring the system into a redesigned, balanced state (Lewin, 1951). This change may occur through several different approaches. One, the change forces may sway the restraining forces to their way of thinking. A second way is through mandates. A third way may be through the removal of the restraining forces. Of these three approaches, the first seems to be the most lasting. Once this change is internalized, Lewin believed, the system stabilizes in the new configuration. This theory applies to all systems, not just an educational one, and it can occur at all levels of the system.

The difference between Lewin's theory and the Kentucky reform lies in the fact that Lewin believed the system would eventually refreeze, and indeed, most organizations would do so. However, when state government is involved, continuing chaos may well become the norm rather than the exception. Certainly, this continuous change can have some unusual effects on a state's educational enterprise. It is the purpose of this chapter to examine the concept of continuous improvement mandated by the state and the dramatic effects that change has on the players and stakeholders within the local system.

Voluntary or Mandated
Improvement

Research seems to support the idea that voluntary change has more lasting effects. It seems that when individuals who are involved in the change see a need for the change, it is more likely to become internalized. This seems to be holding true in Kentucky.

In looking at the state's impact on the institution of education, the issue of mandated or voluntary improvement needs review. In Kentucky, change was mandated. Yet within the mandate many schools volunteered to be the first up to bat, in that they wanted to make change, and the law gave them the incentive to step out and become the vanguard of the movement. Usually these schools were in situations where the teaching staff felt instructional changes were needed if their children/students were to get the best possible education.

Others believed the whole thing would go away and these educators decided to wait it out, believing they would never have to make any changes (improvements) at all. Many of these schools, while earnest in their belief that the way they were doing things was really the best way, were still holding on to their traditional approach and, in fact, many were doing a creditable job with the students under their care. Many other schools, though, were performing poorly and still they believe the reversal of the mandate will surely come. These schools gambled and it could be that they will win if legislative bills now before the Kentucky General Assembly are passed.

Paper Mandates

Educators for many years have dealt with top-down regulations, policies, and orders and have become accustomed to dealing with "Paper Tigers," writing reports on paper that cause the state agency to be satisfied with the local progress. Because of this history of dealing with top-down mandates, and due to the lax or total lack of supervision, local administrators and teachers begin to feel that all that is needed is to wait a while and feed the bureaucracy the paper work and everything will soon revert to the status quo. President Bush, in announcing <u>America 2000: An Education Strategy</u>, stated that American schools must be transformed for the sake of the future of the children and the nation. The days of the status quo are over. Fullan (1993) reiterates when he says, "Today, the teacher who works for or allows the status quo is the traitor. Purposeful change is the new norm in teaching" (p 14).

In change situations like Kentucky's, however, there is no way to revert to the old system, the status quo, since the way things were had been obliterated by court decree and the legislature had written a completely new set of rules. Yet local educators, believed because the system had "always" operated this way they would not readily accept the fact that a new day had dawned and that they would be forced to make level two changes in their schools. This was evidenced in many ways: by teachers refusing to serve on councils; by principals choosing not to move into school-based decision making (SBDM) frameworks, until the last possible date (the law mandated that all schools, with a few exceptions, must be school-based by fall 1996); and, by school boards resisting changes that would assist and encourage teachers and schools to move toward the mandated changes.

The Need for Debate

Because of these established educator (paper tiger) perceptions, the need for a serious debate about mandated versus voluntary change needs to take place on the national stage. It is time to recognize that piecemeal, incremental change, that has little status and practically no supervision, has done an innumerable amount of damage to the credibility of state government and governmental agencies across the nation. According to Kretovics, Farber, and Armaline (1991), "If education is to succeed, it must be restructured to enable teachers, administrators, parents, and community members to address collectively the problems that face their schools" (p. 295). It seems rational that frivolous rules, laws, and policies of the past need to cease and that issues important enough to be legislated or mandated need the follow-through necessary to bring about full implementation. After a while, even the most dedicated finally become cynics of the frivolous—the paper tigers.

Some Pros and Cons

There are pros and cons on both sides of the issue of mandated change versus voluntary change, and certainly the following list is not all inclusive. However, it serves to identify, to clarify some of the issues of the debate.

VOLUNTARY CHANGE	MANDATED CHANGE
PROS	CONS
1. Enthusiasm	Little enthusiasm
2. Implementation	Resistance to implementation
3. Positive attitudes toward the change	Poor attitudes toward the change
4. High level of acceptance	Lower level of acceptance
5. Involvement from staff	Minimum levels of involvement
6. Commitment to sell the change	Little or no selling of the change
7. Carry-over of enthusiasm to parents/children	Negative carry-over to parents/children
8. Camaraderie among staff/students	Little camaraderie among
9. Open structure	Controlled structure
10. Willingness to share decision making	Fear of loss of power
11. Desire to learn new concepts and strategies	Little or no desire to learn anything "new"
12. Cooperation among staff	Little or no cooperation among staff
13. Trust among faculty, staff, administration, and community	Little trust among faculty, staff, administration, and community
14. Effective internal and external communication	Either ineffective or no internal and external communication
CONS	PROS
1. Too little change	Adequate change for mandate
2. Random change	Structured change
3. Powerlessness of change agents	Legal authority to change
4. Lack of motivation	Controlled motivation
5. Lack of buy-in by some stakeholders	Forced buy-in
6. Unconducive educational structure	Compatible structure

According to James P. Comer (1980), when administrators and teachers are given the know-how, they eagerly share their skills, thereby gaining human, management, child development, and relationship skills.

Schools, including staff and students, must believe there is a need to change, and this desire and push must come from within themselves. Cooperation, participation, communication, and trust are essential elements of change and cannot be mandated.

First and Second Level Change

Not only are voluntary-mandated issues important to continuous change, but the level of the change itself becomes important, if the change is to endure the test of time. First level changes take place in education, as well as in a host of other institutions, all the time. They, too, are continuous. But the underlying problem with such endeavors is that they are almost always short lived. In other words, they are band-aid or bandwagon approaches to change, and their duration is usually a few years at most. Fullan (1993) states that "unless deeper change in thinking and skills occur there will be limited impact" (p. 23). What is needed in education is enduring, level two or structural change, that can survive long enough to be proven a success or failure.

Fooling Around the Edges

Much of the change that has come in education, alluded to before, takes place as small change, referred to as incremental change (Raywid, 1990). These changes, even though some are quite important to some segments of stakeholders, is first level change (Fullan, 1993). This change could be considered issues or changes that are on the fringes of education, such as paving a school parking lot or implementing special programs for selected groups of children. These are often needed changes, but do little or nothing to improve student learning (Raywid, 1990). They are like the dog skirting the edge of the pond rather than jumping into the middle and creating deep structural change. Workable solutions are hard to conceive, harder to put into practice, and the strategies used need to focus on things that really make a difference (Fullan, 1993).

Digging the Roots

Second level change, restructuring, is the deep water of change (Fullan, 1993). It goes beyond attempts to fine tune the system and directs its efforts at basic changes in the entire structure. Such changes are aimed at the "roots" of the system rather than the superficial. This level of change is long enduring, is slow to develop, needs much reorganization, and requires basic paradigm shifts and considerable professional development.

Change Resistance (Resistors)

Change, in any of its many conditions, is almost always met with resistance (Fullan, 1993). There are many people whose roles and attitudes may need to be modified and who may present resistance to change. This resistance takes many forms, but there are six basic factors of resistance that are often evident and which need to be dealt with if smooth transition is to take place. These six factors are: loss of power/prestige; obsolescence of knowledge-skill; fear of the unknown; limited resources; organizational structure; and, professional organizational agreements (professional negotiations) (Urs, 1990).

Loss of Power/Prestige

Loss of power/prestige is a major and common fear of individuals in positions of power (Lunenberg, 1990). Loss of power/prestige may cause people to behave in unusual ways. These individuals may change into controlling, manipulating micromanagers. They may become more controlling, more authoritarian, less willing to share information, more possessive, and more threatened by those who are attempting change. They feel that by keeping a tight reign they will keep their power/prestige.

Obsolescence of Knowledge-Skill

Unfortunately, it appears that as individuals move "up the ladder of success," become administrators, they see less of a need for updating skills and keeping up with new concepts and theories. The more things change, the less comfortable they tend to feel. Patterns are comfortable; change is uncomfortable. The more out of date their knowledge becomes, the more they try to keep things the same. Change may be resisted by any individual or group who is mandated to learn and perform new skills and roles (Gorton & Thierbach-Schneider, 1991). Obsolescence of knowledge-skill also causes fear of loss of power/prestige. They may be afraid that teachers will realize how out of date they are, and because of this, try to maintain the status quo.

Teachers also have a fear of change due to obsolescence of knowledge-skill. Teaching children is a full time profession. It becomes more and more difficult to keep current on trends, theories, and strategies as the workload increases. Teachers therefore tend to become comfortable with what they have been doing and find it very difficult to change. The amount of time needed to implement change may also account for some of the resistance at the school level.

One aspect of knowledge and skill not covered under obsolescence is a lack of original preparation (Meyers, 1996). Many teachers have never had the opportunity to learn about governance, budgeting, or decision making. In such cases the new information, new training, has to be provided to overcome the void in those individual's preparation program.

Fear of the Unknown

Fear of the unknown is a powerful motivator. As Fullan (1993) states, "Under conditions of uncertainty, learning anxiety difficulties, and fear of the unknown are intrinsic to all change processes, especially at the early stages" (p. 25). Talbert (1995) reiterates this view when she says that experienced teachers described their restructuring efforts as "scary." This fear alone has the potential to stop progress in its tracks. Education has existed in basically the same way for hundreds of years. Once the door to the classroom or the "door"" school is closed, it may become "business as usual." Now, though, with team teaching, collaboration, shared decision making, and sundry other changes, educators can no longer hide behind closed doors. Kentucky has shown that effective teachers and administrators will rise above new mandated programs with either no or little training beforehand. They have shown, as F. D. Roosevelt said, "The only thing to fear is fear itself."

Perhaps educators need to ask themselves what they are afraid of. Behavior is determined by thoughts and emotions, which is affected by our fear. Once it can be determined exactly what the specific fear(s) is, then it can be determined if it is realistic or unrealistic, and what steps may be taken to conquer it. The authors worked with a teacher who had served thirteen years in one building and had come to the reality she needed a change. However, when the opportunity arrived to make a change, she began to fear the move. She was afraid that being put into a new situation in a new building, she would not be successful. These fears of inadequacy almost prevented a good teacher from making a change which enhanced her career.

Limited Resources

Lack of monies and materials has been an albatross to education from the beginning. There never seems to be enough to do the job. As Sykes (1996) states, the lack of supporting resources multiplies the uncertainty of reform. Teachers are famous for spending hundreds of dollars out of their own pockets to see that all children have an equal chance. Kentucky has made great strides in developing a financial system which promotes educational equity. But this still does not stop some schools and school systems from having much more that others. Kentucky also has mandated several programs which it has failed to fund or has only partially funded. School districts cannot continue to operate under state mandates which are paid for out of local monies.

Organizational Structure

The structure of the organization may also have an effect on its ability to change. The more hierarchical a structure, the more difficult it becomes to implement lasting, level two change. School systems have a definite chain of command, which has traditionally been an authoritarian, top down bureaucracy. Kentucky is attempting to put more control at the local school level by mandating school-based decision making councils (SBDM). Much research has been done supporting the idea that decisions need to be made at the level at which they are implemented (Bergman, 1992; Conley & Bacharach, 1990; Meadows, 1990; Mullen, Symons, Hu, & Salas 1989; Lieberman, 1988). However, mandating such change may be compared to legislating/mandating morality.

Professional Organization Agreements (Professional Negotiations)

Professional organizations produce yet another source of resistance to change. Some states have labor laws that allow for professional negotiations, others do not. Kentucky is a state which allows local options. However it is done, these agreements often preclude teachers volunteering time, effort, or energy beyond the contract. These agreements may hamper many change efforts. Pay for extra assignments, like committees, may cause certain mandates, like SBDM, to fail before there is enough time to gauge its success. These agreements also have the possibility of stopping creative teachers from trying innovative techniques and have a powerful influence on teacher attitudes.

Change Builders

With change, and the resistance that always accompanies it, there needs to be a well designed and highly organized program to enhance, encourage, and reward participants as they move upward toward the goals and objectives of change. Kentucky not only provided these concepts in their improvement plan, they also included coercive (punitive) plans for those individuals and schools who failed to meet the goals of improvement. The rewards were in the form of recognition, satisfaction, and finance (money). For schools who exceed the base line established for individual schools, a bonus of several thousand dollars was available on a per teacher basis.

Those schools which failed to measure-up had multiple forms of coercion. They had to notify the parents of their students that the school was performing poorly, offer to transport children to another school of the parents choice, develop a school improvement plan, accept the services of a Distinguished Educator (Lindauer, Petrie, & Malone, 1996), and forfeit tenure status for all faculty until the performance level established by the state was restored.

There are basically five ways that change can be encouraged, whether the change is mandated or voluntary, and while approaches may be varied with the type of change initiated (voluntary or mandated), careful attention to these plans will enhance the change outcome. The five are: involvement, information, staff development, decision-making, and use of power.

Involvement

While all five have advantages and disadvantages, it seems to the authors that involvement offers the best chance of success in bringing about positive change at the site level where face to face relationships and influence can be brought to bear on the daily needs and problems of the improvement process. In this mode, the leader(s) can get-down and get-dirty with the troops in a way that cannot be done at other levels and, of course, is impossible with legislation from the state level. In this approach the leader's knowledge/skill power is used to combat the insecurities and fears of the participants with successful mentoring at the early stages. It is usually the leader, cast in the role of mentor, who holds the ship together in the first stormy sea of change. In this condition, participation provides security, enhances the environment, and provides the encouragement to initiate the first steps toward continuous improvement. It should be pointed out that this approach allows some leaders to emerge who have the skill, security, knowledge, and charisma for leadership and may not be the status leader, the principal of the school. Many times more than one leader may emerge.

Information

Along with involvement, the flow of information is critical. It is only as ideas and information reach the implementation level that events begin to move toward experimentation, solutions, and eventual improvement. Information must be two-way, sending and receiving (Hoy & Miskel, 1993). Both ends must work continually to insure that the information sent and received is correct. The sender must check and confirm the message was received as intended, while the receiver must confirm the message was decoded as intended. Feedback between the sender and the receiver, which must also flow both ways, determines if the information was correctly received or if it needs to be changed or clarified (Lippitt, 1982). The larger an organization, the greater the need to insure communication of information does not become a problem. Only through constant monitoring can open lines of communication be assured. Often clear lines of communication are difficult when systems as large as a state are involved. Kentucky has not been the exception.

Professional Staff Development

Normally, staff development plays a critical role in the implementation of change. However, in many instances of change experienced by the authors, planning for professional development is an afterthought at best and ignored altogether at worst (Darling-Hammond & McLaughlin, 1995). The limited success of instructional revolution is in part due to the pavety of attention paid to reeducation (Wilson, Peterson, Bell, & Cohen, 1996). Kentucky included this concept in the legislation but failed to provide the necessary time frame for much needed professional development prior to the implementation of mandated programs. Any change requiring new skills of participants should be accompanied by an in-service program (Hunkins & Ornstein, 1988). The non-graded program was one such program, implemented before an adequate professional development program could be instituted. Consequently, many Kentucky schools have yet to implement adequate changes to "make the difference" that children need.

A second aspect of professional development is the adequacy of such preparation. If the professional development is such that it is only introductory or survey in nature, many recipients, teachers in particular, tend to feel they have gotten the information needed and become immune to the in-depth development they actually should have in order to make deep and continuous improvement to their programs. This inadequate training combined with an attitude of, "Oh! We have already had that," is a deadly mixture and often does more harm than good. Sykes (1996) suggests that education's "one-shot workshop" is shorthand for superficial, faddish inservice education and has little effect on what goes on in classrooms. In a five year study by McLaughlin and Talbert (1993), it was found that teachers who developed sustained and challenging learning opportunities became part of a network of individuals who found solutions together.

In Kentucky's rush to get the change program moving, the state fell into the trap of inadequate professional development, and will for some time deal with the negative attitudes and unacceptance. The 1996 Kentucky legislature is currently debating the merits of continuing the non-graded program as it was instituted only six years ago. That debate is due, at least partly, to the inadequacy of professional development in the early days of program implementation.

Decision Making

Decision making also plays a role in the change process, both at the local and state level. Again, Kentucky set about insuring the change process and continuous improvements in her schools by making level two changes: these involved changes in the governance or decision making processes of its schools. While the laws are intertwined in many ways, the change in governance at the local school level rather than at the district level provided the most dramatic change of all. The incentive for faculty of many schools to readily accept the opportunity to implement changes desired by the legislature and to implement them rather quickly was provided by allowing local teachers and parents to become involved in meaningful and decisive ways.

First of all, boards of education were limited in their responsibilities and, secondly, the office of the superintendent was redesigned so that local schools had decision making power in ten basic areas: 1) personnel decisions; 2) instructional materials and student support services; 3) curriculum; 4) staff time; 5) assignment of students; 6) school space; 7) schedules; 8) instructional practices; 9) discipline and classroom management; and 10) extracurricular programs. School councils had the authority to make changes in these areas which they believed would improve student learning. However, along with this responsibility came accountability. Individual schools became accountable for the success or failure of their students. This one change allowed many schools to implement new, research based teaching strategies, not only to improve the potential for all students to learn but also to make school a happier, more pleasant place to be.

Use of Power

Continuous improvement requires effective leadership. Hersey and Blanchard (1988) suggest leader effectiveness is determined by the interrelatedness between leadership styles and the situation. The effective leader behaves differently in different situations (Evans, 1972). This effective leader has the ability and influence to accomplish things. This ability and influence, or power, whether personal or organizational, is characteristic of leadership. Personal power is derived from the personality and ability of the leader. Positional power is drawn from the leader's position in the organization (Hersey & Blanchard, 1988; Stimson &

Applebaum, 1988). However, dividing the power into two pieces, personal and positional, limits the choices a leader has in attempting to influence followers. A more feasible division of power was suggested by French and Raven (1959), who identified five bases of power: coercive, reward, legitimate, expert, and referent.

Coercive power is the perceived ability of the leader to provide sanctions. Reward power is the perceived ability of the leader to provide rewards. Legitimate power is based on the perception that the leader has the authority or position to make decisions in the organization. Expert power is based on the followers' perceptions that the leader is competent and has the education, experience, and expertise to make decisions. Referent power is based on the perceived attractiveness or liking the followers have for the leader (Lindauer, 1993).

Expert and referent power are considered to be dimensions of personal power, while coercive, reward, and legitimate are considered dimensions of position power (Hersey & Blanchard, 1988; Stimson & Applebaum, 1988; Stogdill, 1974). Natemeyer (1975) in reviewing the research done on power base, surmised there was not a best power base, and suggested that the appropriate power base may be largely affected by situational variables. As referred to elsewhere in this chapter, the change situations may offer persons, other than those in positions of power, opportunities to gain leadership status, and as long as conflict does not arise, this emergence can be developed to strengthen the school.

The Leadership Void

When change is imminent, leadership or the lack thereof, becomes important to the organization. This is true in government, the military, business, industry, and certainly in education. Kentucky was no exception.

Status Leadership

Positional or status leaders are no longer able to depend on their positions (principal) to provide the base for leading the school. Councils, teachers, and parents are now actively engaged in deciding the needs of the local school. Administrators who had been trained as managers often knew little about instruction and curriculum, were many times mismatched in their experiential background, and were caught by surprise at the rapidity with which they were expected to initiate of state mandated change.

Leadership Flight

This required change caused many administrators/leaders to retire, others to ask for reassignment, and still others to begin the process of upgrading their skills and knowledge. An informal survey of Kentucky's principals conducted in 1993 by the authors, showed 72% of those responding planned on leaving the principalship in five years or less. Other principals have chosen to leave the principal position for other less stressful assignments (The Gleaner, 1993).

Preparation of Leadership

Continuous improvement forced the Kentucky colleges/universities to re-examine the programs they were using to prepare school managers/ leaders. The need for continuous improvement was now causing the change process to stretch beyond the K-12 level and into the undergraduate and graduate levels of the educational enterprise.

The Changing of the Old Guard

Joel Barker (1990), in his works Power of Visions and Business of Paradigms, indicates that Paradigm Pioneers, those men and women who see and become comfortable with change, are able to move with the change forces and make a contribution to new ways of thinking/doing. Others, he maintains, should get out of the way because they become blockers. In continuous improvement situations, this factor is even more highly emphasized, because in education, as in most institutions, the unit/school cannot move beyond the vision and ability of the leadership. To be effective, principals must be visionary, resourceful, proactive, energetic, and have well developed interpersonal and communication skills (Barth, 1988; Manasse, 1982; Mazzarella, 1982; Murphy, 1988). Again Kentucky's schools were no exception. In schools where administrators had the vision, were knowledgeable, and provided the leadership, dramatic advances were made and improvement became very apparent. The lack of this leadership ability, the lack of energy on the part of some, and the stress of dramatic change with its inevitable increase of workload, caused a changing of the old guard. Superintendents, principals, and teachers decided that they were candidates for retirement, sunnier climates, or for renewed tenure in the classroom. That, too, is a part of the outcome of continuous change, continuous improvement, and no doubt was part of the reasoning of the legislature from the very beginning. Regardless of the motive or the outcome, the "old guard," to a large extent, has now exited the scene.

The infusion of leadership in a leadership void can bring about dramatic change, and this is happening in Kentucky. Preparation programs have gone from preparing approximately 90 percent male administrators to almost the reverse. Women now dominate the students in administrative preparation programs in approximately an 8 to 2 ratio. The once highly delineated preparation programs for school administrators has taken on a new face with a variety of innovative and leadership oriented offerings.

Educating the Patrons, Students, and Parents

One of the most difficult tasks of educators anywhere has been communicating to others what is happening in education. Unfortunately, education has always been held accountable for all the ills/problems of society. But, in reality, these are society's problems and not education's problems. Historically, education has been charged with solving them. Until society accepts the concept of continuous improvement and people as lifelong learners, education is trapped in a model which can only be partially successful.

Since the advent of KERA, teachers and administrators have fought long and hard to explain the changes, involve parents and community, and support what they are doing. The Kentucky reform brought with it extended days and weeks for teachers who saw the benefits for the students. These newly empowered professionals began working extended days and weeks. Fifteen hour days and six or seven day work weeks became the norm for these dedicated individuals, changing the perception many had of educators of being hourly employees to being professionals. But battles are hard to win, and each fight takes a toll on the participants. Many of the changes in Kentucky are so alien to what the parents experienced, it is very difficult for them to understand. As our nation moves into a new century, education must commit to continuous improvement, not only to accommodate the current technological/communication society, but also to prepare its children in ways that allow them to adapt to an uncertain future.

The Politics of Change

One of the problems of state mandated change, or perhaps its very strength, is that once the train starts to move it is hard to stop or derail. Change can become the end rather than the means to an end. The very nature of politics is to respond to pressure groups and lobbyists, to get re-elected, and to appease the electorate. Educational groups, as well as many other patronage groups, find it difficult to slow the political winds of reform.

Pressure Groups

Nowhere are these more evident than in Kentucky's continuing struggle to bring about continuous improvement in the education of her children. Pressure groups organized almost immediately to play an important role in the decisions of the 1990 laws. The "Right" organized to oppose much of the instructional programs and curricular changes identified by the legislature, parent groups began to decry the loss of perceived quality, and teacher groups decided to resist planned improvements by passive means, as well as by pressuring their local politicians. Meanwhile, other constituents organized to support the efforts of state government to improve the system. Today, little change has been delivered by these groups, but each session of the biennial legislature brings change ever closer to fruition.

Currently, the legislature is considering a reversal of some regulations and the revision of several others. Some "fine tuning" is necessary; however, major shifts too soon can become very detrimental. One of the biggest changes being proposed is to the non-graded primary from required to a volunteer program. Another proposed change is to remove the multi-age and multi-ability grouping requirement from the list of critical attributes. Both of these issues go to the very heart of a non-graded primary. As it has been stated before, there has not been enough time to assess the success of any of the 1990 mandated programs. Another change brought about by pressure groups, which has caused considerable problems, is a regulation requiring minority membership on SBDM councils, if a school has a minority population of 8% or more. How do you mandate membership on an elected council? It appears to the authors this is an oxymoron. Yet another change being considered is the appointment of a council member by the local board of education. The impact of such a ruling is yet to be determined.

The Need for Institutionalization and Continuity

The advantage of the continuous change concept is that it allows continuous improvements to be addressed. However, the problem with it is that it fails to provide time to truly assess the success of innovation and improvement. Schooling, unlike industry or business, is a long term enterprise. Students are not made, or improved, in short order as is an automobile or a computer; it takes years, even decades, to help a child grow into a responsible, caring, productive adult. Until programs have been studied over time, improvement may not be evident and cannot be evaluated. One of the problems of education in this country is that educators are "band wagon enthusiasts," waiting for the next trend to come along so they can get off the last one. We, as a society, need to give serious thought to the effects such policies and behaviors are having on the education of our children. Too, we have to begin to understand that education is not the answer to all of society's ills. The evidence strongly indicates that when parents are concerned about their children's behavior and about their education, students do well and discipline is a less serious issue. What is needed in our search for continuous improvement is an element of stability and endurance so that the positive improvements, the successful programs, can become institutionalized. That can only happen when we provide enough time and continuity to allow institutionalization to occur.

Proving-Up

American educators have operated the most successful schooling enterprise in the world (Berliner, 1995). They have the ability to continue on that course, but only if they continually search for ways to improve the system. That improvement, though, must be based on sound research and responsible regulation. Assuredly, old institutions that have become bound by bureaucratic red tape need the impetus of dramatic, even catastrophic, change, otherwise the system becomes stagnant. After the quake of change and its aftershocks, stability is needed once again, so a new norm can be achieved.

Unfreezing and Refreezing

Returning to Lewin's theory of change, the unfreezing of the system has taken place, the chaos has occurred, and it is now time for the refreezing process to play its role. We can fine tune much of the educational enterprise but we must also provide an adequate amount of time for the system and society to discover and understand just how well we are doing.

States make fundamental structural changes which cause and/or allow many other changes to be instituted. The move to SBDM is perhaps the best example of this structural change. With schools operating on a SBDM basis, many important and improved changes can take place. And continuing improvement is both possible and probable. While mandated change has some drawbacks, it can, if carefully thought through and well designed, empower a whole host of continuing improvements in education.

References

Barth, R. (1988). Principals, teachers, and school leadership. Phi Delta Kappan, 69 (9), 639-642.

Bergman, A. (1992) Lessons for principals from site-based management. Educational Leadership, 50 (1), 48-51.

Comer, J. (1980). School power. New York: The Free Press.

Conley, S., & Bacharach, S. (1990). From school-site management to participatory school-site management. Phi Delta Kappan, 71 (7), 539-544.

Darling-Hammond, L., & McLaughlin, M. (1995). Policies that support professional development in an era of reform. Phi Delta Kappan, 76 (8), 597-604.

Deming, W. (1986) Out of the crisis. Cambridge, MA: MIT Press.

Evans, M. (1972). Leadership behavior: Demographic factors and agreement between subordinate and self-description. Personnel Psychology, 25, 649-653.

French, J., & Raven, B. (1959). The bases of social power in D. Cartwright, Studies in social power. Ann Arbor: University of Michigan, Institute for Social Research.

Fullan, M. (1993). Change forces: Probing the depths of educational reform. London: Falmer Press.

Gleaner, The. (1993, June 20). Henderson, KY. p. A-3.

Gorton, R., & Theirbach-Schneider, G. (1991). School-based leadership challenges and opportunities (3rd ed.). Dubuque, IA: Wm. C. Brown Publishers.

Hersey, P., & Blanchard, K. (1988). Management of organizational behavior utilizing human resources (5th ed.). New Jersey: Prentice Hall.

Hoy, W., & Miskel, C. (1991). Educational administration theory, research, and practice (4th ed.). Random House, New York.

Hunkins, F., & Ornstein, A. (1988). Implementing curriculum changes-guidelines for principals. NASSP Bulletin, 72 (11), 67-72.

Kentucky Revised Statutes. (1990). Frankfort.

Kretovics, J., Farber, K., & Armaline, W. (1991). Reform from the bottom up: Empowering teachers to transform schools. Phi Delta Kappan, 73 (4), 295-299.

Lewin, K. (1951). Field theory in social science. New York: Harper & Row.

Lieberman, A. (1988) Teachers and principals: Turf, tension, and new task. Phi Delta Kappan, 69 (9), 648-652.

Lindauer, P. (1993). Teachers' perceptions of principals' leadership effectiveness and school-based decision making council meetings' effectiveness in selected elementary schools in Kentucky. Doctoral Dissertation. Southern Illinois University.

Lindauer, P., Petrie, G., & Malone, B. (1996). The new modern czar: Kentucky's distinguished educator program. Eastern Kentucky

Educational Review, 2 (1).

Lippitt, G. (1982). Organizational renewal: A holistic approach to organizational development. Englewood Cliffs, NJ: Prentice Hall.

Manasse, L. (1982) Effective principals: Effective at what? Principal, 61 (4), 10-75.

Mazzarella, J. (1982). Portrait of a leader. Principal, 61 (4), 28-31.

McLaughlin, M., & Talbert, J. (1993). Contexts that matter for teaching and learning. Stanford, CA: Center for Research in the Context of Secondary School Teaching, Stanford University.

Meadows, B. J. (1990). The rewards and risks of shard leadership. Phi Delta Kappan, 71 (7), 545-548.

Meyers, E. (1995). Changing schools, changing roles—redefining the role of the principal in a restructured school. IMPACT II. NY: The Teachers Network.

Mullen, B., Symons, C., Hu, L., & Salas, E. (1989). Group size, leadership behavior, and subordinate satisfaction. The Journal of General Psychology, 13 (64), 116, 155-169.

Murphy, J. (1988). The unheroic side of leadership: Notes from the swamp. Phi Delta Kappan, 69 (9), 654-659.

Natemeyer, W. (1975). An empirical investigation of the relationship between leader behavior, leader power bases, and subordinate performance and satisfaction. Doctoral dissertation. University of Houston.

Raywid, M. (1990). The evolving effort to improve schools: Pseudo-reform, incremental reform, and restructuring. Phi Delta Kappan, 72 (2), 139-143.

Singh, J. (1990). Organization evolution: New directions. Newbury Park, CA: Sage.

Stimson, T., & Appelbaum, R. P. (1988). Empowering teachers: Do principals have the power? Phi Delta Kappan, 70 (4), 313-316.

Stogdill, R. (1974). Handbook of Leadership. New York: The Free Press.

Sykes, G. (1996). Reform of and as professional development. Phi Delta Kappan, 77 (7), 465-467.

Talbert, J. (1995). Changing schools, changing roles—redefining the role of the principal in a restructured school. IMPACT. NY: The Teachers Network.

Urs, J. (1990). Technology management in organizations. Newbury Park, CA: Sage.

Wilson, S., Peterson, P., Ball, D., & Cohen, D. (1996). Learning by all. Phi Delta Kappan, 77 (7), 468-476.

Chapter 15

TOTAL QUALITY EDUCATION: AN EPILOGUE

Marylyn Granger
Alabama State University

The one thing that we can be sure of in an uncertain world is that change is constant, it is fluid, and inevitable. Every organization in our society continuously changes and fluctuates in unending cycles. Primary examples of these changes are seen in the worlds of business and education.

We are presently on the threshold of what could be the most exciting epoch in American education (Schmaker & Wilson, 1995). The fact that many educational innovations were born in business organizations, which affected management styles and strategies, is disconcerting to some educators, but enthusiastically embraced by others.

In a vastly changing global economy, organizations are finding that hierarchical models, which tap little of the mental talents of most workers, won't allow them to remain competitive (Schenakat, 1993). Indeed, the human capacities that companies are beginning to realize their workers' need are the very qualities humanistic educators have supported all along as desired outcomes of schooling (p. 64). Nevertheless, our educational organizations have been receiving poor grades when compared with the (product) student outcomes observed in other countries. Perhaps this is because today's educators are inundated with countless "answers:" active learning; constructing meaning; teaching for conceptual change; cooperative learning; etc. (Schenakat, 1993). When you add, MBO, Site Based Management, Block scheduling, Inclusion, and other considerations such as: special programs for the handicapped; learning-disabled; and at-risk students, educators, parents and teachers are becoming more and more frustrated and unhappy with our educational outcomes. Thus, you have a loud and clear cry for increased teacher and student testing, and the concept of accountability which many believe will solve our educational problems. Since these methods have not netted us with anticipated positive results in the past, says Schenakat, how then can educators transform American education in the ways necessary to prepare students to flourish in the new high-performance organizations continuously evolving in our society? (p. 65)

To answer these questions, Rankin (1992) believes many educators who are interested in educational reforms and new directions in assessment are seeking to determine whether ideas for improvement in education can be found in increased understanding of the work of W. Edwards Deming who helped industry improve quality through better management.

W. Edwards Deming gave Japan the tools for developing quality over 40 years ago. It has only been within the last 10 years that U.S. industry began to follow his methods. Now there is a movement to apply the Deming method called Total Quality Management (TQM) to schools and government agencies (Richie, 1992). In educational organizations, TQM is often referred to a Total Quality Education (TQE).

Deming's 14 Principles

Rankin (1992) believes that many administrators are interested in educational reform, new directions in assessment, and total quality management (TQM) issues. They seek to determine whether ideas for improvement in education can be found in increased understanding of the work of W. Edwards Deming and others who have helped industry improve quality through better management. The changes in management are deeply rooted in cooperation through a win/win approach for total system optimization.

The implications for education have been embraced by many who feel that the problems inherent in our educational systems have not been adequately addressed. Deming's approach has caught the attention of educators as a means of defining, implementing, and evaluating outcomes.

Rankin (1992) has converted Deming's management focused principles into educational focused principles as an approach to view educational processes into workable plans. These 14 principles are:

1. **Create Constancy of Purpose**
    Several implications for education are seen. Customers must be clearly defined: Are they the students, the parents, the community or society, the board members, business,

higher education? Is the middle level school a customer of the elementary school.

System boundaries must be clear: Is the system the school district or a single school? If it is the school, then either the school must become autonomous from the district or the district office must become a full party to the transforming system and committed to all the 14 principles. If the system is the district, then all schools in the district must be in the program.

The system must improve so that the customers receive quality education, benefit from continual improvement, and act in support of the system. Educational output must be clearly defined, and where possible it must be measurable, although some of the most important aims may not be measurable.

2. **Adopt the New Philosophy**

In education, total commitment is also needed. Existing methods, materials, and environments may be replaced by new teaching and learning strategies where success for every student is more probable. Differences among students and teachers are addressed and used. From the top down, including all components of the educational system, there must be total commitment to putting new processes into effect.

3. **Cease Dependence on Inspection to Achieve Quality**

The need for mass inspection after a process is completed can be decreased by designing the process so that quality is built into the product in the first place. Educational systems often do more screening and sorting of students than teaching and learning for students. This problem is an example of dependence on final inspections.

Educators should monitor the teaching process as it occurs and use feedback to adjust teaching methods and materials as needed. Less reliance on remediation should be necessary if proper mediation occurs during initial instruction. In addition, mass inspection through standardized tests can result in overemphasis on actual items tested, cheating, and increased variance; and can limit educational achievement to those objectives most easily measured. Educational measurement is more likely to be used to improve the teaching and learning process when it occurs as part of the ongoing instruction rather than at some annual testing period.

4. **Consider Total Costs. Do Not Trust the Low Bid on Each Item**

In education, this principle may be appropriate to the purchase of textbooks and tests, computers and other equipment, and supplies. Multiple suppliers can increase output variability, and may lead to consideration of contracting for custodial, transportation, cafeteria, data processing, and other services. It suggests greater use of distance learning via interactive television, or even contracting for some instructional services. The important thing is to consider the total costs and benefits of the alternatives, not just their initial cost.

5. **Improve Constantly and Forever Every Process for Planning Production and Service**

Many superintendents and principals put great pressure these days on teachers to improve scores on standardized tests. Often the result is not real improvement in the quality of education or the number of students succeeding, but in increased performance on a small number of easily measured targets.

The focus of improvement efforts, under a Deming approach, would be on the teaching and learning processes, using the best research to suggest strategies, then trying them out, studying, and acting on the results. There would be attention to both failure and success, and changes in the processes would be prompter and more targeted.

Statistical control can be used in education as well as in industry, but with techniques appropriate for educational variables and conditions. Greater emphasis would be placed on ensuring that all students improve and that minimum quality standards are met and constantly raised along with improvements in teaching methods. Substantial improvements would be needed in the measurement of those Yearnings that are measurable and in managing for the attainment of important Yearnings that are not measurable.

6. **Institute Training on the Job**

Teacher training often occurs after school, on the weekend, or in the summer and away from the work site. Such training may be connected directly to teaching problems, but often it is not. The school day should provide time for training that is directly related to plans to improve instructional quality.

Much training is needed in the proper use of assessment. There may be some greater costs to allow for such training, but in the long run, educational quality gains should more than make up for the costs.

7. **Adopt and Institute Leadership**

An understanding of Deming's "System of Profound Knowledge" will be needed. In addition, leaders must eliminate processes and systems that impede the attainment of improved quality; e.g., quotas, standards, performance appraisal, ranking of staff, and management by objectives (MBO).

Education is full of quotas, standards, rating systems, and MBO systems for educators. Educational leaders will need to eliminate such processes and learn to improve the system itself: its outcomes, processes, and inputs. They must learn the same skills as leaders in industry, and they must learn to carry out the same responsibilities.

8. **Drive Out Fear**

This is probably the one principle that has greatest impact on all the others. Employees fear loss of promotion opportunity, loss of job, criticism, low ratings, being held responsible for results when they do not control the process or the inputs, and not being valued or appreciated. Such fears lower productivity, produce inaccurate information about problems and results, remove honest and open responses, reduce innovation and risk taking, and may produce cheating. Fear can hamstring employee effort and creativity. Fear must be eliminated or markedly reduced.

These same fears are present in the education system. We must recognize that nearly everyone does the best that she or he can under the existing circumstances. The focus of our improvement efforts must be placed on the processes and on the results, not on trying to make people accountable. If the quality is not there, the fault, most likely, is in the system, not in the teachers and other workers.

Educational leaders must remove worry and fears, and work with employees on improving the processes. The improvement tasks in education are hard enough if we all sheathe our swords and work cooperatively; they are impossible under conditions of fear and mistrust.

9. **Break Down Barriers Between Staff Areas**

   This principle is closely allied to the first principle, dealing with constancy and unity of purpose. Competition among functions must be replaced with cooperation so that total quality is maximized and total costs are minimized.

   In education, this principle applies to interdepartmental cooperation. It also applies to interdisciplinary instructional efforts such as teacher teams, writing-to-learn programs that involve several subject areas, and student investigations of problems and issues that require the application of yearnings from different disciplines. In addition, it suggests the sharing of resources such as computers among the staff.

10. **Eliminate Slogans, Exhortations, and Targets for the Work Force**

    Teachers and principals are intelligent, dedicated workers who can have internal motivation and can craft carefully-designed processes to improve teaching and learning. Lasting increases in effort derive from sterner stuff than slogans.

11. **Eliminate Numerical Quotas for the Work Force and Numerical Goals for Management**

    Superintendents often set numerical targets for principals in terms of attendance rates, failure rates, test scores, dropout rates, etc. One fundamental problem is that knowing both the target and the current performance may show the size and direction of the discrepancy, but it gives no clue as to the method of improvement. In addition, variances in intake and resources are often ignored. Cheating in reporting is encouraged, and other important aims may be ignored or underemphasized. Finally, attention is directed away from those processes and methods that can facilitate instructional improvement.

12. **Remove Barriers that Rob People of Pride of Workmanship**

    Merit pay is a major barrier. It destroys teamwork, fosters mediocrity, increases variability, confuses people with the other input resources, and focuses on the short term. Daily or weekly production reports are also barriers to be removed. They may produce immediate profits, but can kill the organization in the long run. The system should emphasize intrinsic motivation, rather than extrinsic rewards.

Ideally, educators would all be self-evaluating, self-rewarding, and self-directive. Intrinsic motivation that is supported by the system is the best bet to engender pride and quality of workmanship. Merit systems are often statistically random in the long run, are held in suspicion by educators, tend to divide rather than unite, and are often no more deserved by one teacher than by another.

13. **Institute a Vigorous Program of Education and Self-Improvement for Everyone**

    Life-long learning by employees is important, but it need not be closely tied to the immediate system function. It may provide retraining for a new job. Or, it may make the worker a more vital, interesting, inquiring person. Such qualities transfer to both workmanship and employee contribution to the quality of the work environment. A self-renewing institution is more likely found where there are self-renewing people. Corporate investments in such education may have short-term costs but will also have much greater long-term gains.

    These conditions apply at least as well to the educational community as to the industrial community. Inquiring, vital educators who are up-to-date in their field and on current world issues are more likely to find quality solutions to instructional problems, and will surely make learning more interesting for students. The educational system should view the continuing education of its staff member as an investment in educational quality for students.

14. **Put Everybody in the Company to Work to Accomplish the Transformation**

    Establish top-down understanding and commitment. Send senior staff members to Deming workshops. Provide statistical training for managers and Deming system training for statisticians. The system cannot be implemented piecemeal; all 14 points must be implemented; they are interdependent.

    Educators with some sophistication are leery of adopting an entire philosophy; they prefer to choose improvement strategies from many sources. But with Deming's approach, it is necessary. All the key parties in a school district must have substantial understanding of the system, and many of them will need specific training in advance of any decision to go forward. They must know the consequences of an agreement to transform their district using these principles, and be eager to do so. This requirement also implies that the program must provide adequate training and other resources for implementation.

Richie (1992) contends that TQM or TQE requires educators to adopt a "New Belief System." A belief system that is embodied in an understanding of how "quality is defined, and how quality is built into the system at every point in the process." However, some educators find it difficult to eliminate the "old" and embrace the new. In addition, there are others who view Deming's idea that "quality" lowers cost, reduces waste, improves productivity and increase costs (for example) is met with skepticism or disbelief. These critics believe that government or educational management techniques are not entirely transferable to the worlds of school boards and government agencies. However, when the 1980s found some schools and government agencies "faced to operate on a 'fee for service' basis, trying to cope with tax cuts, funding shortfalls and arbitrary personnel cuts, many of these organizations began to realize that reducing waste, lowering costs and improving productivity now applies to them." It always has (Richie, 1992).

Brandt (1992), in a conversation with Enid Brown (a consultant on quality for industries and schools), obtained additional clarity and comprehension on Deming and school quality. Ms. Brown contends that:

1. Dr. Deming's work applies to every organization in the world. It applies to corporations, universities, service organizations, countries, families, and certainly to schools. Deming's work provides a conceptual framework for understanding any system.

    The 14 Points apply to any organization, profit or nonprofit. For example, when you talk of cost, there certainly are financial costs in education, as well as other costs. In families and interpersonal relationships, there are nonfinancial costs. So when Dr. Deming says that a quality way of living is the most cost-effective in the long run, that principle applies to any type of organization.

2. Fortunately, we are beginning to value our diversity—although much of this is only rhetoric—because we still

measure, grade, reward, and track as if there were one ideal. Or we base decisions on "averages" of people.
3. Why do we try to force everyone to be the same? And learning to read is not necessarily sequential. You can learn different things about reading at different times. So if we know that a group of 1st graders may be learning quite different things even though all of them are perfectly healthy and normal, why do we have a 1st grade? Why do we have a 2nd grade? The notion of grade levels is just one example of how we constrain our ability to tap intrinsic motivation and learning.
4. We have handicapped, learning-disabled, at-risk, special needs—whatever you want to call all these students who are examples of natural, normal variation in our society. We seem to feel that we've got to label all these groups as special causes—but they're not.

There's a very important point here. Some educators think that Dr. Deming is always seeking ways to reduce variation. In manufacturing processes that makes sense. In people processes it may not. To standardize everything would be one of the worst things we could do. We could reduce variation by eliminating people that do not fit the perfect profile, but that is not what we need. We must provide for the whole broad range of people and find ways to make them all successful, to experience joy in learning.
5. One of the most important areas of Dr. Deming's work for education is the idea of intrinsic motivation and extrinsic rewards. There are so many activities and practices in education that falsely assume the benefits of extrinsic motivation (forces of destruction, as Dr. Deming calls them): gold stars, merit pay, judging people, MBO (management by objectives), grades, numerical goals, and quotas. Such things cause humiliation, they hurt people, and they channel people into doing things for rewards. And to say, "Well, if only the teachers would teacher harder; if only the students would work harder; if only people were more motivated," is begging the issue. All human beings are born with an intrinsic desire to learn and grow. We can destroy it, but it is there at birth.

We look at many at-risk kids and we say that they are not motivated. They are as motivated as anyone else. We have not learned how to tap into some motivations, so we write some people off because they are "different." They do what makes sense; we haven't figured out what makes sense to them. We are not **listening**. It's a common cause issue—absolutely common cause—and we treat it as special cause.

Holt (1993) supports Brown's views in his statements on our American school system and reform. Holt believes that: "the American school system is remarkably resistant to change—and perhaps especially to the kind of deep-structure change that must accompany Demingism." In a Deming model, Holt also believes that reform is a matter of taking each individual case and developing its "internal goals.... In short, the capacity of schools to develop their internal values is seriously constrained when the external values are expressed as received dogma, detached from the context of the particular school and its constituency."

If Schenakat (1993) is correct in his educational assessment that indicates that Deming's Quality is our last but best hope, then we must also consider that learning organizations **should**: nurture people; alter the way that schools and organizations work for adults; transform our ways of knowing—about teaching, about our content, and about systems and theories.

In the final analysis, data show that what we have been doing in our schools has not worked for the benefit of all students.

If rises in test scores (teacher and student) additional per-pupil expenditures have not had a significant affect on most school's performances, then perhaps it is past time for us to look at certain characteristics of schools that do appear to positively and significantly affect school performance. If TQE is the answer, then how can educators embrace, adopt and implement Deming's work? The following steps may answer this question.

The implementation process should be managed by a TQE Steering Committee. This multidisciplined group often includes school board members, senior administrators, and teacher, staff, and parent representatives. Their role is to provide direction and resources to ensure the successful implementation of the continuous improvement process.

Below are listed some of the primary responsibilities of the TQE Steering Committee. Note how many of these responsibilities relate directly to the elimination of barriers throughout the school system via the formation and management of TQE teams:

- Learning and using the statistical methods to drive and steer the

continuous improvement process;
- Developing short and long range plans for the TQE process;
- Building a sound TQE implementation plan, and auditing the school's progress versus that plan on a periodic basis;
- Selecting major improvement projects, teams, and team leaders;
- Nurturing and reviewing progress of the TQE teams;
- Ensuring that TQE teams get the support they need to be successful;
- Reviewing and implementing final TQE team recommendation;
- Securing specialist support (either internal or external) to help in the implementation effort;
- Communicating "success stories" from inside and outside the school to energize the TQE effort and build enthusiasm;
- Putting audit systems in place to hold improvements and gains; and
- "Asking the right questions" that demonstrate their understanding and dedication to the transformation effort..

Next, a multidisciplined TQE project team is formed to be the workhorse for improvement within the Total Quality Education (TQE) process. In these teams, the Steering Committee brings together the following:

- People and skills from various backgrounds and groups within the school system, creating an opportunity for starting to break down systematic and historical barriers between and among those groups;
- Powerful statistical tools and techniques;
- Demonstrated school leadership understanding, priority, and action to provide the resources and support needed for success;
- Clearly defined TQE project assignments that represent major systems improvement opportunities;
- A high degree of challenge and visibility for the team participants; and
- An opportunity to "make a difference" for each team member..

Systems problems by their very nature cut across functional, curricular, grade, and school group lines. Therefore, one best way to attack systems problems is to pull representatives of those groups together at the same table.

The Implementation Stage is characterized by "expansion." The Steering Committee expands the involvement of people throughout the school system via more training, more improvement projects, more processes under study—all leading to more improvement! Implementation

Stage activities may include:

- Implementing a system for regular feedback to school groups and customers/community groups on improvements;
- Developing internal resources, and using those resources to expand training in statistical methods and teamwork;
- Implementing a process for selecting, assigning, and managing additional TQE project teams on an ongoing basis;
- Inviting the local community and business organizations to join the school's improvement effort;
- Implementing a TQE Supplier Relations Program;
- Implementing procedures for getting staff, student, and parents' input and suggestions on: . Education programs;
- Continuing improvement efforts;
- Problems or issues for future TQE Project Teams;
- School policies; and
- etc.

In the final stage of the TQE Implementation Process, the Board of Education and Administration move toward the self-sufficient management of continuous improvement. The need for external consulting help becomes minimal as TQE is integrated into the regular systems and practices of the school. In the typical school, Integration Stage activities include:

- Institutionalizing teamwork;
- Periodic school environment surveys, and feedback to participants;
- Efforts to "derail" any learning tracks in the classroom;
- Parenting and continuing education programs for parents and others in the school community;
- Integrating TQE and continuous improvement as high priority items in all plans, budgets, meeting agenda, and correspondence produced by the Board of Education;
- Involving external suppliers and customers in process improvement efforts, and in new designs for curricula and educational programs; and
- Experimenting with alternatives to traditional tests and grades to measure and "reward" learning.

Conclusion and Implications
The facts all point to a crisis in education. Our students are behind other countries in math, science, geography, and foreign languages. We face

high dropout rates, rising costs, drugs, and violence. These factors increase social problems and interfere with learning. Unless these problems are addressed, our competitive edge in world markets will remain at risk.

We all realize the problems. We all want improvements and seek changes. The issue, now, becomes how to accomplish the change. With continuing studies being done on Total Quality Education, this model may provide a positive direction for these changes and improvements. Now the issue is whether or not school leaders will take action and embrace this model.

References

Brandt, R. S. (1992). On Deming and school quality: A conversation with Enid Brown. Educational Leadership, 50 (3), 28-31.

Freeston, K. R. (1992). Getting started with TQM. Educational Leadership, 50 (3), 10-13.

Host, M. (1993). The educational consequences of W. Edwards Deming. Phi Delta Kappan, 74, 382-8.

Rankin, S. C. (1992). Total quality management: Implications for educational assessment. NASSP Bulletin, 76 (545), 66-76.

Richie, M. L. (1992). Total quality management and media services: The Deming method. Tech Trends, 37 (6), 14-16.

Schenkat, R. (1993). Deming's quality: Our last but best hope. Educational Leadership, 51 (1), 64-65.